To the Mountains and Back

To the Mountains and Back

✦

Outgoing Email 1998–99: Reflections on Politics and the US Economy in a year leading up to the Millennium

Andréas Daniel Fogg

iUniverse, Inc.

New York Lincoln Shanghai

To the Mountains and Back
Outgoing Email 1998–99: Reflections on Politics and the US Economy in a year leading up to the Millennium

iUniverse books may be ordered through booksellers or by contacting:

iUniverse
2021 Pine Lake Road, Suite 100
Lincoln, NE 68512
www.iuniverse.com
1-800-Authors (1-800-288-4677)

ISBN-13: 978-0-595-38629-1 (pbk)
ISBN-13: 978-0-595-83009-1 (ebk)
ISBN-10: 0-595-38629-6 (pbk)
ISBN-10: 0-595-83009-9 (ebk)

Printed in the United States of America

Contents

Preface

Some of the themes touched upon in this book follow, in no particular order. Some of these points will be obvious to many readers. However I attempt to draw conclusions and inferences from them. For instance, the television mass media deliberately selects out news which it does not want the public to think about, like the opinions of the vast majority of scientists who study global warming. Neither does the mass media treat of the arguments amongst economists re the reality of global warming nor what can and should be done about it. Neither is there any relation drawn between US foreign policies, oil scarcity and EPA auto fleet mileage standards. Here as elsewhere the oil companies' and American Auto companies' lobbyists seem, despite protestations to the contrary, to dominate the selection and analysis of the news. Which is to say that too often there simply is no news analysis. It apparently is above the pay grades of many of the so called pundits, and also considered to be above the competence levels of most of the American viewing audience. Any analysis which might sacrifice short term corporate particularly oil company profits seems to be dispensed with as politically incorrect, unmentionable.

Another theme that I come back to throughout the book involves a critique of the way mainstream democrats have handled tensions arising from the civil rights movement that was pushed so far forward by the Revered Martin Luther King Jr. and his many allies. My position here is that the Republicans have been exploiting these tensions to the nth degree and have been able to get away with this exploitation, which has allowed them to seize control now of all three branches of government, significantly because the Democratic leadership continues to implicitly place, on seemingly ideological grounds, virtually all of the onus for the lack of Black and Hispanic achievement parity upon White bigotry and underfunded predominantly Black school districts. Too often, to the Democrats, the discriminated against are totally blameless, all of the onus falls upon Whites and the White working classes who are implicitly being asked to forgo upwardly mobile job and educational opportunities in favor of their less successful brethren. The Democrats need to correct this misperception of their position. All this in a context in which good jobs at sustainable wages are being phased out due to computerized efficiencies and the threat or actuality of outsourcing.

Other themes touched upon deal with the atrophy of socialization (normal growing up processes) caused by the couch potato syndrome, too much TV watching. This lack of normal growing up experience then impacts upon our society's ability to realistically resolve anxieties and tensions associated with interracial interactions and the lack of the development of strong conceptions of individual self esteem.

Some of the harms associated with the rapidly growing gaps between the very rich and ordinary people are described and analyzed, instead of being merely suggested to be obviously harmful. Questions treated include, in what ways is this gap harmful, psychologically, morally, and macroeconomically? How long can the US economy allow itself to be driven largely by home equity loan and credit card economic demand functions? This part of the manuscript could be described as qualitative sociological economics.

Other topics include Darwin and Social Darwinism, sperm banks, organ banks, donors and their effects on the quality of life. There is a review of Stanley Kubrick's last film, Eyes Wide Shut.

The book is a journal or diary covering November 1998 through the end of 1999. It touches upon the Kosovo intervention, the impeachment of President Bill Clinton, emphasizing the Republican successful attempt to waste the people's and the governments time with this minor scale scandal, while the numbers of the medically uninsured were not diminished and global warming continued hand in hand with the sales of ever less efficient SUVs.

The title refers to the fact that it has been written during vacation travels between skiing in the mountains of northern New England and then back home to an urban area on the outskirts of Boston, Massachusetts. That is these travels involved temporary immersion in small town rural life followed by returns to my base. Somerville, where I dwell, is an intriguing city which borders Cambridge and Boston and remains a vibrant working class community, in recent years experiencing considerable levels of gentrification that is professionals moving in from out of town and the suburbs. This gentrification process has resulted in steeply rising housing valuations both in Somerville as well as in much of the entire state

Meanwhile the diary entries in some sense reflect or perhaps foreshadow the as yet unknown problems that have since been suggested re the Catholic Church by some of her parishioners.

I occasionally throughout the book resort to the use of fictional anecdotes or vignettes which have a tenuous at best or no relationship to reality in order to illustrate some point or other.

Readers who wish to see more current and gratis samples of my writing are welcome to access my blog which has been online since early December of 2005. The blog, no pun intended, can be found at <u>defoggingthedata.blogstream.com</u>

This manuscript contains lots of other points too numerous to mention. For instance, it advocates potentially studying for compensation as early as the high school, certainly at the college level. That is it advocates the idea of rewarding good scholarship with cash, making the point that athletics are over rewarded in the society, academics particularly in high school, not given enough public rewards. Another section critiques the mass media prevalent conception of the "significant other" concept, which it is argued incorrectly seems to suggest that the meaning of significant other is identical with spouse or "main squeeze."

January 2006

Part One: Fall

Subj: Fiction, Mother Nature sending humanity negative feedback? Immacu-
latetroutfishinginAmerica
Date: 11/9/98 12:02:28 PM Eastern Standard Time
To: the editors (The American Prospect, The Nation, The New Yorker)
From: Andréas Daniel Fogg November 5, 1998

Letter from Somerville
  Is it possible that all of these vicious storms are nature's way of telling humanity that our current policies in regard to carbon dioxide emissions are extremely
dangerous and should be changed?

  There appears to be a sort of dearth of significant consciousness such that
enormous numbers of subjects are simply not thought of perhaps as a result of
certain standards of political appropriateness which are implicitly imposed on the
populace by the mass media specifically the TV networks. Therefore significant
contributions to the quality of life and personal consciousness can be accomplished simply by introducing a sense of history and thus continuity into every-
day discourse.
  Further, contributions can be made by references to the politically incorrect,
since the media's most important influence may amount to what it deliberately
omits.
  Again, the assumption that a so called "significant other" must be someone
with whom one is sexually involved is crucial, humanly subversive and wrong.
Likewise the assumption that each person is allowed only one significant other is
also wrong. Both media assumptions remain uncorrected and unchallenged. The
goal of the system seems (at this point, to me) to be to desexualize behaviour
between men and women, so that associations between men and women should
have no more sexual impetus than sexual relations between men and men. Or, if
there is an implied sexual relation between a man and woman with whom he is

not sexually or emotionally involved, then it is assumed that such a relation must be the equivalent of a passing "one night stand."

November 7, 1998

It has been suggested that the results of blood tests might be significant determinants or predictors of human procreative fertility, i.e., that the results of some tests might suggest relative or total procreative incompatibility. If this is the case, and this information is not widely known then the results of its widespread dissemination would likely have an enormous impact upon the qualities of the so called romantic sexual love complex. That is, the desirability of finding a "perfect love" or a love at first sight (sort of experience) would likely be diminished. Of course the goal of finding the perfect love with perfect compatibility, perfect complementarity, probably involving a psychological sort of "loss of self in the other" would also likely be diminished in overall emphasis. Such a goal of course is one of the psychological mechanisms which fuels the imperative toward the sort of experiences emphasized and rationalized in the book Trout Fishing in America by I think, Richard Brautigan. That experience might be roughly characterized as immaculate procreation through autoerotic orgasmic experiences, not a terribly happy accommodation through which most would want to travel through life's travails. It is also almost surely likely substantively a huge load of horseshit. It would appear that the only substantive genetic inheritance that can be immaculately passed on involves facial appearance and other physical characteristics. It is questionable at best whether any emotional or intellectual faculties are capable of being passed on "immaculately." Indeed it is questionable whether any characteristics can be so transmitted. Of course for the auto eroticist, hope springs eternal. Such themes are prevalent in literature, although the only other example that comes to mind involves a partial memory from a series of books about India, the title I remember is "The Jewel in the Crown" I am sure that is not right but it's something like that. There was a phrase therein to the effect that "the kingdom will be OK so long as royalty continue to "cast the fishing nets"." I interpreted this phrase as amounting to an equivalent of the Trout Fishing message. It is also of perhaps a rationalization for the Catholic celibate priesthood, which defers competition between the women of the community for the sexual favors and of course marriageability of the "spiritual leaders" of the community (religiously defined).

The thought in practice, I suggest (in the HIV era), is that the priests will attempt to practice celibacy and end up covertly practicing autoeroticism, which the rationalization holds will allow the "holy ghost" to immaculately trigger selective ghostly, divinely given conceptions.

The whole rationalization however makes it difficult for fathers to intervene to aid their immaculately conceived sons, since they have only appearance to go on and since the context of their conception involved deferred emotional and physical support and contact between father and mother. Hence the whole subject of paternity involves high degrees of remembered lonely frustration. It is questionable how many individuals effected by such thinking ever allow themselves to actually experience a full fledged heterosexual experience. Hence they are likely to live their lives constantly affirming themselves to be "on the make" and therefore never really having the time or the inclination to enjoy the company of other or even one male friend (and often, in practice, of even one woman). It would seem that under the regime of this way of thinking, heterosexual men must be forced to apologize to their female partner or partners for even thinking of spending time with another male, (and, if they spend time with a woman they feel that they have insulted all the other women that have indicated attractedness, hence they end up for the most part as loners and childless, for which fact they are personally, and society is as well, the poorer) that is time that they are not absolutely required to spend in order to support the woman and children. To actually admit to enjoying spending time with a member of the same sex, is, it is suggested indicative of a basically deviant orientation. So much is the deviant given the status of being "forbidden fruit" that the merest suspicion that a man enjoys talking with or visiting another man when he doesn't absolutely have to, such a suspicion is enough to convince many conventionally un-hip straight women that such a man (is) sexually perverted. (And of course to spend time with more than one woman, to "play the field" as it used to be known is to risk being labeled a promiscuous womanizer, Lothario? Don Juan, sort of person who believes himself to be "God's gift to women, as an extremely flirtatious ex girl friend of mine used to accuse me of thinking myself—but it was OK for her to spend time with other guys.)

Thus it is that women and men who are most ideologically committed to upholding the appearance of heterosexuality do so largely in order to convince themselves of that of which they are actually personally in some doubt, since if they actually had experienced the compulsive quality of full fledged successful heterosexual experience, they would have no need to punish errant behavior since they would know that same sex experiences cannot compete against a deliberate unblocked heterosexual seduction. In fact by constantly demeaning the homosexual corpus of experience, they make it seem more attractive to young people who have not yet experienced full fledged heterosexual fulfillment.

Local corporate bonuses and managerial salaries

The narrator suggested, in a memo to mid level and upper level management, that corporate bonuses be assigned not just on the basis of overall corporate performance, but also on the basis of individual "branch" performances. The general manager pointed out that if such were to be the case, then if a general manager erred by some significant margin in holding or manipulating inventory, that then, the branch might suffer a diminished "branch" bonus. So that if there were a branch bonus it might be effected by the consequences of local managerial decisions. So that therefore there should be no locally based bonus. But while I acquiesced at the time, the question arises "why shouldn't local managers have an incentive to improve the performance of the local office? In such an evaluation, positive points could be given for cooperative activities which involved local sacrifice of immediate profits in favor of overall corporate profits, whereas simple negligence and shortsightedness could be penalized. Meanwhile overworked non managerial associates being pressured into donating large amounts of overtime in order to accommodate the profitability goals of management, who (the managers) are neither required nor asked nor pressured into providing overtime would have the compensation that to some extent at least, their extra work will be recognized and rewarded in a manner far more palpable than the usual rhetorical thank-you's that typically are accompanied by management pocketing the lion's share of the spoils, a lion's share that typically is not known to associates, neither does it seem to be reduced when the board of directors feels compelled to hurt the performance of company stock by reducing the magnitude of the dividend, if the managers were taking a salary hit in such circumstances there is no doubt that it would be in the interest of company morale for the associates to be informed of such a sacrifice by the "bosses." Since no such communications have ever been made it is probably safe to assume that no such sacrifices have occurred.

November 8, 1998

Is it in any way important to distinguish qualitatively between working class and lower middle class lifestyles, orientations, ideologies, characteristic occupations?

For example, is it fair to characterize the working class as being involved in basically productive endeavors, whereas the lower middle class tends to be involved in manipulating, supervising, managing or administering those who actually produce, and in addition to manipulating the producers, actually taking credit for the work, perhaps also being willing to appropriate significant amounts of the value actually generated. At the university level the distinction amounts to those who actually teach and write and those in "administration" to whom the actual faculty is in some financial sense indebted. In the context of the university world, faculty members are members of a working class. The fact that in the over-all society university faculty members are usually considered to be middle class, because of what used to be status if not income, does not detract from the fact that relative to administrators, faculty members are actually productive workers. The distinction I am looking for is between those who actually work and might feel guilty about claiming some of the value generated by those who actually pro-duce and work, and those who are quite willing to pursue the control of subordi-nates as personal job oriented objectives and to claim larger pay checks than those who actually do the work. It is these individuals who are triggering layoffs in hopes of improving corporate bottom lines, these individuals who would prefer to empower machines while laying off workers or destroying private lives through the imposition of onerous overtime burdens.

It is these individuals who acquiesce in the deterioration of economic demand both at home and abroad which occurs as a result of competitively generated wage stagnation, which stagnation probably in large part accounts for the rela-tively low levels of productivity growth during the present decade. After all, there is little motivation to produce goods and services for which there are insufficient buyers. And much of the American demand pool as such includes individuals mortgaging their futures in futile attempts to keep up with Madison Avenue gen-erated images of the Joneses foisted upon an all too gullible public by socially irre-sponsible but systemically crucial mass media television networks. (It would be interesting to quantitatively determine what percentage of American consumer spending involves the carry over and acceptance of ongoing accumulating credit card debt.)

Of course the declining wage spiral and the escalating international and inter-state competition to provide more and ever more corporate welfare subsidies and tax breaks should not be attributed merely to ill will on the part of the managerial class, however its' personal characteristics should be described. There are real eco-nomic forces which are compelling these trends to continue and even to expand. It is these economic forces or mechanisms which need to be legally effected, muted if you will, so that the demand pool, the wage pool will be allowed to increase rather than forced to shrink. Note that with the increased level of com-puterization, cybernization if you will, many jobs seem to be technically less demanding than they used to be. As a result, with machines doing more and more of the work, the rationales for providing higher and higher pay shift from being based merely on skill to being based also on interpersonally based qualities (that is rewards increasingly may constitute rewards for valued interpersonal behaviour). If this observation is indeed true, then it begins to appear that being "liked" by one's fellow workers is beginning to be far more important in determining levels of pay than it used to be. And if this is indeed the case, then it would appear that the struggle to define what behaviors are appropriate and acceptable also acquires a new significance, a significance that it didn't used to have. Again, if these observations are true, it would appear that those whose orientation is most fundamentally characterized as inner-directed are likely to earn lower levels of compensation than are those more accurately characterized as other-directed. This conclusion follows from the likelihood that the other-directed are more likely to be attuned to the needs of their coworkers, even if they are less creatively productive or even less productively oriented in terms of nose to the grindstone work.

Again if this is the case the society may need to find ways to nurture and reward those who march to the beat of different drummers, the inner-directed, if they are not to fall by the wayside.

November 9, 1998

Fiction

Did I mention the perhaps psychologically critical issue of the stolen or appropriated baseball glove? No, maybe? Well, the narrator used to play pickup hardball usually at the Murdock house, with the Murdock boys. When he was about eleven or twelve, I think, he left his glove at their house one time before going home. When he returned, after presumably a few days, his glove had the Murdock sister's name written on it in magic marker. How this occurred, or who wrote this name on the glove remains unclear. Also unclear is whether it occurred by accident or deliberately. Dr. Murdock, as I have pointed out, is a Freudian psychoanalyst. Symbolically, psychologically, however, it appears to have gotten in the way of the narrator's ability to "play the field" which is a euphemism in social life for dating a variety of partners without making a commitment to any one of them.

I once heard a Russian writer describe himself on the radio. He said, "I am a writer, therefore, I am a woman…" Of course he meant psychologically, I presume. His point about writing, I suppose, is that writers take a less activist, a less directly confrontational, less directly manipulative and controlling approach to events. Instead they prefer to obviously write and let others act upon the basis of what they have written. This seeming passivity might be interpreted as woman like, in conventional gender characterizations. At any rate having lost his baseball glove does not seem to have hurt the narrator's ability to write, although it may have contributed to a loss of self esteem, a diminished sense of self esteem that made for a sort of social awkwardness, perhaps being unable or unwilling or afraid to confront the Murdock's about the theft or appropriation contributed to the development of certain symptoms of psychiatric illness, feelings of paranoid persecution, the feeling that people were out to get him, that have significantly bothered the narrator through much of his life. But then the world is not always equally hospitable to everyone, it can be particularly cruel to those who are willing to express sentiments or facts that reflect disadvantageously upon themselves. You will rarely, I submit, find a supervisor or manager who will voluntarily admit to any fact or facts which reflect badly upon themselves. Yet the ability to think critically about oneself may be an essential ingredient in most good writer's personalities. I suspect that most good writers do not make good managerial material. Yet the managers, full of self confidence and esteem from their educations, educations that are largely based upon and formed by the work of writers, get paid the larger salaries. I submit the question, "what would supervisors and managers be without writers?"

Merits of two party system/bi-polar disorder vis-à-vis schizophrenic disorder
Date: 11/21/98 3:12:46 PM Eastern Standard Time
to: the editors (The American Prospect, The Nation, The New Yorker)
from: Andréas Daniel Fogg

Letter from Somerville November 10, 1998

That the Democrats alone, without input from a critical Republican Party, then out of power, would almost certainly not have been likely to initiate any significant welfare reform during this decade. Therefore, the fact that seemingly effective workable welfare reform appears to have been implemented should be credited to both parties, since the Democrats insisted upon the maintenance of a reasonable workable safety net by utilizing their power as a minority legislative party and the fact that they held the Presidency. Without the Democrats it is likely that Republicans of a vindictive mean streak would have shredded the safety net and the demand side of the economy altogether. But the alliance of moderate Republicans and compassionate Democrats working with an economically savvy Democratic President carried the day. (Of course it remains to be seen how things go as the program unfolds.)

November 14, 1998

Notes: obstacles in the way which make it difficult for poor people in poor countries, which make it difficult for them to work. First they tend to be personally and economically insecure. That is they do not trust their employers neither their managers nor their supervisors. So they may either carry weapons—to defend themselves against imagined attacks or sometimes rightly suspected excessive exploitation, or let their coworkers (and/or their supervisors) know that they have weapons available. Then they may seek to establish a sort of quasi Marxist distinction between themselves and the other workers and management. That is workers have everything in common with each other and should unite together against management. If a long standing worker agrees to influence a new worker to conform to the needs of management, then that worker is a turncoat, a traitor to the other workers. In other words worker intra group loyalty transcends or should transcend any company loyalty. This view is a sort of primitive leftish quasi Marxist ideology which when carried to extremes amounts to the effective sabotage of that individual's work ethic. If this view spreads throughout a nation or culture it may in effect amount to that society's effective assumption of low productivity and poverty, unless some other effective services are produced, and possibly even in that eventuality. Without some sort of disciplined work place some minimal level of obedience, of subservence of the individual initiative to some sort of disciplined production process, human culture, in the face of a temporary productive glut is likely to degenerate into a sort of anarchic meaningless pleasure seeking experience that is devoid of, that knows not either need for neither the rewards of deferred gratification. And the view that all discipline is merely an evil capitalist plot foisted upon the working class by a greedy capitalist class effectively refutes and condemns all such discipline as unnecessary and an affront to what should be. It also effectively gets in the way of processes which might generate sufficient production as to allow for effectively a significantly higher level of global and national prosperity that is the establishment of a higher minimal standard of living which might be shared by even the poorest individuals and countries.

November 15, 1998

Through the movies, through the movie stars, members of the audience may and often do acquire ideas of reference which are usually held in order to enhance their personal self esteem. Occasionally, the relation between an actor and a member of the audience transcends the idea of reference category of experience and becomes roughly equivalent to what used to be described as a relationship with a significant other. Typically, I suspect, the reason why actors may turn down certain roles which might reflect badly on their public image, their public persona if you will, is that if they accept roles in which they depict evil or weak characters, that as a result their viewers who regard them as significant others will become alienated. Therefore, it is suggested that in the event that significant movie actor personalities accede to acting in a variety of roles such that their true intentions must be plumbed directly before a personal assessment can be accurately made, that in that event the public's reliance upon superficial appearances as sole criteria for public social acceptance might be challenged and as a result, social interactions might become more satisfying in and of themselves and less seen as poor substitutes for what the self esteem starved member of mass society sees as their true objective namely association with people who are truly socially in, truly socially stars.

November 16, 1998

Bipolar or manic depressive syndrome or disorder as being caused partially by low levels of self-esteem. That individuals suffering from symptoms of this disorder may seek to elevate their own levels of (poor) self esteem by attempting to degrade the self-esteem of their putative emotional partners i.e. friends if you will. Individuals suffering from schizophrenic like disorders in which actual reasons for having high self esteem exist, but in which such high self estimates are deliberately suppressed or hidden from the self (and others) in order to avoid attack or rejection from family, friends or other significant others, such individuals suffering from schizophrenic like disorders make perverse sorts of partners for the manic depressive eager to elevate himself by putting down his "friend" since if he is able to make someone of genuine worth feel poorly about himself, then he may be able to believe, so long as the schizophrenic does not effectively reject his labeling, that he is superior to the schizophrenic. Since it is part of the schizophrenic's "illness" that he be able to shield himself from beliefs that are self laudatory which might cause him to suffer social or even physical attacks from those who see themselves as rightfully above him on the social status pecking order, he becomes a willing coconspirator with the manic depressive whose attempts to subvert the schizophrenic's self esteem are actually on one of the schizophrenic's own agendas. Of course the schizophrenic probably has other agendas as well, such as the wish to achieve without suffering retaliatory attack or without being destroyed by envious competitors and also being able to achieve some minimal level of personal and familial self fulfillment such as being able to marry, have children and sustain a minimal standard of living in which the children are able to live some sort of normal fulfilling life.

The manic depressive who nurses extremely inappropriate feelings of emotional and/or sexual possessiveness toward his or her partner may in threatening circumstances issue supposedly serious threats of rejection or mock threats of either violence or actual death in order to deter the feared loss of the loved relationship (through his displacement by a competitor). In Erich Fromm's terms, such love was given a particular label which I cannot remember, perhaps it was symbiotic, which can mean parasitic. The reference is from Fromm's book The Art of Loving if I remember correctly. If such an individual is either a latent homosexual or an actual homosexual or bisexual or merely has resigned himself as to the futility of ever achieving sexual fulfillment with a member of the opposite sex (perhaps he lives with his mother and his father is either passed on or moved out of the picture and so his mother fills the role of a spouse with whom sexual relations are taboo) in such a case in American society at present he is likely to suffer from generally imputed poor self esteem. The so called pro gay movement attempts to elevate such individuals esteem difficulties by attempting to defend its members against the imputation that their lives are less than full or less than adequate. However it would appear that homosexual individuals experience statements or gestures or actions that occur in public between heterosexual partners as refutations of their movement's attempts to defend and even praise their mode of adaptation. Hence if a homosexual has a friend who is not currently involved with a woman or has not been for some time he is likely to experience the onset of such a relationship as a threat to both his relationship with his friend as well as to his sense of self esteem which was based upon a shared understanding that a woman was not and is not necessary for either partner's happiness. Hence you have gay advocates for same sex marriage legislation pushing the rationalization that, as I heard on the radio the other day in regard I think to proposed legislation in Vermont, that "the institution of marriage is in a process of evolution." This is of course possible. However opponents of the proposed legislation could point out that the institution of marriage is also potentially subject to devolution and which label is appropriate is precisely what the debate is about.

This sort of micrometric picture of the struggle between manic depressives and schizophrenics also can be viewed as characteristic in part of the struggle between members of the middle and lower middle classes and the working and so called under classes. That is, a principle goal for members of the working and under classes is to elevate their own levels of self esteem. Whereas a principle goal for the members of the middle and lower middle classes, and the upper middle and upper classes as well, it goes without saying, is to maintain the levels of self esteem that they had inherited from their parents. Occasionally, of course the upwardly mobile succeed in instigating a more or less significant element of doubt into the self images of and levels of self estimation of those from higher societal origins. These elements of self doubt may also arise in part as a result of too much identification with a partner of incommensurate personal self esteem or overall status, or so it would seem. (Love is not the same sort of thing as is identification.)

When this occurs on a societal level of magnitude sociologically speaking, the result can involve a retaliatory impulse to punish the upwardly mobile, those from the so called poorer levels of society.

Level of status of the participant observer likely to influence his ability to elicit the most crucial and revealing information. That is when a participant observer is up front identified as an anthropologist or social scientist from a think tank or university (i.e. "This is Mr. Fred Smith from Cornell University. He is going to study you. Please give him your utmost cooperation.) who's avowed purpose is to obtain and record and reveal publicly crucial information that may reflect adversely on the level of prestige and self esteem of the actual or potential informants, that in such a case such crucial information may either not be forthcoming at all or it may be revealed only sparingly. On the other hand if the participant observer is not identified as such and if his assigned level of self importance within the research setting in question is not such as to inspire fear or for that matter particularly respect in the participants whose views are the object of the research, then it would appear that qualitatively different sorts of information are likely be obtained by such relatively unobtrusive participant observers.

November 19.1998

Perceived demand or marketability for military expenditures versus environmental and educational expenditures;

The so called market for military expenditures in the US is driven by a sort of national insecurity, a sort of fear of attack from poorer countries. This sort of fear has a natural constituency, a natural basis, although as peace extends its tenure, if peace extends its duration, as people grow accustomed to disputes being resolved short of military means the perceived need to expend large sums of the taxpayer's dollars on military readiness and sophistication is likely to diminish. However, in the interim as well as in the long run, novels, movies and even TV advertisements may be productively utilized by special interest organizations (like the Sierra Club, the Environmental Defense Fund, the Natural Resources Defense Council, CARE, Catholic Charities, The Red Cross, UNICEF, UNESCO, United Way, Physicians Without Borders, National Education Association, to name a few) which operate in the public interest and who have every right to purchase time on the public airways, whose causes can quite legitimately be advanced by either television networks, movie studios and/or publishing houses (all three of which could conceivably be given tax incentives to advance such causes). The point is that funding for clean air and clean water is a goal of whose desirability the public needs to be convinced. Whereas the danger of military attack is known by all. Hence if more tax dollars are to be spent for legislated expenditures toward educational or environmental ends then the public needs to be convinced of the need for such expenditures. It will not do for sanctimonious liberals to opine amongst themselves as to what should be done largely it seems in order to be able to assure themselves that they are superior to the irresponsible selfish conservatives and those members of the working and middle classes who refuse to follow their lead. In a democracy spending is for the most part not justified by fiat but rather by consensual agreement. Such agreement must be subject to debate, in regard to educational and environmental spending there is no question that there is currently vast opposition to such spending. Yet I have never seen any of the organizations mentioned above publish an ad in a magazine or broadcast even one television commercial. Such a televised expression of public interest advocacy could theoretically have an enormous impact in part because heretofore the only such expressions that I have seen have been anti smoking ads. Most other ads involve blatant appeals to make their producers wealthy by encouraging individual consumption.

Wage increases may constitute an antidote to an inflated stock market caused by an over-swollen money supply;

That a larger money supply may be less inflationary when a larger proportion of that increased supply is part of the wage pool thus stimulating demand. If the wage pool is not encouraged to soak up enough of the increased money supply, then the result is likely to involve inflated stock and bond prices, inflated because the share prices are unlikely to be supported in improved price/earnings ratios.

Generative origins of bipolar and schizoid syndromes

Note that bipolar syndrome is generally likely to arise in children grown to adults, especially in men, in cases where the child wins the competition with the father for the mother's attention. For example, this result might occur if the young adult grows or is seen as likely to grow to be significantly physically larger than the father, or if the mother in practice, after and during adolescence comes to be more frightened of the child's disapproval than of her husband's potential anger. In the opposite configuration, the husband wins the competition with his "child" or children either because the husband turns out to be larger physically than the grown up children or perhaps because the husband had defeated his father in competition when growing up and so vigorously resists being eclipsed by his own children—threatening them for example with expressions of intense anger when he senses significant increases in their expressed levels of autonomy and self esteem. The children of such bipolar syndrome holding fathers, particularly the male children, are likely to develop schizoid like syndromes which involve literally hiding their stronger qualities and accomplishments since they realize that any significant levels of success are likely to be greeted by their father or father figure with nominal approval but also anger and effective emotional rejection if not threatened random violence. Such hidden qualities can include nothing more significant than the fact or believed fact that "mom (and/or dad) really loves me more, she is merely afraid of and dependent on you (the father)." If an adolescent believes such a fact to be true the implications for his actions are likely to coalesce in adolescence and early adulthood rather than during the ages of one to five as Freud suggested. Similarly in girls the schizoid secret may be that she thinks and believes perhaps correctly, that the father "really finds his daughter more desirable than his wife (the mother)." A young woman who holds such a view may feel it necessary to suppress her femininity to the point where she appears mannish in nature and perhaps enters into lesbian like relationships or instead opts for the status of permanent old maid spinsterhood.

Fiction

For example, the Murdock sons both grew up to be significantly larger than their father who had walked with a significant limp. Certainly the older Murdock son exhibited the sort of threatening manic depressive like behaviour during his younger years described above toward the narrator if no one else. The younger Murdock son (and the narrator, who was a sort of quasi sibling) existed under the threat of his older brother's disapproval, the older brother functioning as, I suppose, a sort of manic depressive threatening surrogate father figure who probably induced the described schizoid like symptoms into the younger brother, i.e. let the belligerent older boy win. The narrator's father, on the other hand had had, he reports, had a quasi incestuous relationship with his mother during his childhood, and his mother had repeatedly verbally criticized her husband in front of the family, and he grew up to be significantly larger than his father, so that the narrators father was well aware of the dangers inherent in allowing his wife to freely reward her son's accomplishments either verbally or emotionally. Any such expressions, indeed after the son moved out of the house to go to college, any moves on the son's part to form spontaneous potentially sexual relations with a nubile woman were greeted even at long distance over the telephone, with seemingly psychically informed expressions of verbal anger and hence implicitly disapproval. The father used to say, quoting the book of Ecclesiastes I think, that for "everything there is a season and a time to every purpose, under heaven." But as far as his son was concerned, that time never seemed to arrive. Perhaps the father felt that he would be unable to maintain his intellectual relation with his son, the son had graduate training in both anthropology and sociology and the father had a PhD. in sociology and was a law professor, or perhaps on some unconscious level the father feared that the arrival of his son's children would signal the end of his justification for existence, his will to live. Whatever the cause, the narrator never seemed to get any professional recognition for his writing and yet schizoid like nursed the belief that his writing was in fact extremely important on the professional level, on the so called cutting edge of the fields in which he worked, if you will. Still it could not really be said that the narrator was hiding this belief from himself. Rather if the belief were true, that if his work was in fact of extremely high quality, then the blame for his negligible social and professional life needs to be placed on his correspondents, including his father, who have failed in most cases to respond to the narrator's pieces of writing which he shares with a variety professional journals. So the correspondents have failed to respond and while the narrator suspects paranoiaclly that his work is being published unbeknownst to himself, he recognizes that this is a self aggrandizing paranoiac like suspicion and so keeps it to himself. He does not, in manic like manner, brag about his accomplishments, although given half a chance he would very likely do some serious damage to the manic like self esteem of some of his friends, especially those friends, including his father, who regularly minimize or ignore what he considers to be the true value of his contributions to social science and humanity. (Note that the narrator's father neither encourages nor discourages autonomy and innovation in the narrator's writing, rather, it is taken for granted.)

Psychotherapy and the bipolar/schizoid relation

Note that the psychotherapist may regularly play the complementary role in her relation with her patient. For example if the patient suffers from a schizoid like need to hide himself, the therapist may play the role of the manic depressive esteem deflator. Or if the patient suffers from the belief that he is really a fraud, that is if he realizes or suspects that his position in life is due to threatening coercive gestures that he has made or is continuing to make, then the therapist could conceivably play along with his constructed attempt to maintain a high self image, for example, reinforcing his likely in fact over achieved level of attainments as legitimate i.e. saying for example, "of course you earned your position, of course you earned your grades, of course you deserve your salary…" Whether such a strategy actually helps the manic depressive is another question. However it is well to keep in mind that most manic depressives are in fact threatening individuals who punish those who do not grant them the sort of acknowledgements that they feel they need and are justified in holding. Hence the therapist (or for that matter teacher or professor) dealing with a manic depressive is in fact likely to feel personally threatened and so not feel particularly guilty about puncturing the bubble of esteem with which such individuals tend to surround themselves. (Editor's note: the author is and was aware that for example Beethoven is generally considered to have been manic depressive; and that many if not most schizophrenics often seem zombie like, perhaps overmedicated and unremarkable. So that these observations tend to pertain mostly to himself and a limited number of others. For example, if Beethoven were alive today and living in a secular western society, his illness and likely his music would have a different edge. because he would likely be receiving some sort of psychotropic medication.) Perhaps that is why the world is filled with many more mediocre individuals than with those who are truly excellent. The mediocre tell us that they are excellent since they know we will not believe them and so will not feel threatened in our levels of self esteem. The excellent in fact constitute threats to the self esteem of the mediocre and so either tend to hide their lights under wraps or else to quickly either whither and fade or be destroyed in full public view. Theoretically it is possible of course for an individual of excellence to hide the excellence under a pseudonym while advancing himself under the persona of declared excellence. The narrator has labored under the view that this latter course of action has been followed by his previously described father. However, it is clear that the belief that one's father is an excellent high achiever covertly, writing under a variety of pseudonyms, while it is a view encouraged by the narrator's father through a series of suggestive remarks, is clearly a view which aids the narrator's self esteem (through prestige by association), and it encourages the narrator in his decisions to intermittently utilize pseudonyms and in his efforts to continue to write in the absence of any encouragement from those who would be his professional colleagues and potentially peers and friends, should they choose to recognize the worth of his efforts.

November 21, 1998

Fiction; the narrator's parents

His mother had been for the most part a physically weak person. At one point it was revealed that her sister, five years younger, had been stronger than his mother when they were children, having been able at a relatively early age to outfight (the mother). So in terms of primitive psychology, primary process psychology if you will, it appears that the mother needed and looked for in marriage what is termed in sociology as "a protector," that is someone who is large and potentially threatening who will threaten or apply some sort of pain directly to those who might consider attacking, either verbally or physically, the protectee. According to Goffman, that is why prison inmates form alliances. And indeed the analogy seems to apply on the so called street as well. The people who get mugged tend to be people who have not formed alliances with other males or persons willing and able to administer retaliatory pain. Clearly these alliances can be either sexual or merely emotional, merely affiliational. The point is however that whatever their basis, they must be mutually rewarding. So that if someone's partner is attacked, his friend must care sufficiently so that some significant retaliatory action occurs. However, the premise of such alliances needs to be clarified and clearly mutually understood.

For example, the protectee is likely to have no more rights and freedom than he or she insists upon retaining. Hence the narrator's mother found herself in a somewhat ideal relationship with her husband, in fact, after he became crippled with polio. As noted, the disease forced and forces him to walk with the aid of a cane which potentially serves also as a weapon. Hence his excuse for carrying a weapon around with him at all times is obviously, that he is crippled. Yet his limited mobile capacity enables him to assume a psychologically threatening stance in relation to those with whom he interacts. This is particularly the case since his upper body, always quite strong, has grown even stronger as a result of years of walking with the cane, sometimes canes, so that in the event that he or a friend of his were attacked, he would be unable to run away, as the law often seems to require, and would also because of his great personal strength, in all likelihood, be capable of administering a lethal blow to the head of any assailant (with the cane). On the other hand, being significantly disabled by the disease he also seems vulnerable to potentially devastating sneak attacks, so that the mother and his children and friends, who see him and interact with him regularly in unguarded moments, feel free to write, think and act pretty much as they choose, although in the event that writings are shared with the father, the writer, the narrator, for example, risks incurring displeasure. At the same time, unless work is shared, whether it is writing or painting or music, it does no good to anyone and cannot constitute a justification for a mutually reinforcing intellectually based alliance or relationship. Meanwhile, the mother, who is a somewhat alluring female figure, functions also as her husband's protector, shielding him from the sexual advances of younger male collaborators who may occasionally be inclined to attempt to advance their career causes by making advances toward an older man who is apparently otherwise quite happy to share his considerable expertise in a variety of fields with both men and women.

Justifications for socioeconomic mobility: need for more self esteem vs. merit
Date: 11/30/98 12:03:25 PM Eastern Standard Time
to: the editors (The American Prospect, The Nation, The New Yorker)
from: Andréas Daniel Fogg
Letter from Somerville November 22, 1998

When a society bases its decisions vis a vis social status on the perceived need for personal advancement as opposed to merely achieved merit, then a disproportionate emphasis is placed upon personal aggressiveness, indeed occupational advancement is likely to be assumed to be an indication of personal aggressiveness rather than of any particular merit, certainly as the skills required to perform crucial societal tasks become relatively easier to accomplish, because of computerization, socioeconomic status may well come to reflect ruthlessness more than skill, competence or wisdom. If the highest quality work is done more out of loyalty or for the goal of achieving respect or earning affection, rather than for the end of pulling down a large paycheck, then our understanding of how work is to be motivated may need reevaluation. In this regard it is important to distinguish between work involving the facilitation of virtually any information, that is content neutral work, such as work which makes communication of any sort possible, such as developing the Internet and e-mail, versus work in which the content of that which is communicated constitutes the relative value or lack thereof of the work. The latter sort of work may not respond well to pecuniary motivation, this being the case since the magnitude of the reward offered for content based work is likely to have a direct effect on the quantity and quality of work in such areas that has yet to be produced. So if there is a large reward for a book for example, the writer may be inclined to continue in that vein, in order to earn more similar rewards or he may be inclined to change direction, or he might have changed direction if he was not responding to the market cues. The question arises whether content producers need best to follow the mass market or to lead it. And the answer to that question is that they should probably attempt to lead the mass market and that such attempts may not result necessarily in large scale rewards if successful. Think, sports and the content-less mechanisms of computer technology earn some of the largest mass market monetary rewards, whereas poets earn pauper like wages and many struggling writers earn nothing. Yet in the end, whose contributions are more important?

What if someone, a writer for example, feels no particular need for a boost in his own self esteem? What if he feels no wish to supervise or manage or control his fellow human beings? What if he is content to limit his contribution to writing materials which he distributes but which no one is required to necessarily read? Does that mean that he should not be paid for anything like the market value of his work whereas those "supervisors and managers" who are indeed eager to "take the responsibility" and assume the privilege of manipulating workers are paid in exorbitant amounts?

In the ultimate scheme of things items which are offered but not forced on people are more valuable than objects which are required to be consumed or which are force fed through compulsion inducing advertising.

If pushiness is regularly rewarded and valued over stoicism, then genuine humility is likely to become a scarce commodity.

November 24, 1998

Musings about professional sports stadium roulette, the competitive bidding game;

What if it was or could be outlawed? What if a private owner of a professional sports franchise when in need of greater profits and greater community financial support, what if such a group of owners or a single owner was required by law to first attempt to raise needed funds by either borrowing at prevalent interest rates and/or by issuing an IPO (which stands for I think, Initial Public Offering) that is offering to sell shares of his team to the public which shares would pay perhaps some dividend (presuming that they reached some agreed upon value), so that the members of the community, who wished to finance in this case the desired new stadium, could express their desire concretely by buying a part share of the team. Such a move would constitute in fact a measure of voluntary individually subsidized community support and in fact might assure the continued location of a franchise in a given location, presuming that enough local residents were willing to maintain a controlling interest.

At the same time it may be well worth considering the possible question as to what would happen if corporations of a manufacturing nature dispensed with the option of playing one location off against another in order to see who can be coerced into giving up the most tax breaks. What if that sort of competition as well were declared to be illegal and what if each time a corporation considered relocating, the only question they were allowed to consider was "how much of their outstanding stock is held and will be held at the time of the proposed move by residents of the proposed new location?" What if it was simply deemed illegal in the United States or for that matter in the entire world for communities and states to alter their tax policies in order to attract corporate residents?

Two scholars specializing in population growth and the significance of weapons of mass destruction, speaking on the radio just now, seemed to claim some credit for the fact that the world population level seems to be leveling off, since they had been writing on the topic for several decades at least. A listener expressed astonishment that they should claim some of the credit for this development, as if academics were presumed to have no ego needs whatsoever, as if intellectual public pronouncements presumably do not have an effect upon global unfolding developments. Apparently professional intellectuals' works are taken for granted by large numbers of the membership of mass society. Such a taking for granted attitude may begin to explain the reluctance to fund preparatory public educational endeavors and the lack of respect with which so many members of the university based academy seem to be regarded by the typical consumer in secular mass society.

November 29, 1998

Some degree of public ownership of professional sports franchises required as a prerequisite for the utilization of publicly licensed media;

From some certain date, that thereafter all professional sports franchises which would continue to seek to profit from the use of publicly licensed broadcasting facilities, facilities that is, which service the public markets, from such a date such franchises must place on the public market shares equal in value to 49 percent of their total extant shares and that in the event that ownership of such franchises seeks to increase its' profitability by extracting public benefits from local communities or states in return for relocating to said community, that such extractive competitive corporate or company generated extortive depletion of a local tax base's funds shall be prohibited by state, national and international legislation and be punishable by significant fines and/or imprisonment of responsible corporate or company officers.

—That the present situation is such that members of virtually any corporate management team seek to maintain their market share and justify their salaries and privileges, a substantial proportion of which, it is alleged, are sustained by such corporate (welfare) extractive procedures, by claiming that their relatively larger salaries are justified by their "people skills" which often tend to allegedly consist in adherence to a supposedly higher, purer level of sexual morality. These higher levels of income in turn tend to be boosted higher, by way of comparison to the exorbitant levels of pay given out to professional athletes who participate in sports which the mass television market favors, which levels of pay are substantially sustained by profits given back by television networks, a substantial portion of which profits arguably rightfully belong to the public and therefore should rightfully be taxed at a higher rate than that at which they are in fact taxed (it is argued) at present (?); certainly higher than the top rate for personal income.

Societal systemic imbalance caused by tax policies toward media functions;

This argument is based on the notion that a systemic imbalance is being generated in the society by virtue of the fact that the privilege of serving the consumer market by broadcasting a wide variety of news, sports and entertainment "products" on television and radio is being given away far too cheaply and that the alleged fact of cheap give away licenses and corporate taxes that are also in the process of being lowered, presently I am under the impression that the top corporate tax rate is below the top rate for the federal personal income tax, that these facts may constitute a substantial causal component of the increased magnitude of the gap between the so called deserving extremely wealthy elites and the working and shrinking middle classes. That is, again, professional sports franchises have vast television generated profits available to them which the athletes have succeeded in taping through judicious bargaining. The corporate elite and American society as a whole feels a need to match these salaries so that those who work at the less remunerative occupations whether within corporations or for that matter in agriculture and small business, education, law, medicine etc. feel that through a process of identification with the highly paid elites, whether in sports or in the major corporations, that they too can participate in what they fantasize these enormous salaries can yield. Keep in mind that in a consumer oriented society happiness comes to be defined as being rich enough to be able to purchase in virtually unlimited quantities the finest most luxurious and expensive consumer commodities that are available. These commodities include in the fantasists' minds, beautiful people serving as agreeable and amenable sex objects who are satisfied through the purchase of innumerable expensive consumer commodities.

I note a fictional informant who once expressed the view that he was gratified that "the same people are rich today as were rich thirty and fifty years ago." This same individual, we will call him "Fred" has expressed admiration for the ideas of Adolf Hitler. He also, interestingly enough, claims to be a second cousin once removed of a famous Yankee Republican politician. It seems to be tremendously important to this individual that top management continues to receive exorbitantly large salaries, as if the magnitude of the salaries amounted to a sort of crucial component of his view of how power should be distributed in society. In this view women respond first of all to men who have lots of money. In this view it is largely inconceivable that any "decent looking woman" would be willing to show loyalty to a poorly paid man, even if he were very smart. This view is familiar to the psychiatrists and psychologists, it is the view that women are essentially more interested in money than in love, or that if they are interested in love they also show a willingness to betray love in return for money. Most people don't like to talk about this view of women, or for that matter of men—the same view can be applied toward men by women, I might add, yet it may be serving as a partial justification for the growing gap between the very rich and the rest of us. The so called "perpetual adolescent" male may be thinking "there is and should not be any higher objective, as far as I am concerned, than succeeding in big time so called 'major' sports. I am angry and disappointed that so many non white men are succeeding in those sports. It makes me uncomfortable that so many of those Hispanic and African American men are getting very rich but I have no idea whether there is anything wrong with their getting all that money, after all, there is no denying their athletic skills and abilities, I just wish that white athletes were getting the money. I wish I had that money myself, but to tell the truth, I have no idea whether having such an income would in fact make me happy, in fact, I merely assume that having that much money would be the best thing that could happen to me. Since the mass market sports stars are getting all that money, I feel that it is important that the "true leaders of society" that is those who are "most responsible" for the success of our major corporations should be able to compete and win in competitive consuming, in displays of conspicuous consumption, so that some white men will be able to defeat the non white professional athletes who I admire yet resent so much." This as far as I have been able to determine is how Fred thinks. Fred is unusual in that he is willing to express some such views out loud, that is enough of them so that the narrator is able to fill in the blanks. Fred might well deny that his views are effectively summarized above. The allegation is that whether Fred and lots of others in the society know it or not, many of them hold some or all of the above attitudes and that these attitudes are sustaining and justifying both the growing gap between the very rich and the working and shrinking middle classes and the decreasing percentages of the American GDP per capita devoted to public education. Note that the view is that women "want" not sex, not affection but rather to be lavished with more expensive consumables which they can display so as to be able to win old lingering struggles with their siblings and adolescent peers, struggles as to whom is more important, who gives way to whom, who stands where on the communal and societal pecking order. And the thought is that those truly in possession of merit, of God's grace, if you will, can actually dispense with physical pleasure, indeed that the ability to completely control one's physical cravings and drives, except for those which involve procreation, constitutes evidence of personal superiority, evidence that such an individual is "above all that sub human animal stuff." Hence the need to pillory and attack those who are suspected of occupying positions of leadership and status in the society yet have not succeeded in sufficiently repressing their drives toward women. Note that there have been relatively fewer attacks on individuals for alleged inappropriate homosexual behaviors. It may perhaps be noted that there is a branch of the Republican conservative group, the so called "Log Cabin Republicans" which may well be willing to turn a blind eye to such activities, believing, the narrator suspects, that sex between "consenting male adults" is superior to the exploitation of the "economically and physically weaker women," who, it is archaically believed, "really don't like sex anyway."

Normative effects of television viewing as the primary mode of communication and cultural transmission;

Note that the so called "virtuous viewer," the socially appropriate viewer, does not attempt to make actual interpersonal contact with the objects of their fascination who appear either in the movies or on television. Hence the norm of not touching, of literally refraining from touching those who archetypically hold our attention is established through the widespread cultural experience of utilizing television watching as a means of staying culturally and economically oriented. This norm is then replicated by the economically elite as a sort of justification for their own economically elite status i.e. we don't practice sexual harassment, in fact we're above the use of sex for other than purely procreative purposes. Recreational sex is for undeserving people who, (we don't like to say this out loud because it makes us look racist), do not fully have control over their "lower" natures. Unless of course we are talking about same sex experiences which improve our job security. But we don't like to talk about those either. Basically the appropriate participant in what can loosely be called television culture believes in looking at attractive people as much as possible and, wherever possible, avoiding having to touch or be touched by anyone. The problem with this orientation is that touching experiences are crucial to the regeneration of physical and emotional vitality, indeed arguably touching and resultant sexual arousal in moderation can lead to the retardation of the aging process itself.

Racial antagonism, distantiation, admissibility of PJones suit, sperm bank donor
Date: 12/7/98 10:24:56 AM Eastern Standard Time
To: the editors (The American Prospect, The Nation, and The New Yorker)
From: Andréas Daniel Fogg
Letter from Somerville December 1, 1998

Notes: that interracial antagonism between males stems in part from personal confusion on the part of the participants as to what level of personal status should be "claimed." In White/Black interactions, which tend to occur relatively rarely, the identities of the participants are often unknown. Hence it is potentially possible for an African American man to "pose" as a highly paid professional athlete who as such probably possesses a higher level of status (and wealth) and personal self esteem than the presumed level of status and accruing income accompanying his White counterpart. Hence the Black man must face the dilemma, should he attempt to put the White man down or treat him with respect, leaving the door open for potentially friendly relations. The dilemma is difficult because if the Black man leaves the door open for friendly relations he runs the risk of either being ignored or he appears to be vulnerable to an implied or stated racial slur. If he puts the White man down, which he usually does (or attempts to do), he has a temporary feeling of euphoric superiority, but he reinforces any feelings of racism that might exist in the White man and, he does not advance to any extent any sought for socioeconomic advancement (for either himself or his African American peers) in a multiracial society which so far continues to be economically dominated by Whites.

Impeachment, Paula Jones case and the Supreme Court;

Anthony Lewis suggests in the current TAP (The American Prospect) that the Supreme Court erred when it allowed the Paula Jones suit against President Clinton to proceed during his term. I had been under the impression that the President and indeed Senators and Congressmen, if not members of the Judiciary, had some sort of limited immunity from prosecution that is immunity from prosecution for non impeachable offenses. Such immunity would, it would seem, be designed to shield them from being preoccupied by petty politically motivated, perhaps wholly contrived law suits that would amount to the utilization of criminal or civil charges to accomplish a new form of "political mudslinging" and harassment.

December 6, 1998

The sperm bank donor as Darwinian hero, humanistic and religious antihero;

This is a relatively new can of worms that probably needs to be opened. A whole series of observations needs to be made. For example, a year or two ago a female feminist named I think Catherine Mackinnon (?) observed and was published to the effect that all heterosexual acts of coitus involved, included, could be characterized as "acts of rape." These statements were published and reviewed in the New York Times as intellectually respectable contributions to the presumably intelligent discussion of what the relations between the sexes were supposed to be and what they might become. It should be suggested that Ms. Mackinnon's statements to this effect were facilitated by, were rendered possible and conceivable in part because of the existence and availability of sperm donor banks. Note too, that the existence of such banks allows humanity to retreat from heterosexual intimacy, allows for such acts to be classified as undesirable, unnecessary, inconvenient and unwanted, yea even unnatural. So that in a brave new world where reproduction need not involve even affection, certainly not physical contact, children will (may) be the result of economic and genetic calculations. Not only will "God" have nothing to do with getting their two parents together and in the right frame of mind, but also there will have been no physical love present at their creation.

The narrator labors under the impression that such in vitro children have been generated for some numbers of years now and that donors are often selected for both good looks and intelligence, so that it makes sense that these children as well as those created more naturally may be gravitating toward the better colleges and universities or perhaps merely toward the larger urban areas. It is likely that during the courses of their childhoods and adolescences that someone may come to suspect that they are different, perhaps the mother is likely to drop some hint, after all presumably the mother knows whether her children are natural or in vitro children. Such hints in turn may generate significant levels of interpersonal anxiety which may become exacerbated into full blown diagnosed mental illnesses. Such diagnoses in turn can inhibit the individual from attempting to have children or from forming a stable relationship with a member of the opposite sex. All this because the mother sought total control over the male sexual reproductive input. This is the can of worms that I am attempting to open or reopen. In Darwinian terms, the selected sperm bank donor likely thinks of himself as superior to other males (who are not donors). After all, he has succeeded in spreading his seed far beyond the possible achievements of males who are not selected. And his children, presuming that they tend to look like each other, to the extent that they look like each other enough, may physically function as legal alibis should one of them become a defendant in a criminal court proceeding i.e. "you saw the defendant leaving the scene of the crime on the day and at the time in question. I see. Are you sure it wasn't the gentleman or lady presently standing in the back of the court room? Oh, you aren't sure, they look so much alike. No further questions, your honor...." Hence such individuals may begin to appear as threatening potentially dangerous potentially criminal monstrosities all the more so remember because they were not conceived "in love." Ah, the wonders of modern genetic science and technology. Yet to the primitive Darwinian theorist, he who would equate human evolution with the evolutionary processes of the so called less advanced species, the sperm bank donor is a hero, never mind that he may be obnoxious, precisely because he regards himself as superior to other males, even "God's gift to women," and that the procedures and norms that he and others like him help make possible (indeed are advancing and promoting) may be contributing to the destruction of the qualities and pleasantries of interpersonal heterosexual public lifestyles for the rest of us. In other words, if homosexuals insist on equating heterosexuality with rape, such an insistence amounts to holding a belief which denies that sexual lust is capable of being melded with love and which accuses all heterosexuals of being the equivalent of criminal sexual offenders. That is give them an inch and they take a mile. The movement toward tolerance for so called gay people has been turned on its head to the point where they are accusing so called straight people of being degenerates. Surely some sort of compromise short of this dramatic and emotionally debilitating and destructive reversal is both possible and desirable.

December 7, 1998

A Darwinian definition of success;

Note that in a Darwinian evolutionary scheme of values success would be constituted not by the person with the most "toys," neither the most money, neither the most movies produced nor books published, neither would the label be applied to a person who considered themselves to be the "happiest." No, according to the Darwinian schema success is defined, the label is applied to persons whose genes go on to survive and dominate the species; in other words, on a simplistic level, over the short term, the most successful individual is he (or presumably she) who has the most children. Note too, that the sperm bank donor while seeming to fulfill his Darwinian mission, imposes the pain of childbirth on innumerable women while at the same time depriving them of what, before the radical feminists and gays had their say, used to be called "the joy of sex." The idea that sex can be a joyful, romantic experience has now, it is suggested, become politically incorrect. The MacKinnon view has already been noted. Note too observations on Saturday Night Live in which actors note sarcastically that "so and so actually likes sex." The narrator is acquainted with a member of management at his place of employment who has remarked, with the authority of a member of management with great job security, "Have you ever looked at the faces of people when they are actually having sex? They seem to be in pain!" This interpretation presumably is taken after viewing films of actor's simulating sexual experiences, simulations which are characterized by a painful realized violation of the actors' privacy.

It should also be noted that the criteria for choosing sperm bank donors are unclear and not discussed in the public realm. Some donors are it is rumored, medical students, some, it is rumored, are Nobel Laureates. Low budget donors may be merely willing and deemed relatively normal. Whatever their characteristics, they constitute implicitly a defined group of "winners" who may in the long run be causing the society to lust after an unrealistic and dysfunctional definition of success.

Identification with movie actors may induce paranoia
Date: 12/19/98 2:53:57 PM Eastern Standard Time
To: the editors (The American Prospect, The Nation, and The New Yorker)

From: Andréas Daniel Fogg
Letter from Somerville December 9, 1998

First, consider, why would someone identify with a movie star? Perhaps because they receive so much attention and are so very well paid. But note that they tend, often in the pursuit of realism or if you will, social realism, to portray extremely intimate behavior, behaviors that most ordinary people would prefer to perform either behind closed or locked doors or else under the cover of darkness, that is behaviors that most people would seek to shield from the public view, that is for which performance they would seek privacy. Of course I am speaking primarily about how sex is depicted in the movies. And in general, for some considerable number of years the cinema industry has attempted to portray sexual behavior with, if you will, no holds bared realism. Of course what is displayed is in most cases merely simulated sex that is actions which entail physical intimacy i.e. physical contact, often nude or semi nude physical contact, embraces, kisses, deep kisses. But actual passion, actual physical sexual arousal, the depiction of real desire is more difficult to portray, particularly when camera crews, lights, directors and of course cameras surround the actor and usually actress. So what we usually get is the depiction of physical intimacy, French kissing, for example, that is done on someone else's commands i.e. "lights, camera, action…." without any real hope of having it mean something to the participants. What this paradigm of behavior teaches to the viewing public is that intimacy without desire is highly rewarded and that the emotions associated with allowing oneself to be intimate in exchange for large amounts of money all the while being filmed for public indiscriminate viewing, that those emotions and feelings are valued and well reimbursed by the society and therefore appropriate for utilization and imitation by ordinary viewers. And one wonders why the society so often seems to be a joyless place.

December 12, 1998

What about the advisability of staging a confrontational televised "teach-in" on the subject of global warming, inviting proponents and opponents of the thesis that excessive levels of carbon dioxide in the atmosphere are causing significant levels of global warming and that said alleged global warming is having catastrophic effects on the planet's accrued levels of storm related damage, not to mention the increased significant probability of flooding of sea level land areas. Note that participants would needs reveal publicly any stock ownership in carbon dioxide producing enterprises as well as any direct occupational links which might suggest that a conflict of interest is present which might tend to bias their supposedly objective scientific opinions. Such a teach-in could be broadcast nationally in the United States as well as translated for broadcast in other countries.

That the essence of being a socially acceptable, "cool" "hip" member of a mass society lies in not having any perceptibly unique opinions. The basic notion that seems to be required as a precondition for social acceptance lies in not violating the precept that all opinions are of equal value. To in any way imply that one's opinion might be superior in quality to the opinions expressed by mass media outlets (for acceptable opinions) is to label oneself deviant and socially unacceptable. Indeed, the mere fact that one has stated an opinion that might serve to educate or teach media spokesmen what they might say next, suggests that one is socially anomalous, that is that one does not fit into any preconceived social roles that the society is capable of understanding. The basic premise of mass culture is that in fact all opinions are of equal value. To state an opinion whose quality is such that the immediate inference is that the speaker, or writer is significantly smarter than either the media spokesmen or for that matter, the academic powers that be, is to suggest that such a speaker or writer is someone whose very existence constitutes a threat to the basic presumption of the mass media audience, namely that it is futile to talk back to the media outlets since they are by definition the smartest and best arbiters of what is possible and allowable. Hence anyone who has an opinion that the media elite are unwilling to broadcast tends to keep such thoughts to themselves, since as the members of the working class tend to say "thinking only gets me into trouble."

But the nature of the trouble, it is suggested, tends to be generated by the would be speaker, since to offer an opinion that might challenge the definitions of timely and appropriate thought propagated by the media, amounts to the commission of a rebellious, often guilt generating act against the powers that be and indeed against the very definition of personal insignificance upon which mass culture rests.

Fiction: family names or surnames;

    There is an individual, we will call him Ted who had an unusual surname. Now the reader will please bear with the writer here. No political incorrectness or racial slur is meant or intended. The surname is used because although it means in itself a racial slur, the name is essential to the story. Ted's last name is "Nigger." And he always seemed to be making friends with people who had very impressive last names

Like, for example, one of his friends was named "Zimmerman," which means in German I think, "superman." And another of his friends had the name of a Presidential family, one had the name "Captained" another had the name "Gold" in it, another was named "Allen Moses." You get the idea. Often too he tended to become friends with young men who were also named "Ted" but instead of having surnames which seemed to slur their owner's status, as he did, they tended to have names which implicitly enhanced their own status, such as those described. And it was these friends who insisted that he be known as "Ted Nigger" whereas they merited the status of being the basic essential clearly known, just plain "Ted." So that if someone said "Ted, what do you think?" Ted Nigger would know that they did not mean him. If they meant him they would have called him Ted Nigger, you see.

It is also vaguely important that Ted Nigger was, well he had blond hair that was slightly kinky, I guess, a roundish nose, clearly not aquiline, but really quite white skin, although, it sometimes seemed a little grayish or even greenish, it is difficult to say, he looked a little different from most Caucasians, perhaps the skin was of a slightly different quality. And sometimes he looked older than other times, sometimes dramatically so. At any rate TN felt that he was basically accepted as friends by these perhaps you might call them codependents, on the condition that his role be defined as the less than important "sidekick" component of the duo, i.e. someone who was there to lend support, to make the leading part of the duo look more important, since he had clearly an intelligent supporting friend, who most people shied away from associating with on their own due the stigma associated with Ted's last name, which as is well known, suggests that that name's holder was descended from people who had been slaves, that is, had little family status indeed negative family status. And hence one need not wonder why genuine African American peoples have difficulty holding acceptable leading roles in society, since their physical characteristics themselves suggest that they are descended from slaves, rather than from socially prominent families.

That the principle that "to think is dangerous" actually has come to constitute a so called 'categorical imperative;'

In other words those individuals who think, speak and write critically about what is happening in society and about the law itself, such individuals actually in a sense are violators of a categorical imperative against all critical thought. The rationale for this imperative, I suppose, is found in the question, "what if everybody questioned whether the status quo was OK?" to which an implicit answer is, "why there would be chaos!" Hence this imperative suggests, there must be penalties associated with critical thought. But if these penalties are rigorous, the thinking continues, then certain rewards are needed as well in order to induce some intelligent criticism, because clearly society needs critical input if it is to continually refine and correct itself. It is not enough, as the members of the Federalist Society of Lawyers proclaim, to discuss "what the law is." New and better laws must come from somewhere, they are not merely miraculously spontaneously generated. And most legislators are so busy getting reelected and following the polls that the inspiration for valid and needed new laws is unlikely to be found amongst their ranks, although some of them may be inclined to read certain critical materials put together by academic and free lance critics and writers which would tend to suggest what is presently lacking in the organization and values of the society. But such potential critics suffer, as it has been suggested, from negative sanctions put upon them by members of the mainstream society who tend to be most intent upon defending what is and what was against what might be since, their reasoning goes, what might be could all together amount to a series of less satisfactory outcomes, a regression or devolution rather than a progressive evolution. Hence the eternal conflict between liberalism and conservatism. It would appear however, that of the two solutions i.e. first that there should be no support for critical activities and second that critical activities should be sustained and encouraged and engaged in conversation with by conservatives, that the second is to be preferred.

December 13, 1998

Privatizing Social Security;

Privatizing all or part of the Social Security Trust Fund, that is giving people the option of putting some of their funds in the stock market seems on the surface like a good idea, and the temptation to invest would likely be great. However, one should keep in mind that when the baby boomers start retiring in large and larger numbers, there is some real possibility that significant withdrawals from the market could trigger a crash, which might devastate those who had sought to rely on the market earnings for their retirement savings. A situation might well arise where those who jumped out of the market first would salvage most of their earnings whereas those who sought to ride out the crash might eventually end up losing much of their nest eggs. Further, as it is pointed out in a Nation article, privatizing even part of the Social Security Trust Fund without raising social security taxes would seem to necessitate lowering benefits, whereas what is probably desirable is to raise benefits.

A different definition of who is a Jew;

A Jew in the positive sense is he or she who remembers or is able to visualize or feel empathy, that is, who remembers or understands what it is like to have either been a slave, or to have lived with great hardship, and therefore seeks to ease the burdens of the oppressed peoples of the planet. Such a definition minimizes without totally precluding from relevance the number of times that one blesses God, also the sincerity with which one prays to God. Such attempts to placate God are considered perhaps personally satisfying, and probably satisfying to God and to anyone who considers himself to be God as well, but they basically are ways to avoid the problem of how one should behave economically and socially toward one's fellow human beings, of whatever religious orientation. This definition of who is a Jew is unlikely to please all Jews and it may well include under its umbrella significant numbers of peoples of nominally different religions. It is clearly, probably, more of a statement of political, ideological values than it is a religious statement. But then I am presently far more interested in political and economic realities and their moral implications than I am in considerations of religious ritual.

December 14, 1998

Aging, divorce and sexual promiscuity;

A relatively small number of personal observations suggest that several divorces perhaps accompanied by a significantly liberated promiscuous sexual life style on the part of women, that such a combination has resulted in at least several cases, in an acceleration of the aging process that as such has resulted in significant premature aging. On the other hand it also appears on the basis of a small number of observations, that isolation, repressing even the possibility of the experience of wanting, of sexual desire, in whatever direction also may result in premature aging. That is, an individual who is so hounded by his or her partner, so hounded, that is that they refuse to allow themselves to interact and react to multiple other persons even on a platonic level, such a person is also likely to experience probably depressive symptoms and premature aging.

Part Two: Winter

Anomic panic in the public sphere, the conditions of media production and guilt
Date: 12/21/98 10:08:38 AM Eastern Standard Time
To: the editors (The American Prospect, The Nation, and The New Yorker)
From: Andréas Daniel Fogg
Letter from Somerville December 19, 1998

Legitimate needs for privacy and voyeuristic media culture

Note that most people have a legitimate interest in concealing their sexual actions from the view of both the general public and indeed of anyone other than the immediate participants. This need stems from the need to avoid triggering jealousy, anger and envy. The assumption that one's sexual behavior even in marriage should be disclosed to the public view or even should be a matter of public spokespersons' legitimate inquiry, this assumption rests on the view that human beings are not subject to envy or any of the weaker emotions and that therefore there is in fact no need for sexual privacy. Note that in the movies and soap operas, sexual interactions typically take place either in daylight or with the lights on, rarely are the lights off, rarely the participants naked or semi clothed and in bed. Perhaps this is the case because the voyeuristic thrill is dependent on the lights being on, so that the "action" can be filmed. Whatever the reason, probably inadvertently, the assumption or definition of appropriateness has been extended by implication, from the widespread depiction of sexual behavior in full, well lighted public view, the definition of what is appropriate has come to include the idea that sexual behavior should not be hidden, should not be cloaked in privacy. Indeed it appears that those who would seek to conceal the nature of their sexual interactions seem to be implicitly guilty of a normative infraction, as if to have something to hide cannot possibly be justified, since it is a state of being that the media refuses to acknowledge can be justified.

December 20, 1998

Note that the precept that there should be a separation between church and state may or may not amount to a state of affairs wherein the actions and decisions (and allocations of funds) of the state may be characterized by either no values or values of questionable sociological justification. The question needs to be raised, in fact, whether in declared absence of religious values, seemingly quasi Darwinian so called sub human values, are moving to the fore by way of default. That is, when religious values, which also can be humanistic values, fail to be either rationally or humanistically sufficiently justified that is justified other than through the appeal to their supposedly divine sources, then such values are likely to be superseded by Darwinian values such as amount to the notion that might makes right or more concretely that distributing the genes of talented individuals takes precedence over needs for individual happiness, family emotional support and indeed individual and group held sustainable mental stability.

Note that the utilization of sperm banks amounts to in effect the triumph of lesbian values. I.e. procreation through in vitro fertilization allows women who harbor homosexual desires (either latently and unbeknownst to themselves, or manifestly) for each other to procreate without having their jealousy of a potential male partner be challenged by the actual participation of a male partner in a real act of sexual intercourse. Hence the triumph of the "scientific immaculate conception." Hence also by extrapolation, absent new, sufficient economic and cultural and emotional incentives, the end of the heterosexual family that had been based upon the economic dependence and social subjugation of the female partner.

The justification of the "traditional" heterosexual family can be based either on a divine rationale or it can be justified through references to data and psychological, or social psychological (social scientific) argument. It would appear that as leisure time increases in a society that is growing increasingly wealthy and that successfully manages to distribute that wealth and by implication that leisure time throughout its' different strata, that as such leisure time increases, individuals increasingly become unwilling or less willing to accept divinely sanctioned normative definitions of what sorts of behavior are deemed acceptable and what sorts of behavior are deemed unacceptable. That is, as wealth and leisure increase, individuals increasingly are likely to question ethical prescriptions which are justified merely by claims that either "the Gods" or "the one true God" "says" that such and such is how things are supposed to be. At the same time, appeals to live the way "their parents and grandparents lived" increasingly tend to be rejected as inapplicable on the implicit grounds that grandma and grandpa and mother and dad did not have the leisure time available to them that is available to the newly "enfranchised," newly wealthy and therefore relatively "free" members of the younger generation. Therefore, such newly affluent individuals are likely to reject the mores associated with their traditional religions unless, that is, strong and effective rational argumentative appeals are made that are based upon clearly defined values that are stated and defined and which it is claimed are likely to be lost if the leisure time is squandered to too great an extent in nihilistic activities. For example, consider a novel or film in which a glamorous movie star who had had multiple marriages, divorces and promiscuous affairs, appears without her makeup, looking old, or in which her liposuction bills are displayed, or in which the negative psychological consequences to her children of the multiple divorces are indicated. Or consider a film in which the effects of chronic excessive alcoholism upon the liver are displayed. Such morality novels and films used to be popular in the US but appear to be less popular or politically correct in the contemporary. Still, the narrator watches little TV rarely goes to the movies and rarely reads novels or even book reviews, so the current depictions of morality in US media are largely unknown to him.

The effects of increased leisure time on the political process in Iraq, and by implication in Israel and the potential Palestinian State;

These sorts of observations about divine definitions of what is right and the effects of increasing levels of leisure time on the people, however, would also seem to apply to the Islamic world and more particularly the Islamic and Arabic world and even more particularly to the Iraqi world, wherein, it is suggested, Saddam Hussein's dictatorship is propped up by his ability to repress the ultra religious while at the same time allowing a significant amount of modernity and modern secular leisure to flourish. Thus it would appear that the secularists in Iraq need Saddam's terror because they are unable to justify their own lifestyles to the ultra religious and so would be likely to suffer persecution, perhaps very likely educational regressive suppression, were a religious, democratically elected, regime to assume power. If this is the case then it would appear that a promising course of action would involve attempts, on the part of enlightened, scientifically educated, democracy seeking secularists, that is attempts to forge a political consensus with traditional religious Islamists which would allow the two groups to move forward together toward the assumption of power in a government which would not need to assume an anti-Zionistic stance in order to deflect rampant criticism from itself.

Non-violent civil disobedience in Israel-Palestine/up from slavery/sexual dysfunction
Date: 12/29/98 11:34:18 AM Eastern Standard Time
To: the editors (The American Prospect, The Nation, and The New Yorker)
From: Andréas Daniel Fogg
Letter from Somerville December 22, 1998

Notes: that vaginismus may be more common than is ordinarily acknowledged in the media. To judge from depictions and discussions of sex on television and in the movies, vaginismus is not a problem for significant numbers of couples in society. If as I suspect it to be, it in fact is a significant problem, it's existence could in part be accounted for by a fear of acquiring HIV, and by a wish to have (only) a "successful and happy and genetically correct child," and by heightened levels of rivalry and antagonism between the sexes caused by the normative introduction of women into the competitive work force, followed by the thought that perhaps the screeners of sperm banks are likely to be more successful prognosticators of who would be a good father than the woman herself. Also, if it is in fact a common problem, its presence might begin to explain the current popularity and trendiness of fellatio.

Note that as women have become potential and actual career rivals of men (and often rivalrous toward their sexual partners), the role of heterosexual spouse or partner tends to be defined less as emotionally supportive. This externally, societal suggested, even perhaps imposed "relative lack of emotional support" makes the achievement of sexual intimacy on a regular continuing basis much more difficult than it had been prior to the normative seemingly required introduction of women into the work force.

Therefore, for all these reasons it would probably be an extremely good idea to do a survey of a representative national and international sample(s) of psychiatrists, psychologists and psychotherapists in order to determine the magnitude of incidence of the vaginismus phenomena.

Suggested topic for a science fiction story;
Hominid aliens from an advanced civilization located on a distant planet travel to Earth where they set up sperm banks. Upon obtaining sperm, however, they perform genetic engineering machinations upon their specimens, creating

children whose personalities and intellectual characteristics are more to their liking than those of more ordinary humans.

December 24, 1998

Notes: that sometimes it seems that either the writer's family "contains" him or her, or, the writer manages to "understand and contain and describe" his immediate and extended family.

The intellectual wish to sexually penetrate a woman is qualitatively different from having the actual sexual desire to do so. Often the wish precedes the desire, in which case impotence, and/or vaginismus often blocks success, particularly when physical contact for purposes of genital arousal are shunned in part because they are usually not shown in the visual medias (because they take too much air time)(and because they therefore are not available as examples capable of being imitated as appropriate). External heterosexual genital contact (with either no clothing or minimal clothing), short of penetration or even attempted penetration, can often result in mutual genital arousal which, if not squandered, can allow for successful coitus. Forgive me if I sound like either Dr. Ruth or Master's and Johnson, but I fear that those individuals' works leave considerable problems unaddressed. Real people do not have plastic genital organs.

Note, too, that sexual activity is often not shown in the dark, or even in semi darkness, in the media perhaps in part because of the widespread fear of "vampires," which in turn feeds on a combination of a fear of social interaction with people who look like famous dead people whose photos have been distributed, and the widespread distribution of such photos. Hence, anyone who looks like someone who had been famous is immediately suspected of being a vampire and hence the possibility of physical, sexual contact at night may be subliminally avoided. Since the number of famous visages is increasing at a near astronomical rate, increasingly everyone is capable of coming under such suspicion. In this regard, however, it should be noted that people who demonstrate excellence of any kind, however, are particularly likely to be suspect, since folk wisdom (?) has it that those of genius typically may be "rewarded with eternal life" (note the similarity between "eternal life" and the idea of the "undead" associated as characteristic of vampires).

December 28, 1998

Note that while it is the case that all non converted Jews are somehow descended from former slaves, and every year attempt to remember the bitterness of the slave experience during the holiday of Passover, note that not all peoples who have been slaves are equally ennobled by the experience. That is, slavery is a psychologically degrading experience, an experience whose quality is affected in part by the brutality of the specific slave masters involved. And note that in the process of being emancipated from slavery, a people can find the will and accept leadership which might allow them to rebuild their moral fiber. Or alternatively, it might find itself having great difficulty rebuilding its moral fiber. One thinks of Louis Armstrong as a great rebuilder and sustainer of the human and African American spirit. James Brown, who sings somewhat approvingly of himself as a "sex machine," may be either calling out for help or more than likely leading society along a nihilistic path that it is suggested is far from being helpful to anybody. Unless, that is, it is seen as symptomatic of the same sort of polymorphous perversity described in Woody Allen's recent film Celebrity which I managed to watch yesterday evening. That is, Brown seems to be suggesting that a man can also be polymorphously perverse, perhaps even to some extent multi orgasmic. The implications of such a phenomenon are often not discussed, indeed the phenomenon itself is not acknowledged to exist.
However, individuals as prone to sexual arousal as the model in the film, able to be aroused by virtually any sort of physical contact (it is as if she is suggesting that her entire body is an erogenous zone) may be likely, in practice, to flaunt their ability to arouse others while at the same time eventually retreating and avoiding actual experiences that would seem to require regular actual conventionally defined sexual interactions.

December 29, 1998

A purported belief in God and the interpretation of events;
Note that those whose public roles depend upon a claim to the effect they have access to knowledge of the will and intentions of the "one true God" are often reluctant to question the rightness of their prescriptions in the event that God or Nature deals them some sort of negative feedback. The dilemma always is, for example, do my feet hurt because God is punishing me or merely because by unrelated chance I have picked up some sort of case of athlete's foot? Social pressures are likely to suggest that punishments should be interpreted as mere chance rather than as a message from God to the effect that some significant action has been strongly disapproved of. Are Sheik Yassin's feet swollen and hurting merely by chance or perhaps because he is not sufficiently understanding of

the dilemma of the Israeli Jews, because he is too prone to advocate violent resistance and unwilling to advocate for example nonviolent civil disobedience, a course of action that worked exceedingly effectively in the United States in a different context, and a course of action which would likely be met with a much more lenient and gentle response on the part of the Israeli's. Note that the putative justification for the admittedly repressive Israeli actions involving pretrial preventive detentions and often actions that either are or are close to being psychological if not physical torture, that the implicit justification for such actions is that Israeli society is currently involved in deliberate violent attack, an attack that in effect constitutes the imposition by rejectionist Arab Palestinians of an undeclared but nevertheless very real state of war.

Non violent civil disobedience advocated in the Israeli-Palestinian struggle;

If the rejectionist Arabs and Palestinians were to opt instead for nonviolent civil disobedience as a matter of deliberate policy, the absence of terrorist violent disobedience, the absence of suicide attacks, would remove the need for the preventive detentions and the "shakings and hoodings" and other forms of violent interrogations used by the Israelis in attempts to uncover and stop attempted, planned violent attacks.

Aggressiontransmutesintosexualprovocations/payingviewerstostudyeducationTV-viaPCs
Date: 1/3/99 9:40:43 AM Eastern Standard Time
To: the editors (The American Prospect, The Nation, and The New Yorker)
From: Andréas Daniel Fogg
Letter from Somerville December 30, 1998

As or if racial, class, ethnic, nationalistic, religious or personal conflict become transformed normatively from assumed acts of violence to presumed acts of nonviolent civil disobedience which are designed to modify legal guidelines which affect the processes of socioeconomic mobility as well as the distribution of relative socioeconomic benefits and salary levels in general, then, if such a transformation takes place, as seems substantively to have occurred in the United States, acts and statements of sexual provocation, gratuitous invitations to sexual intimacy that are designed to arouse but never be fulfilled, acts which usually occur in the visual medias and which do not necessarily reflect the intelligence of the performers (rather may reflect the intelligence of those who program the teleprompter) but which may also occur interpersonally, such acts may be used as a means to intimidate, to captivate, to inhibit individual's abilities and willingness to socially contact others, to share opinions and make new friends and contacts. To the extent that media figures succeed in becoming any given viewers everything they have succeeded in maximizing their power and control over that individual or those individuals. This idea is also applicable to any charismatic figure, whether the communicative link occurs in public or private social space.

December 31, 1998

Note: the possibility of transforming television audiences into paid viewers, so that welfare recipients might be required to watch a given number of hours of television a week or day. If televisions incorporated computers as some now do, then brief quizzes could follow programs in order to determine if viewers had in fact paid attention and hence deserved to be paid for their efforts. It is a theoretical possibility that deserves consideration, if only because it seems so outlandish. Yet in fact television viewers are fulfilling various important societal functions which make them responsible citizens. And if viewers were paid to watch TV, there would be an additional incentive to improve the quality of programming, such an incentive is currently actually not present, and the incentive is merely to catch the interest of the viewer regardless of what attention getting device is employed.

January 2, 1999

Note the recent NYTimes story to the effect that only one of the major television networks is actually showing a profit. This statement might suggest to the naive that individuals involved in the other networks are not individually earning exorbitant large salaries. Indeed it is likely the magnitude of their salaries that is keeping their networks from clearing profitable bottom lines as corporations. The argument for taxing the revenues of both corporations and indirectly the incomes of individuals personally profiting from their involvement with the industry is that in fact television exists to serve the people, whereas at present the onus of responsibility seems to have been turned around. That is, people feel an obligation to watch television in order to be cued in as to what is new, what is happening, what is "in," what is politically correct and socially appropriate. Indeed it could be argued that many people begin to feel the effects of changing cultural mores, that is the effects of culture shock, or more correctly of future shock, for which remedy they seek the guidance of the TV "wise men." The implicit thought seems to be that because society has empowered these people to broadcast directly to millions, that therefore these people must have important valuable things to communicate, that they should be listened to. But in fact, it is not particularly clear what the criteria are which are used in deciding what normative messages are endorsed and propagated by the mass media.

Occasionally, clearly, public sensibilities are outraged by a statement or comment that some media personality makes either on or off the microphone. But in general the media cater to the opinions of the lowest common denominator, the vast majority of the citizens in this massively large and diverse society. And the vast majority of the citizens are counted in either the shrinking middle class, or the lower middle class or the working class. Of course this generalization is not entirely true since it appears that some considerable amounts of programming appeal to the relatively wealthy. This makes sense since advertising pays the salaries of the media writers, actors, producers and directors. And effective advertising appeals to those who have disposable income to spend, or to those who can be induced into going into debt in order to give the appearance that they are fulfilling the norms for expensive conspicuous consumption that the advertisements and drama both propagate and indeed suggest need to be honored through purchases regardless of such purchase's effects on the security, magnitude or even existence of the consumer's nest egg.

Watching television is sold to the public as a pleasurable use of leisure time whereas in fact it has become a psychologically enervating that is energy draining, emotionally exhausting sometimes desperate attempt to find a way to achieve financial and psychological security. Whereas in fact watching the media is defined as something that one does when their work is done, in actuality it amounts to a de facto form of work, work that the anomic, normatively disoriented nonreader desperately pursues in an attempt to discover what this decade's definition of appropriate and generational "cool" consists in. Since increasing numbers of individuals find themselves unable to find the time and energy necessary to identify and focus and concentrate on reading materials that might help them find a way to "make it" in contemporary society, they increasingly turn to television and movies as resources of last resort. And typically what television and movies offer, it is hypothesized, are suggested poses which the unempowered might assume in order to give the impression that they have positive identities, that is that they don't have negative identities. In fact what is involved in watching television or movies involves the viewer's deliberate subjugation of his own ability to even think of responding to the messages that are propagated. Whereas a spokesman for the economically unempowered, Jesse Jackson, suggests to his audience members that "you are somebody" the message the TV viewer implicitly accepts in order to psychologically rationalize his interest is precisely the reverse namely, "I am nobody special." In fact, even the interactive call-in programs, in which the host "accepts" calls from random members of the viewing audience, involve, for reasons of time conservation and I suppose propriety, an emphasis on the anonymity of the caller's identity. Typically we do not know the caller's last name, but even if we did know his last name or her last name we usually don't know anything about their religion, how much money they make, their political loyalties, their political concerns neither about their personal histories. Therefore their opinions are predefined as of equal importance as those of any other caller; that is their personal identities are irrelevant. Indeed the only "persons" whose "identities" are allowed to actually appear on television or the movies, with a few exceptions, are literally fictional persons, that is actors portraying either real people (who aren't deemed as photogenic as the actors), or actors portraying fictional characters. While journalists are allowed to appear on television on talk shows, the shows often are unable or unwilling to consider or discuss the underlying problems that the country faces for to do so might well risk insulting the vast majority of the viewing audience whose typical assumption involves the idea that "I am as good as anyone else, and I refuse to consider suggestions to the contrary. It is not my fault that I am not as successful or as socially adept as the so called stars" whose lives are programmed and written to represent and embody the wish fulfillment aspirations of the vast majority of the earners' pool.

With some exceptions, serious writers and thinkers do not appear in the media. In general real people who have received higher educations are anathema to the program schedulers since they tend to make much of the audience feel less than adequate. Every once in a while Donald Trump, the real estate magnate, appears on the tube or in the movies, but his very name has a sort of assumed, fictionalized "stage-like" quality. So much of the media reality involves people with stage names who have literally disowned and in a sense destroyed or murdered their pasts in order to become what the media define as "real." The effects of this destruction of past real identities of societally defined significant people has implications as a sort of negative paradigm that the society has adopted at its own peril. In the late sixties a college professor of philosophy, Arthur Danto, used to say that it is logically possible to begin your life starting "now" that is in the present. He was also fond of quoting the poet Holderlin, whom Hitler recommended to his Nazi troops. Now Danto, as far as I know, was and is not a Nazi, he currently writes an art column for The Nation, and in the late sixties I remember that he seemed to be against the Vietnam War.

But what of this idea that successful people change their names and "drop their pasts?" Where does this leave one's relations with his or her parents, siblings and childhood friends? Does one have a responsibility to just drop all these old accoutrements of one's self? And if one does so, what then? What if the well paid public relations oriented relationships which the "stars" seem to content themselves with are not forthcoming? What if they are? How supportive can someone who is indifferent but paid to be a friend be?

On the other hand, parental figures can and often do impose a continuation of the original parental domination pattern on their children, no matter how old they are. A typical parent, father, for example, will refuse to acknowledge that his son or sons are equal despite all evidence to the contrary, refusing to compete in the presence of the mother in areas in which the son has excelled, perhaps in which the son has even currently outperformed the "old man." Such paternal figures may refuse to involve themselves emotionally in relationships in which they see that anyone, even old friends or their own children, might prefer or even merely equally enjoy the company of his spouse as compared to himself. Such is the level of insecurity of such individuals that they may be unwilling to recognize the double standard that they force their children and friends to accept. That is, the paternal male says, "I can enjoy talking and flirting with your girl friend(s), with your wife, but if you begin to evoke emotionally warm responses from your mother, or my wife, then I feel the need to put you at an emotional arms length. It is tremendously important to me, says the patriarch, to feel that I am the central actor in what is going on, at least in front of my wife. I cannot and will not allow anyone to upstage me in front of my wife and if they find it necessary to do so, I will not allow them to be my friend. When I say to someone that I "love" them what I really mean is that I love them so long as they play no better than second fiddle to my concert master. But perhaps I am exaggerating the relative incidence of such parental orientations. Perhaps also the characterization amounts to a snap shot of a fictional ideal typical patriarch whose insistence on his own centrality in what is after all his own life's drama amounts to a forgivable reluctance to accept less than the star billing that he seems to believe he had held in his prime. In any case, this amounts to a long-standing dilemma that has been a recurring phenomenon in western civilization since certainly Shakespeare wrote King Lear and probably going back to the Bible.

The difficulty lies in the fact that this individual is one of the only members of the social science establishment who responds to the narrator's formal correspondence, all the other editors to whom he corresponds, but has not been introduced, ignore him. And this individual responds only on the personal level, refusing in almost all cases to discuss with the narrator any of his substantive ideas. It is surmised that this is the case because to do so he might seem to have to adopt a "second fiddle" like position. Of course this surmise could be incorrect and involve an unjust and unfair imputation, in which case an apology may be in order. Still some of these ideas, it is suggested cry out to be discussed if not read, in the public sphere. And they are unlikely to be published in the open until they are first discussed privately.

Granted, they needn't necessarily be discussed with the author, but I am merely pointing out that the refusal to acknowledge or confront any of these substantive ideas amounts to a decision, in football terminology, to "punt." The narrator has been, professionally speaking, out in such cold for over twenty years, twenty-six years since graduating from college.

Gemeinschaft vs. Gesellschaft: the extended vs the nuclear family

Note the relevance of these observations regarding father/son conflicts to Tonnies' Gemeinschaft/Gesellschaft distinction along with the likelihood that extended families in which filial piety, that is the duty to always show respect and obedience to one's elders and especially one's father tend to be characteristic of less complex "village based" traditional small scale communities in which both father and children continue to live in close physical proximity, if not in the same household. In such contexts, it is argued, it remains difficult for even sons or daughters grown to adulthood to either contradict an elder about anything significant or for that matter in some cases to even make the elder appear diminished by virtue of the child's levels of accomplishment. It is only, it is argued, possible in more complex cultures such as are found in more urban areas, for children to achieve independence from their parent's authority since in cities nuclear families, that have achieved marked levels of autonomy from the parental levels of authority found in Gemeinschaft like extended family cultures, tend to be encouraged. But in modern American society there remains a continuing conflict between those who have overthrown the influence of their parents at one extreme and those who want nothing more than to do just exactly what was good enough for Mom and Dad and Grandma and Grandpa. Of course when the parental model differs from the grandparental model confusion may set in. For example, if the parents had told the grandparents to avoid interfering in the child rearing, an attempt to emulate the parents may lack a putative justification or rationale for declaring or achieving autonomy.

But in general it would appear that it is only when young adults are free to make decisions either supporting or contradicting their parents, that only in such circumstances does society become capable of achieving either increased levels of technological accomplishment or impressive artistic, musical or literary accomplishments. It could be argued that allowing the nuclear family to have autonomous status is a prerequisite to high levels of economic growth and cultural sophistication. Note that communist political totalitarianism tended to, (and seems to persist today) in Cuba, North Korea as well as the People's Republic of China, to substitute the authority of party leaders in place of the authority figures found in extended families in peasant like village cultures. When these totalitarian figures, whether they are communist, or pseudo socialist or orthodox fundamentalist religious, assume unchallengeable positions within a society, the ability of that society to utilize multifarious sources of ideas that may either support or be critical of the status quo becomes imperiled, freedom begins to diminish and fear grows. It is argued that the media in the US currently has assumed a position of far greater importance and economic valuation than is good for the society. It is further argued that the number of persons filling low wage jobs that should properly be described as "dead end jobs" has actually increased, that the exact number of persons occupying such jobs is meticulously kept from the public view, never discussed on the talk shows, since the numbers are likely to be frightening, leading to a likely conclusion that "there are not enough good jobs available to go around." Which conclusion while it may not be accurate is certainly frightening. And, since the media does not tell viewers how to get out of dead end jobs, preferring to pretend, in most cases, that the viewer is not in a dead end job or that he or she actually likes being in a dead end job, see for example the Coors beer commercials featuring the happy beer man, and so has no need to figure a way to achieve a different career. In a Taco Bell restaurant, it says on the wall "why would anyone want to work anywhere else?" Hence the idea that some sort of structural change is necessary in which income is transferred from the hands of the media elite who tend in most cases to narcotize the society, into the hands of the economically unempowered or the economically less empowered. Hence the idea that watching the media ought rightfully be considered work for which some compensation might well be due is suggested. And it is further suggested that the power of the media programmers, since they would in this scenario be creating hopefully useful work for the disenfranchised members of society, that their power would needs be subject to hopefully socially responsible external review. That is, that poor ratings, which in this case would amount to low levels of compensation, would constitute bases for negative annual salary oriented reviews, perhaps indeed it would be the case that watching mindless violent escapism would not pay nearly as well as watching more serious educational materials, but that in any case watching and understanding educational materials would be possible and duly noted and would serve as justification for recognition that would include economic remuneration in addition to what has often become presently an economically meaningless certificate.

Note in passing the rumor that at least one European state, perhaps Denmark, has unilaterally made virtually all higher education free to those who qualify for it, that is all higher education is paid for with tax dollars. But the idea suggested above goes farther and suggests that, at some level as yet to be determined, media based computer assisted educational challenges when adequately met, should be financially rewarded depending upon the relative level of accomplishment of the individual student. I am thinking that perhaps others have already thought of this idea, perhaps Paul Starr, for example, who lists a course on the electronic policy network that he currently is offering at Princeton.

January 3, 1999

In an earlier issue of TAP SherrieTurkle, I think, discussed the possibility and desirability of sustaining community oriented computer centers in economically depressed areas. Imagine if such centers offered gratis to anyone a computer name, a private password (personal identification number) and the possibility of registering either a conventional credit card or a combined ATM bank card/ credit card in connection with said nexus. Then, a schedule of gratis computer based learning program/courses, starting at the level of remedial reading, then to elementary school, junior high school, high school level, but moving up through college and even theoretically beyond could be offered to any theoretically deprived or discriminated against individual (or for that matter, any individual). Significant accomplishments would be rewarded with deposits to the students credit card account. The advantage of this learning mechanism lies in the area of avoiding negative peer pressure. That is, the student just seems to be minding his or her own business, playing with a computer. He or she doesn't appear to be threatening the ascribed or achieved dominance of any other individual peer or of the members of any other group. Neither need he or she fear repeated failure and defeat in the eyes of the members of dominant, supposedly superior groups or for that matter in the eyes of their own group. I.e. thereby avoiding debilitation associated with attitudes that might be characterized by the following statement: "I ain't going to do this stuff if 'whitey' is going to beat me every time."

Impeachment proceedings and Clinton's relationship with Hillary
Date: 1/6/99 10:55:23 AM Eastern Standard Time
To: the editors (The American Prospect, The Nation, and The New Yorker)
From: Andréas Daniel Fogg
Letter from Somerville January 5, 1999

The courts seem to have been riding rough shod over citizen's rights to privacy for some time. Hence it might well be relevant to allegations that the President has bent the truth, if not actually materially perjured himself, as to what possible justification might be present in the actual relationship between the President and the First Lady, that is might some justification possibly exist flowing from the content, the quality of the living arrangements, the sleeping arrangements if you will, that have existed between the President and his wife. That is, in any potential legal proceedings between a man and wife, if the wife refuses or is unwilling to provide consortium, then shouldn't such a fact be relevant in determining the courts if not the community's determination of guilt in any allegations of either infidelity and/or wrongdoing. And, might not the presence of a lack of consortium between the President and the First Lady actually explain the reluctance of the President at first to totally "bare his soul" in regard to the matter of his relations with Monica Lewinsky. If it were told confidentially to the impeachment court that such a lack of consortium had in fact been the case, and that the President's recalcitrance in testifying had been partly due to his desire to spare his wife embarrassment, then one would think that the House's movement to impeach might be dismissed by the Senate and switched to a move to censure, thereby avoiding unnecessary and personally painful and probably damaging Testimony.

Euro's effect on global GDP re producer based deflation/retailbaseddeflation
Date: 1/11/99 7:23:45 AM Eastern Standard Time
To: the editors (The American Prospect, The Nation, and The New Yorker)
From: Andréas Daniel Fogg
Letter from Somerville January 7, 1999

Note the argument as to whether there is a global deflationary trend. The evidence for such a trend may be obscured by a combination of producer based deflation coupled with steady or inflationary retail trends. In any case, the capacity for a deflationary situation seems to be present.

The new presence of the Euro and of the Euro's central bank, which presumably has the capacity to increase the global supply of Euros, by printing them and selling them, so long as this mega currency remains in demand, it will have the capacity of serving as a balance to the dollar, that is it will be capable of balancing anti deflationary attempts to reflate or reinflate local third world currencies which are attempting to counter the effects of deflation by printing more money of their own, which currencies unlike the dollar and euro, are not likely to be in international demand. In such a case, said third world states will not, theoretically, be as beholden to one central bank, or the IMF, since they can always bargain with holders of dollars by threatening to buy euros instead. But this may be a lesser hypothetical point, less important than the basic point which is that the presence of the relatively "hard" euro will have the effect of enabling the growth of third world money supplies.

January 9, 1999

Notes: the positive effects of growing the money supplies of developing states in terms of the Marxist critique of capitalism; the undesirability of letting the precedent of allowing the prosecution of high government officials for sexual harassment while they are in office; a perceived imbalance in the law, i.e. the law seems to be tilting in favor of women's rights in both the spheres of marriage and the work place, so that the very institution of marriage as well as the sustainability of the heterosexual bond both seem to be threatened by the law as much as by liberationist ideologies; observed double standard in the implementation of military regulations against adultery; Clinton being attacked in part because of his socioeconomic class origins i.e. he represents an attempt by a member of the economically disenfranchised class to live by the covert moral standards of the middle and upper middle classes, such as those standards practiced by former representative Bob Livingstone. Note that one of the "perks" associated with membership in the middle class has been that one is allowed to impute immorality to the members of the working class indeed to claim that a reason that the members of the working class do not succeed to the same extent as some members of the middle class, have not succeeded, is that they tend to be, or seem to be, morally bankrupt. Whereas they (the middle class) tend to allow their own members to get away with quite a bit on the grounds that because they are members of the middle class and therefore believe themselves to be relatively financially secure, that is secure relative to the members of the working class, because they are members of the middle class, therefore, they must be morally OK and according to Weber, favored by the so called grace of God.

Note that the members of the working class and lower middle class, who often claim to be members of the middle class, have been called "(wage) slaves in denial."

This is a valuable, apt, extremely descriptive phrase. It explains many observations. It describes a great deal of behavior, sketches many working class attitudes toward supervisors, management and educated people in general. (The narrator wishes that he had made this observation himself. However, he heard it quoted for the first and only time by Christopher Lydon, on the NPR radio program, The Connection. Lydon used the quote, attributing it to someone else, whose identity is not remembered. Neither is the context in which the phrase was used clearly remembered.) In fact it may apply in the sense that the narrator has noticed that many of his warehouse coworkers tend to behave as if to deny the existence of the power which managers and supervisors hold over their (that is the workers') livelihoods. And/or alternatively it could apply to the working class male (chauvinist) attitude which tends to deny that women have any power in their relationships with men i.e. that women exist merely to satisfy their i.e. men's needs for sexual gratification and ego satisfaction.

The precedent of allowing high government officials to be prosecuted while in office for relatively petty crimes such as sexual harassment;

Consider the use that such a precedent could serve in the hands of dedicated fifth columnists in either a cold war or hot war situation. That is, the agents of a foreign power, or for that matter, the agents of a religious cult, which for one reason or another had assumed a hostile attitude toward the United States, could fabricate a case against the President or perhaps a Supreme Court Justice, or the Speaker of the House, or the Senate Majority Leader, to the effect that he had committed sexual harassment either while in office or prior to assuming office, claiming the Clinton episode as a valid precedent which therefore required public attention, resources and time. The legal system would have to, in such a case, deal with not just a fabricated charge, but also likely with fabricated testimony, testimony which might well be fortified with evidence deriving from entrapment procedures.

Deflation and Marxist critiques of capitalism;

Note the basic, correct Marxist insight to the effect that deflationary situations serve as constraints on the growth of production and the possible growth of the overall standard of living of the masses. That is when economic demand cannot be increased enough so as to allow for increased, compensated production, then production must either slow down or cease until unutilized demand capability appears. So that if a mechanism could be found which allowed for the regular increase of demand in relatively impoverished countries, then that constraint on continued, increased global production would diminish or temporarily disappear and businesses and producers would be constrained in their wish to produce only by levels of needed resources and their personal inclinations to actually work; along with of course, their businesses ability to hold market share. But deflation, that is falling prices, would cease to be a structural, endemic problem on the macro economic level. Within given sectors of the economy, of course, relative over production and sectoral deflation would continue to be an inevitable possibility.

That the allowability of husband/wife charges of rape serve to subvert the marital bond;

That is, if a wife is allowed to charge her husband with rape, then the possibility of familial married coitus becomes continually a possible grounds for prosecution so that the motivation for such acts tends to be diminished or even to disappear. It would appear that if a woman wishes to charge her husband with rape, that the result perhaps should involve either an immediate divorce or separation with no financial award (other perhaps than child support) to the wife, since if she was foolish enough to marry a man who would abuse her she has no one else to blame but herself. Otherwise, the male ability to allow himself to be sexually aroused by the woman is likely to be personally inhibited, due to his fear that in the event that she is somehow offended by his behavior or attitude, or perhaps by his political positions, that she will proceed to fabricate or claim to have been raped. Note the number of times that relationships end with the claim that "not only do I not love you, I never loved you! Or I never enjoyed the sex." From this position it is only a short distance to charging the estranged party with rape.

Military regulations against adultery

During the case of the female B52 pilot (perhaps Laura Flynn?) there was a NYTimes article to the effect that married officers had been observed leaving a brothel and that no charges had been filed against them. This story is offered as evidence to subvert the claim that because the President was involved outside of his marriage he is therefore unfit to serve as the Commander in Chief of the military services and therefore should either be impeached or resign his office.

Extreme religiosity, moralism and the debilitating effects of complete homoerotic denial and repression;

Note that individuals who, early on in their careers, tend to assume occupational positions in which most of their interactions with others take place in a hierarchical context tend to be extremely emotionally and sexually needy. Such persons, for example, are likely to have become professors or managers shortly after leaving college or graduate school. And their life experiences therefore likely have not included sufficiently large doses of nonhierarchical relatively egalitarian interactions with peers whose ascribed status is equivalent to their own. Therefore they tend to interpret all of their interactions in terms of whether their co interactor occupies either an ascribed superior or subordinate status. Hence, they are deprived of sufficient opportunities to know what it means to simply be friends with one or more of their peers. In effect they see all interactions as qualitatively determined by preconceived status considerations, rather than by genuine interaction generated emotional events that are relatively sincere, that is not precalculated to facilitate some personal career based advantage. Hence the individual who has not known sufficient egalitarian relationships tends to be perpetually lonely and emotionally if not sexually frustrated; perhaps even, often close to being clinically depressed.

January 11, 1999

To those Democrats who might suggest that Clinton should resign;

It is suggested that the Supreme Court decision to allow the Paula Jones lawsuit to proceed, and the decision of the special prosecutor to harass the President with this investigation sets a terrible precedent for the country as a whole and for the legal system in general. Further it is suggested that the best, desirable remedy for rectifying this terrible precedent, for which the Republican Party, and the Republican dominated Supreme Court are responsible, is to pass and sign into law legislation which would protect high government officials from being prosecuted for non-impeachable offenses on the grounds that to allow such legal attacks is tantamount to placing the actions of government in general at the mercy of any potentially unscrupulous enemies of the people. Further it is suggested that while it seems to be true that the President has bent the truth while under oath in defense of his private life, and that while such perjurous or near perjurous acts are clearly wrong, they are not nearly as wrong as the obfuscatory tactics that the Republican House majority and the Special Prosecutor have employed in their successful attempts to keep this extremely capable President from pursuing what he has accurately and successfully managed to perceive as the peoples' business. That therefore, it is inconceivable that this President should even consider resigning without an accompanying admission on the part of the Republican House majority and the special prosecutor that they themselves have been guilty of committing an even greater wrong against the interests and security of our Republic.

Re allowing a precedent: prosecution of high officials for non-impeachable offenses
Date: 1/11/99 7:53:52 AM Eastern Standard Time
Notes to the editors….addendum
From: Andréas Daniel Fogg

It is suggested that allowing the current precedent in which the courts allowed a high gov't official to be harassed in the courts with charges that he had committed sexual harassment, that allowing such a precedent to stand will result in a basic weakening of our political system because: any official who pursues an active sex life, even within marriage, will run the risk of incurring charges in the event he or she incurs the displeasure of the partner. But even in the event that no sexual interaction occurs, perhaps merely in the event that some compromising situation has occurred, if the courts allow high officials to be at the mercy of sexual harassment law suits, then the freedom of action of political leaders is likely to be severely diminished.

   Also, if you wonder as to the cause of the so called weakened American nuclear family, perhaps you need look no farther than the increased power that the courts have ceded to women. After all, if any husband is seen to be continually at risk of being prosecuted on charges of raping his wife, such cases have occurred, then how much freedom of action of any sort does such a husband possess. He becomes a creature who is utterly at his wife's mercy; a situation, no doubt that the courts and legislators had no intention of allowing to exist. And a situation that seemingly leads to increasing numbers of divorces and separated couples.

   Re: Clinton and military rules about adultery
Date: 1/11/99 7:49:07 AM Eastern Standard Time
To: tap@epn.org
Notes to the editors……addendum

From: Andréas Daniel Fogg

About the time this woman B52 pilot, I think her name is Laura Flynn, was being court-martialed for having an adulterous affair with a soccer coach, who I think was an enlisted man, there appeared a story in the NY Times to the effect that in many cases the military rules against adultery were winked at, in effect had become "blue laws," when those doing the violating were male officers. Someone had taken photos of male officers leaving brothels and lo and behold, nothing was done about this so called serious violation of the rules. Of course Laura Flynn was warned numerous times to cease and desist, but she continued. Then there is the question as to the desirability of said military regulations against marital infidelity i.e. should the penalty be as severe as it is, should the rules be dropped? Just because there is a rule against something doesn't mean that there should be such a rule. That is why some rules atrophy, wither away and become "blue laws."

Don Juan complex, love and "honor," Brazilian devaluation
Date: 1/17/99 3:23:41 PM Eastern Standard Time
To: the editors (The American Prospect, The Nation, and The New Yorker)
From: Andréas Daniel Fogg
Letter from Somerville January 11, 1999

Mass culture seems to discourage independent sociological theorizing, since independent thought about what is right or wrong with the society tends to be stigmatized as arrogant elitism. Hence Riesman's original scheme about contemporary society being primarily other-directed is apt since if most are other-directed, then the question arises, who or what forces or influences are determining the directions that they are moving toward?

January 12, 1999

Notes: omissions in Racine's treatment of the play, Phaedra. First it is too contextless, that is the "history" of the Minotaur problem is ignored as is the story of Theseus' relationship with his father, which is very different from the relationship between Hyppolitus and Theseus. Commentators at a symposium that took place after the performance in Cambridge, made much ado about allegations that Theseus had been a terrific womanizer and philanderer. Only under repeated questioning did the story about how Theseus had abandoned Ariadne, the woman who had led him out of the Labyrinth after he had managed to kill the Minotaur, in favor of his consorting and eventually marrying Ariadne's younger sister i.e.

Phaedra, emerge. Presumably Phaedra was considerably more sensuous than her abandoned sister, since Phaedra is described as having been descended from or perhaps possessed by the goddess of love, Venus or Aphrodite; perhaps also descended from the same woman who had been seduced by the father of the Minotaur, who presumably had been Zeus in the form of a bull.

Fictional development in the contemporary. A character, we shall call him Davey, an undergraduate student of sociology, finds that he is able to begin earning top grades after he has finally managed to lose his virginity. He sleeps briefly with, if I remember correctly, three different women. Immediately his grades improve. One of the women, the third, is also a student of sociology, has a name that is almost identical to that of Davey's mother. Both Davey and the third girl, we will call her Ariana, have blue eyes, although Ariana has light blue eyes, whereas Davey's eyes are dark blue, indeed they are so dark that sometimes they even seem to turn brown.

Their sexual relationship, the actual interactions occurs once or at most twice, however, the two of them travel together to visit one of their professors, a female sociology professor who had married her senior dissertation advisor, the marriage following the professor's divorce from his long-standing wife. They visit the couple in their home. Davey and Ariana are presumed to be a couple. However, Davey is not particularly happy or satisfied with the relationship since the intercourse has been libidinally tepid. It appears to Davey, however, that the top grades that he receives from his professors that term have been at least partly contingent on his relationship with Ariana. That summer, Davey meets a young woman with brown eyes. The two of them seduce each other. There is great passion. Sparks fly! When Davey returns to school that fall, he finds himself unable to resume his relationship with Ariana, indeed, he cannot even tell her that anything has happened neither why he is breaking off with her. Davey's grades begin to return to their previous level of medium quality, that is, he begins to receive Bs and Cs again.

January 14, 1999

The Don Juan Complex as being caused by an attempt to personally deny rather than sublimate one's personal same sex impulses;

The individual in the thrall of the so called Don Juan complex feels it continually necessary to sexually accost numerous, multiple members of the opposite sex in a continuing, vain attempt to prove to himself (ego is usually a male in this complex), that is, to deny homosexual impulses that he actually feels, i.e. to demonstrate that he has no homosexual impulses toward his fellows. As previously suggested, such individuals have often achieved early occupational or professional success, which success has allowed or required them to interact with other males largely on a hierarchical rather than egalitarian basis. Such hierarchical interactions leave the individual feeling largely without the emotional support and reinforcement of his peers, indeed because so many hierarchically based relationships are available to such persons, they tend to shun egalitarian relationships, which might allow uncoerced genuine interpersonal social feedback, and hence allow for accompanying personal growth and maturity. So that such individuals tend to feel homosexual impulses that are likely to be stronger than those of those in more egalitarian situations, because these impulses represent an expression of a need for freely given friendship, which friendship's need is obscured to the individual by his very success within the occupational structural system.

Prior to the systemic interjection of large numbers of educated middle class women into the work force, such widespread profligate, promiscuous Don Juan like behavior has been tolerated in the repertoire of behavior of the economic and political elite in the United States. However, with the aforementioned change in the composition of the work force, and the accompanying change in definitions of appropriate sex role behavior, American society has felt a relatively new need to repudiate the use of occupational power in order to pursue such promiscuous sexual behavior, indeed such behavior which had previously been assumed to be necessary, as for example in the administration of John Kennedy, has been greeted with schizoid like swings of alternating approval and repudiation.

The narrator had originally heard about this Don Juan complex from a cousin of the younger Murdock son, who heard about it while studying in Colorado on a Telluride scholarship program during the summer after his junior year in high school. Note that the sort of prodigiously promiscuous, wantonly promiscuous behavior described as part and parcel of the so called complex was at one point characteristic of the sexual behavior of Negro slaves who were encouraged, it is suggested, to treat their couplings as being almost consciously part and parcel of a Darwinian agenda. Thus it may be the case that when high powered executives make the decision to personally indulge in such behavior, they may be consciously or unconsciously seeking to emulate behavior that has been ascribed to African Americans in both past ages as well as in the present.

January 16, 1999

"Love and Honor"

There was a story on either the BBC or NPR radio about a week ago, about perhaps a Pakistani Muslim and his wife. Apparently a group of Muslims were being attacked by an angry mob of Hindus, perhaps it was in India, and the husband feared that his wife would be dishonored, that is raped, and that therefore he determined that he must literally kill her. At this point, with the mob at the door he attempted to murder her with a long knife, but he failed. The mob came on, the wife was raped, he was killed, the wife survived to tell the story. From this brief account, however, it may be possible to accurately infer that the husband felt that not only would his wife be dishonored, but that he, as his wife's lover and husband, would also be dishonored and that therefore, in order to prevent all this dishonor, he felt impelled to attempt to snuff out her life. But in less exaggerated terms, how many men allow themselves to be alienated from their wives and/or girlfriends in order to avoid the pain of realizing that they are unable "to protect her" from the wanted or unwanted advances of other males. Indeed, how many divorced men and women or seemingly confirmed bachelors and bachelorettes, avoid getting involved in emotional or physical relationships simply because they feel that they are unable to sufficiently control or protect a potential partner from the advances of others. But the truth of the matter is that if one gives in to the impulse to truncate relations, if only by avoiding going to dinner or merely out to the movies because one fears that the hoi polloi will somehow not show sufficient respect, then one is in effect declaring that one will only associate with those toward whom one does not feel either love or respect. One has in effect acquiesced totally in mass mob-like control over the quality of life. Actually, I think, this oversensitivity may well result from the fact that so many of us have allowed ourselves to experience acute episodes of crucial socialization like experiences while watching either television or movies; so that out of a sort respect or awe for such experiences we have become over sensitized to and even fearful of being touched by those toward whom we are not totally trusting (toward those who might be merely acting). More to the point, it may be the case that many of us simply do not know how to respond when we are touched by someone that we do not particularly want to have touching us. The implicit question is, what's wrong with me that you don't want me touching you? Are you somebody special who only lets certain people touch you? What are you some kind of an elitist who does not relate to others as if nothing should be kept private from anybody else? Are you special, not an ordinary "Joe" member of the mass society, who gets what he needs from the TV, has no distinguishing opinions, is not a threat to any of his buddies. If you're special after all, your buddies may drop you as not ordinary enough; and women may consider you to be too strong minded, not subservient enough to be a good mate; you may end up all alone stuck in an office in a University somewhere. Of course that wouldn't be so bad if the pay was decent. If the pay was decent, you could go out to dinner. You probably would have friends of the academic variety. Probably you would be able to talk to other professors and students. And who knows, maybe you would even be able to talk with working people, who might actually have more respect toward a hard working professor than toward an ordinary relatively mediocre blue collar worker.

January 17, 1999

Notes: one reason for the widespread discrimination against African American men may be that so many of them seem to be in the thrall of the Don Juan complex that it is assumed that all of them are subject to it. That is, perhaps because of their initial lowly socioeconomic standing, they feel strong homoerotic impulses toward white economically enfranchised white men. Typically their mechanism of dealing with these impulses is to on the one hand, deny that they exist (i.e. many Black men think to themselves, I can't be feeling this, if I were feeling this then I would be one of those deviants, therefore I must prove that I do not have these erotic aroused feelings by showing hostility toward he or those who have engendered them), and on the other hand, to resist the realization and actualization of these impulses by reactively converting the "positive" feelings into their opposite, namely hostility. And of course sensed hostility coming from economically unempowered males is greeted with at best indifference and usually with outright rejection and where possible often, punishment and/or retaliation in kind, all of which has commonly been interpreted as racial prejudice.

Notes: The NYTimes asserts that the Brazilian gov't has a 270 billion dollar domestic debt. And apparently they are reluctant to impose equitable if not progressive federal income taxation. Hence they must face the option of whether to pay off parts of the internal debt by either borrowing money abroad, which will be a problem if and when they either devalue the currency or allow its' depreciation, or they can elect to print money. But printing money in the absence of increased productivity tends to lead to inflation. That is one reason why Brazil has extremely high interest rates. These rates once as high as 100 percent, reportedly cut to 34 percent recently, of course tend to lower productivity. And of course, without progressive taxation, with what is assumed to be a minimal wage pool, demand is likely to be slack, which slackness is likely to further inhibit productivity, which is likely to cause stagnant wages and inflation in the event that the country attempts to print its' way out of the dilemma.

For all these reasons and probably more, Brazil needs to be told by the IMF and the United States government that it needs to impose a progressive income tax system.

Bretton Woods and German inflation prior to and during the Third Reich
Date: 1/24/99 8:15:27 AM Eastern Standard Time
to: the editors (The American Prospect, The New Yorker, The Nation)
from: Andréas Daniel Fogg
Letter from Somerville January 18, 1999

written at: North Peak Lodge
Sunday River
Newry, Maine

Notes: Drawbacks and merits involved in establishing a system of programmed learning courses in which accomplishments of varying degrees are rewarded with at first merely cash deposit incentives, but later also with the recognized fulfillment of various occupational prerequisites, the granting of relatively selective job interviews. One can also imagine courses in which occupation relevant socialization learning is demonstrated, taught, rewarded and potentially such a course could include disincentives, for instance, as the student proceeded through the programmed learning experience, the program could continually display his or her "current earnings total" and in the event of a seriously wrong or even "bad" answer (such as might be found in a socialization learning program), the student might find that their earnings total had been diminished by the less than adequate or seriously wrong or inappropriate answer.

American society currently rewards all sorts of relatively insignificant behaviors, like checking people's coats at expensive restaurants, or participating in a game show like "Jeopardy" in which levels of unrelated anomalous facts, knowledge of facts subject to quick recall are rewarded, but only the participants who are selected to participate on TV have the opportunity to earn monies, and the knowledge displayed serves no valid or even remotely obvious societal purpose.

Society needs people to have all sorts of skills, of course. But the ability to maintain both civility and freedom may ultimately depend upon how much of society achieves and maintains reasonable levels of knowledge vis a vis basic literacy but also vis a vis history, the humanities, political, particularly democratic, theory. And of course accomplishments in mathematics, computer science, the social sciences and the so called hard sciences are necessary if society is to be able to maintain and increase its advanced standards of living which are based upon both shared understandings of how people should behave and a high level of technological accomplishment.

Too often, it seems, interpersonal misunderstandings or unrealistic and unnecessary perhaps overly burdensome personal relationships get in the way and halt the accomplishment and advancement of individual learning and of course too often learning stops because it ceases to be either an emotionally or fiscally (i.e. monetarily) rewarding experience. That is, the teacher either doesn't care or else actually opposes further accomplishment (see the play The Bald Soprano, by Ionesco) and/or funds are not apparently available, or the student feels unworthy of asking for funds if they are available. If society feels the need to support education it should speak clearly to the effect that funds should be available to those who have a sincere interest (and sufficient talent), and such funds should not be contingent on a student's having a personal relationship of one sort or another with a teacher or professor. I do not mean to imply that interpersonal teacher/student relationships are valueless or functionless, merely that too often, for the less than economically secure, such relationships may interfere in the accomplishment of further learning, causing lifelong learning to be abandoned long before any present possibility of tangible possible rewards appears on the horizon of the future.

Part of the difficulty seems to be that the society values product acquisition more than it values learning and/or learned experiential or cognition modifying experiences. At some point we need to begin to ask ourselves the question "what is really important to us?" Sure we value computer technology with it's speed enhanced communicator capabilities; but how much do we value the actual messages themselves? As a society the reward scheme seems to be very much a winner takes all situation, as far as publication and media productions are concerned. That is, equivalence is drawn between mass market share/payback and a piece of work's value to society. This equivalence is perhaps unfortunate, albeit quite characteristic of pure, free market democracies. It also seems characteristic of a culture in the throes of transitioning from an ethos defined by scarcity to an ethos defined by affluence. Although it is true that John Kenneth Galbraith characterized American society with his book and descriptive title, The Affluent Society, some decades past, nevertheless the United States continues to be characterized by vast discrepancies between the haves and the have nots, all the more so because the impression persists and the data may suggest that despite low unemployment statistics, real absolute deprivation, hunger and poverty continue to exist certainly in the 3rd world, but probably also in the United States. In any case, levels of job insecurity among large numbers of the workforce remain high, so that while many are just above poverty, hunger and homelessness, the fact that these dangerous traps are feared by large segments of the population suggests that the ethos of US society continues to be influenced if not defined by fears associated with scarcity. Hence unless mechanisms are established for rewarding those who build and reinforce society's modern, secular underpinnings, which include much of the individual thought constructing apparatus, i.e. much of the secular humanistic liberal arts curriculum, we are likely to find ourselves in a situation in which wealth holders include a relatively smaller segment of the population which has received an anti-intellectual "customer is always right," trade school like indoctrination in business and management techniques, which education likely includes the implicit ideology that the possession of wealth is equivalent to "class" and (its possession) is the most important characteristic which should be considered in determining an individual's status and value to society. That is, what you know and what you think pale into insignificance before the question, "what do you have?"

Of course in educational endeavors the customer is the student and the student cannot always be right, for if the student is always right, in a sense, he or she ceases to be a student or consumer of educational materials and to the extent that they begin to be "right" they begin to acquire the status of educational provider or the status of teacher or professor. So the question arises, why not encourage learning and reflection by rewarding moderately at first answers and writings, attributable to students, that are in fact valued by the society, in this case, represented presumably by the US and state departments of Education as well as concerned philanthropical foundations who are funded by mega-national corporations seeking tax write-offs.

The questions arise, "management controls what? Speed for its' own sake alone? Production as the ultimate societal end? Consumption then as the ultimate societal end? Are we as a society merely about some choice select minority getting to live "very well" and the many condemned to struggle to live from pay check to pay check? Are we about living well or should our taxes be used to encourage, much more directly than heretofore, educational attainments amongst, not merely the rich and entitled, but everybody?

----

back in Somerville, MA,
Notes: it appears that the hyperinflation that beset Germany during the Weimar period and also presumably during the Nazi period leading up to WW2, might

have been averted if the German government had ignored the Bretton Woods accords which I believe established fixed rates of exchange for the major western currencies, and if the German government had allowed the deutschemark to float and depreciate in value or had deliberately devalued it, it is suggested in hindsight and in light of the recent Brazilian experience with devaluation, other foreign monies would likely have poured into the German economy and it is highly likely that the Second World War would have been averted.

Editors note 051704: I thought Bretton Woods occurred after WW2? Were there two accords? Maybe the point is, if Germany had not followed a path that would come to be required later by Bretton Woods?

Bipolar ideal of invulnerability/esteem derived from socialization through TV
Date: 1/30/99 3:26:33 PM Eastern Standard Time
to: the editors (The American Prospect, The Nation, The New Yorker)
from: Andréas Daniel Fogg
Letter from Somerville January 24, 1999

Correction: The Bretton Woods Conference apparently began in 1944. However, the system if any which governed the value of the deutschmark in its relation to the dollar and the other prominent currencies of the era remains obscure to the narrator.

In other words it is not clear whether currencies prior to the Second World War were pegged to the value of gold, neither is it clear whether they were allowed to be either devalued or depreciated in relation to each other. If depreciation and devaluation were not possible, as I suspect, then the point about a fixed deutschmark seems to remain valid.

Television and movies as encouraging an unrealistic and vacillating ideal of personal invulnerability and self esteem through conditioning identification mechanisms in viewers;

Fiction: when Davey was in high school, living at home, he had several long term successive relationships with girl friends, which involved extensive dating and extensive petting to orgasm, at least for himself, and they seemed to enjoy all that petting since it went on for extended periods, about a year for each girl friend, with dating about once a week or more. Davey and his girl friends attended a large four year public high school with about one thousand students in each year's class. The school as a whole was divided into four sub schools or halls, with the members of the halls attending home room together, eating in the cafe-teria together and only in the upper class years, if I remember correctly, attending similar advanced specialized classes, such as college placement American History, English, Math, Chemistry etc. Davey's girl friends were both members of a Hall other than his own. So that in general during the early years, except in the senior year, he didn't attend classes with them, seeing them for petting and social pur-poses, basically, on the weekends. But one of his best friends was in their Hall, I think they were both in the same Hall, all three in the same Hall. And the girl friends, one relationship lasted from the sophomore year into the junior year, the other from the junior year until just before the senior prom, used to see, talk to and touch Davey's friends and probably other boys. The thought that his girl friend might be touching another guy, might be being "unfaithful" to him aroused intense rage in Davey and he apparently resolved that when he became an adult, he would no longer put up with allowing his "mate" to be or even seem to be in the slightest bit unfaithful. In the meantime he persisted in maintaining these relationships which included kissing, petting to orgasm, but which failed to achieve literal full consummation. But when he got to college and lost his family's social support and to some extent the sense of economic security that he had felt while living at home, he found that his need to maintain a sort of patriarchal con-trol over any potential girl friend resulted in his being unable to establish any sort of heterosexual relationships, involving sexual contact, for some extended signifi-cant period of time. (That is, he felt and was unable to date anybody "success-fully" for several years after leaving home to go to college.) And, he never seemed to completely control those women with whom he actually became involved. In fact, he didn't seem to be aware of even the possibility that one of the sources of his real desire for his high school girl friends might have had something to do with the amount of freedom that they maintained and exercised toward other young men, some of whom were his closest friends.

In retrospect, a traumatic event involved his viewing the film, Midnight Cow-boy, in which the hero is forcibly separated from his girl friend while they are pet-ting, if I remember correctly, and after they are separated, he is anally sodomized by a group of three or four older men, in, if I remember correctly, the back of a pick up truck? Seeing this film brought home to Davey just exactly how econom-ically insecure and vulnerable he actually was. After all, he had no job experience and the hero of Midnight Cowboy worked at first I think as a dish washer before going to New York in order to attempt to make a living as a gigolo. Then there was the film Deliverance, in which a character, played by an actor named Ned Beatty, is also sodomized during a canoe trip in the mountains. Davey, it has been observed looks somewhat like Ned Beatty. So that when people see him those who have seen the movie may well think, "he looks like that guy who was raped in Deliverance. Let's see if there is anything to that resemblance." Apparently everything that happened in that movie happened to James Dickey, the author of the original novel. Although it is unclear whether he himself was sodomized. Still, you can see that Davey does not feel any particular debt of gratitude to those who made the casting decisions for the film. I mean, it seems it wasn't as if they were trying to make his life easier for him.

The theory is that the introjections of television watching experience into the narrator's life resulted in an enhanced unrealistic sense of invulnerability in his personal sense of self. (But because he couldn't seem to qualify as a genuinely important central character, being able to land only mediocre jobs and for the most part mediocre grades, he ended up fearing that his lot would be more like that of the character played by Jon Voight, in the aforementioned film than like the fantasized invulnerability of James Bond. Then, he saw the Spy Who Came in From the Cold which was about a British Jewish spy who attempts to return home after working under cover in then East Germany and, if I remember, gets double crossed and probably ends up dead. So since Davey is Jewish, his sense of invulnerability was not enhanced by this film either.) But, because he was able to watch many shows in which the hero always or almost always won and emerged unscathed from violent conflict, because most action programs and movies involved such ends for those who were able to identify with the protagonist, the viewer usually felt entitled to assume a sense of exaggerated, unrealistic personal invulnerability (so long as he didn't act upon a belief in such invulnerability). And the protagonists in those years were almost always males. The women's function was to enhance the male's ego aspirations. Only bad women were unfaithful to good men. When he left home in the late nineteen sixties, he soon realized that the definitions of good and evil were not as clear cut in the real world as they had seemed from the point of view of an upper middle class suburban high school student who was living at home at his father's expense. In real life, it became clear, nobody necessarily knew whether he was a good guy, destined for happiness and success through invulnerability, or whether he was perhaps on the wrong side of the issues. (To see my point, imagine if you will, one of "James Bond's girl friends" cheating on him, either just for the sake of evening the score, or, for that matter, in order to placate one of his enemies.) After all, in the late nineteen sixties, just who exactly was on the right side was, if you will recall, a matter of some contention.

So that for Davey, the media gave mixed wildly vacillating messages about who was destined for success and invulnerability and who was destined for failure, humiliation and hardship. In the Bond films, Bond always had dark hair, the villains often were blond, or light haired like Goldfinger or the assassin in From Russia with Love. Voight, the victim hero in Midnight Cowboy had light colored, blond hair. Davey had blond hair. And the victim in The Spy Who Came in From the Cold was Jewish. Davey was and is Jewish, although he will argue with you about what it perhaps should mean to be a Jew. So it appears that while the media was programming or perhaps more accurately conditioning the majority for success, it was programming or conditioning Davey with fear and the anticipation of failure, disgrace and perhaps death. Of course having "the nerve which allows one to fail and yet continue their efforts" may be a necessary prerequisite if one is to become a successful, significant writer.

January 25, 1999

Fictional tacit thought processes in the American power elite: "The Bull" (not a professional basketball player) intimated to "us" and the narrator, that he was Jesus. This intimation could have occurred in either a dream, a hallucination, or perhaps it was the product of the misinterpretation of a deliberate metaphorical comparison that was designed to enhance the narrator's sense of self esteem i.e. "I know Jesus, Jesus talked to me, therefore it is important for me to write." "The Bull" drives a gas guzzler for reasons that are justified by his situation. Nevertheless, "we, the power elite," seek to emulate him. Therefore, in order for the society to take meaningful action against gas guzzlers which exacerbate the greenhouse effect, we would have to overthrow our esteem enhancing belief that we have a personal connection with the one, true returned Jesus (and all the other important people who take pride in the fact that they drive gas guzzlers). But we are unwilling to give up these beliefs. To which configurations it is pointed out that the so called "Devil" has horns, just like a bull. And of course Zeus sometimes assumes the form of a bull. Not that I believe in either the Devil or Zeus and I remain somewhat agnostic and skeptical as to the omniscience and omnipotence of Jesus, and for that matter, of God. (Incidentally, the idea, which is surely a basic part of all three of the major monotheistic religions, i.e., that God is omniscient and omnipotent, includes the implication that he, that is God can control the weather and of course, thunderbolts. I mean if God is omnipotent then surely he can control the weather, right? But what better disguise for a Devil, even if he appeared in a dream, as it is alleged, than to suggest that he really is Jesus. (I realize that this comment seems extremely subversive, particularly if one is avidly awaiting the return of Jesus.)

And I really am sick of hearing about how wonderful trucks are as against cars and I feel in my gut that I and the public really need to be better educated as to the current state of the greenhouse controversy. What is holding this up???? I say, "Broadcast a global warming teach-in now!"

January 26, 1999

Delusions of grandeur encouraged by rampant identification with "heroes" in collaboration with the credit card companies which seek to encourage consumerism.

January 29, 1999

Notes: Can it perhaps be the case that the "Nature's God" described in the Declaration of Independence, perhaps the original inspiration for the Deistic religious assumptions of the Founders(?), was not Jesus at all but rather some approximation to the hurler of thunderbolts, a vague approximation of "he who controls nature (and the weather—since lightning is perhaps symbolic of weather is in general). More than likely, the Founders intended to keep the issue unresolved. Yet, as pointed out, within the Christian tradition, it is suggested that there is some overlap between the Christian notion of the Devil and the Greek conception of Zeus, who apparently has numerous "children" in contradistinction to the Christian conviction that God had and will have only one son (or child?) ever.

Ego development and TV mediated socialization, fiction, budget priorities
Date: 2/7/99 12:31:54 AM Eastern Standard Time
to: the editors (The American Prospect, The Nation, The New Yorker)
from: Andréas Daniel Fogg
Letter from Somerville January 30, 1999

Consider the thesis that weak ego development results from a systematic discouragement of reality testing, first, and second, that TV watching discourages reality testing as a direct consequence of its' imposed, forced assumption of a presumed single perspective which in deed does not require neither does it allow for comparing perspectives, neither for resorting to intersubjective verification. That is, intersubjective verification is not encouraged by the media because all of the media "views" of reality are identical, hence to question a media "view" has become technologically inappropriate, tantamount to performing a social gaffe.

Written at: North Peak Lodge
Sunday River
Newry, Maine
February 1, 1999

Points: that the national debt, estimated at 3.7 billion dollars, might be gradually rather than drastically reduced, say, off the top of my head, at a rate of no more than ten per cent per year, so that the rate of growth of the GDP does not appreciably diminish. There is an enlarged estimate of what the budget surplus over the next ten or fifteen years is likely to be. The question, then is a.) Pay off the debt as soon as possible, b.) don't pay off the debt, instead cut taxes for all, including those in the top twenty per cent of earners (and those in the top one per cent of earners), c.)Use the surplus partly to retire the debt and partly to improve the peace of mind of the elderly and those who are looking to assure their own secure retirement i.e. fortify Social Security and Medicare.

The problem with each of these approaches is that none of them do anything to improve the prospects for socioeconomic mobility for those who find themselves in the bottom forty to sixty per cent of earners in the US. These are people who are continually struggling to make ends meet; people who continually fear losing their jobs and who by and large are unable to participate in the finer fun and games that the society offers to those in the top forty and twenty percent of earners. The bottom sixty percent, more than half of the earners in the society, need help from the gov't in order to avoid being beaten down into a psychological stance of hopeless apathy. The gov't needs to make it clear to them that "hope is indeed alive" and not just because Jesse Jackson insists that it should be (and that in rhetoric "everybody is somebody") but that in fact opportunities to better one's situation other than through criminal activities are being made available by the gov't (and through tax breaks, charitable corporate foundations) and not just for the sick and elderly, but for the young and middle aged members of the society who have so to speak, "missed the train." I am, let it be noted, not speaking of sure thing welfare like benefits, I am not speaking of handouts to the poor, but rather of making it clear to the down and out, the members of society who are at or below the poverty line, to the relatively unskilled members of the working and so called under classes, before they get sent to prison, that opportunities to study on computers or in computerized learning centers, opportunities for adults who are either illiterate or semi literate or semi educated will be provided at the expense of the gov't and that significant accomplishments may result in limited financial rewards as well as the opportunity to participate in more advanced challenges both through the computer and in real socially interactive situations. It is suggested that to neglect to pursue the development of such an initiative; to instead neglect the public educational system (for both youth and adults) in favor entirely of fortifying support for the elderly and sick, is to neglect the vital productive age groups upon whom the responsibility for the continued strength, vitality, productivity and competitiveness of the society rests. Parents by and large should be bringing up children, not grandparents. Bringing up children takes time, the television and VCR are not adequate baby-sitters. And the bottom sixty percent often cannot afford to take off enough time from "suggested" and needed overtime in order to establish emotional connectedness with their children. The society pays the price in the form, it is suggested, of increased levels of hyperactive attention deficit disorders, of predicted increased incidence of psychotic disorders and perhaps in the future, in the event of an economic downturn, of increased rates of penal incarceration. (The percentage of the population currently incarcerated is at present disturbingly high relative to the rates of other states.)

The point is that I have seen lots of perhaps ordinary folks buying scratch tickets and ritualistically rubbing them in what appears to be a vain hope of winning by chance what they know might be a few thousand dollars, but might amount to five or ten dollars or merely another free ticket, or even nothing at all. Imagine if participation in computerized learning "challenges" included the possibility of similar or larger rewards. Think of the increased incentive to participate. And think of the improved levels of literacy and learning that would likely result from the encouragement and proliferation of such programmed incentives.

Furthermore, think of the increased level of civility, the lowered, decreased need to scapegoat and hate resented "out groups."

Fiction: A female US Ski Team racer, the winner of at least one major World Cup race—but never an Olympic medal, suffers a psychotic break, is hospitalized for a time, then released while on medication, to live back in her home town. It is not clear if she lives with her parents or alone or with a roommate. She gets a job as a waitress at a pizzeria. The breakdown seemingly had been precipitated by a huge drive to succeed and become famous (and wealthy). But when her achievements fell short of her goal, she was quoted in the press as having once said "I suck." Then, when she won one World Cup race, I think it was a downhill, maybe a super G, she had been embraced at the finish line by the great Austrian super GS champion, Fred rich Kroch, Kroch, a notorious partygoer, playboy and womanizer, the son of wealthy parents, had embraced her publicly.

She had been tempted to take up with him, but despite the fact that she had adopted a professional name, Franny Buckfield, she was unable to shed the hold of her local relatively poor and ordinary Maine friends. She knew what they would say about her taking up with Kroch, not that she couldn't handle him, but they would call her, she feared, knew, a gold-digger and even a "hooker." So, she broke down from the combined stresses and presumably heard some voices, perhaps lost some of that "racer's edge."

But here we see it; society has some limited rewards for Olympic skiing champions (Picabo Street managed to win one or two World Cup titles over the last few years, in addition to having won several Olympic medals, and she got some Chapstick endorsements and presumably her name is on more than a few types of skis). But apparently there is little economic recognition of renaissance like overall diversified accomplishments. So that this talented racer, Franny Buckfield, feels like a failure because she did not win more races instead of feeling or being encouraged to strive for success in fields other than skiing. Afterall, being an accomplished ski racer and a talented professor of say political science might well amount to being more important sociologically, and ultimately in the overall scheme of things, than being merely a world champion and, say, for example, a wealthy playboy.

Rehash of TV and ego development, the lack of a greenhouse debate, Clinton + race
Date: 2/10/99 11:38:28 AM Eastern Standard Time
to: the editors (The American Prospect, The Nation, The New Yorker)
from: Andréas Daniel Fogg
Letter from Somerville February 7, 1999

That speaking to other people in an attempt to determine what has happened is a primary motivation that drives people to have social interactions, to have conversations. That TV and movies present single perspective views of what the director determines should be accepted as the true version of reality. That is, his or her view of reality is implicitly foisted off on the public, in the guise of art or cinema verite, as the truth. Hence the work that would ordinarily go into any concerned citizen's attempts to determine just exactly what the nature of reality is, is bypassed, and co-opted by the media presentations. Only a sophisticated, educated viewer has the intellectual resources to see through the propagandist's artificial almost hypnotically persuasive version of reality. This version is often presented as a sort of fait accompli. Hence most viewers are attracted, on the one hand, to a version of reality that purports persuasively to be "true," and on the other hand, in a world of competing voices, may be willing to accept the imposition of an imposed artificial consensus, imposed that is by the media acting hand in glove with commercial backers. Hence the decision to not discuss the greenhouse effect is sold to viewers primarily on the implicit ground that challenging that decision involves too much effort, and that the authorities must know what they are doing. Hence the impulse to rebel against the established views of reality withers and in its place we find an exaggerated passion for following professional big time sports. Civility may be withering in part as an expression of frustration at the cooptation of citizenship by the media apparatus. That is, people may be feeling frustrated at the tacit realization that the experts have effectively removed them from the political deliberative process.

Truth it would seem may be defined as that which is not subject to debate. In the past, truth has been arrived at as a result of extensive public debate and discussion. Today, the media elite present it to the public too often as fait accompli, all of the major discussion and controversy having been dealt with behind closed "professional" doors. Yet still the suggestion that big money interests may be influencing the outcomes of such discussions fails to draw the attention of the journalists, most of who have apparently themselves become recipients of large sums of cash and corporate benefits and hence are unwilling to break the code of the establishment's silence. It is amazing to me that well into this greenhouse controversy literally no one in the media is willing to devote air time to discussion of either the data or the theoretical controversies associated with it. There is an entire channel on the cable system devoted to the weather, yet the only discussion of the greenhouse effect is the occasional belated mention of the fact that 1998 was statistically the warmest year on record, globally speaking. The Chinese, it should be noted, recently experienced a series of devastating internal floods, to the point where the damage constituted a traumatic national disaster. It is highly likely that, because of these floods, they would be amenable to accepting restrictions on greenhouse emissions emanating from their automobiles and trucks.

Fiction: fatherless young man, a laissez faire conservative supports professional wrestler recently elected governor of Minnesota, says, there is nothing wrong with eliminating the public broadcasting system (which had been advocated by the wrestler governor) from that state, or anywhere, since most of public broadcasting "does not turn a profit," and therefore is not worthy of public support. Ironically, it may be the presence of capitalistic concentrations of wealth which will allow for the transcendence of the hegemony of mass market values. Afterall, in contradistinction to Marx, capital may represent the accrual of power to intelligence. And without such an accrual of power, we might see indeed the end of public educational funding, the end of public broadcasting funding all on the grounds that not enough of the mass market, which after all is dominated by those of, by definition, average and below average intelligence, is willing to voluntarily support such efforts.

February 8, 1999
Written at: North Peak Lodge
Sunday River
Newry, Maine

Fiction: P. the lion, fatherless, is a professional wrestling fan, in part, perhaps because he longs for a father or father figure who will ritualistically "pretend" to beat him, to symbolically take his self-centered narcissistic self esteem down one or two notches. In real life P. the lion purports to own a firearm and has ridden the accompanying intimidation factor to a fairly secure fairly important privileged but non-supervisory position in the company he works for. P. the lion is a staunch Republican conservative, is one of these people who believes in the ultimate validity of the market, that is, he believes that market generated valuations, prices cannot be wrong and that to accept the market's decision's in all cases is the best possible course of action for society. Hence if a former professional wrestler, former Navy seal turned Governor of Minnesota decides that National Public Radio does not deserve the support of the state of Minnesota "because," says P. the lion, "almost none of their programs earn a profit." Then that is probably why the Governor decided to perhaps attempt to eliminate the state's support, he thinks.

But the appeal of the TV program and the appeal of the movie seem to lie in the fact that the views of reality presented appear to be already intersubjectively verified, that is, before any argument or discussion amongst viewers and reviewers has occurred. Hence discussing whether what has been seen is true or accurate seems to be a waste of time. The point is that the better the production, the more convincing its' message. And these messages connect to and convince the emotions sometimes almost hypnotically bypassing the viewer's critical faculties.

So that what the public believes to be true is highly subject to the manipulative intent of media production, network and movie studio corporations. Hence these production companies become the objects of appeals from other monied interests which seek to have their interests supported or if not supported, that their interests should at least not be attacked. And some of these interests are the oil and automotive corporations. These influences also influence many of the publishing houses and newspapers. Also, the individual's perceptions are regularly belittled in comparison to the "views" expressed in movies and TV. That is, the implicit view is, your point of view cannot matter much, because you aren't a TV or movie star, personality or mogul. In this way, even once respected members of the professoriate are also put down. For example, consider the condescending tone of a TV talk show host in the manner of presentation of the question, "and what do you think, Professor?" as if the term professor was somehow a term of derision. It didn't always used to be the case. If a professor sought to convince a TV audience of a view not previously or currently supported by the moneyed interests, he would likely be dismissed unceremoniously with the rebuke "sorry, we don't have the time…" Because time is money." Hence all of the real controversial argumentation goes on, if at all, "off camera," out of the public's view.

Suggested public conversation "game:" Discuss what the media don't want us to discuss and why. Possible subject for a sci fi film: How alien humanoids from outer space have taken over the media and hatched a plot to not discourage global warming. The aim is to seize control of the higher managerial corporate power positions, make the planet warmer, sell more oil and make bigger profits with bigger cars and trucks. Eventually perhaps they hope to trigger an extremely destructive world war in which humanity will perish but they will survive, having disseminated weapons of mass destruction to whose lethal effects they are immune.

February 9, 1999
North Peak Lodge again
Affirmative action, Milton Friedman, Federal vs. Corporate Funding, Inter-racial friendships and the President's difficulties with marital fidelity;

Just having fun. I am thinking it would really be nice if somebody potentially in a position to pay compensation would ask me to write about something that they want me to write about. Anyway, the snow is good today, and my legs are holding up even through two consecutive days of skiing.

The inn keeper tells me that the "National Training Laboratory" is located in Bethel, Maine, not far from Sunday River, that they offer managerial training seminars in the summer for university and corporate people, for people from the US and from countries throughout the world. This NTL is apparently not supported by US Federal funds. Where their funding and accreditation come from, other than possible fees charged to participants' supporting universities and corporations, is not clear. Yet the question remains intriguing. Perhaps indeed there is some central organizing non federal possibly corporate controlling and coordinating organization, as has been hypothesized. I had heard vaguely about the NTL being here before, but I didn't know that they were nonfederal.

But if there are significant nonfederal programs involved in a significant proportion of the US and international economies, then the question arises, what exactly are such programs doing? Why and at whose behest? When Milton Friedman argues that federal economic intervention is either not helpful or actually harmful is he perhaps implicitly arguing for the tacit delegation of power to such central coordinating non federal organizations, perhaps since it is non federal it is immune from sanctions stemming from the violation of certain affirmative action hiring guidelines?

Angry people with poor attitudes and chips on their shoulders are certainly not easy to work with, yet the US federal gov't often seems to require that they be hired if federal support is to be continued. And, too many of the members of the larger principal discriminated against groups (i.e. African Americans and Hispanics) are poor, blame white people for this fact and are angry at white people as a result. If the gov't requires that such people be hired despite the negative effect upon the morale and productivity of the members of groups who are not discriminated against, then overall productivity, morale (educational accomplishments) are likely to suffer.

I went swimming a week or two ago, struck up a conversation with a middle aged African American man in the next lane. Then, we began to swim. In the course of eight or ten laps, at one point, his foot apparently inadvertently touched my leg. (The lanes in the pool are not particularly wide.) For the next two or three hours, I found myself looking at virtually every single young woman who crossed my path as if she might become (my) sexual partner. I do not usually entertain such extremely promiscuous assertive sexual fantasies. Their cause, I surmise, was my physical contact with this African American; it was as if the contact allowed me to partake of (presumably) his point of view. But such an obser-vation probably hasn't been made by others?!?

What is the putative cause of this observed African American higher aggregate blood pressure? Surely it does not involve an ingrained genetic predisposition to promiscuously womanize? If so, such a predisposition could have been selected as a consequence of having lived relatively closer to the equator, in regions where the hotter aggregate temperatures are more inimical to sustained agriculture and hence in environments where a subsistence like standard of living tends to be the norm, where a relatively smaller proportion of children survive and where, as a result, a hereditary premium is placed upon male sexual assertiveness. Of course, if such an observation is valid, which is possible (though also likely to cause embarrassment if not loss of face and hence be politically inappropriate and incorrect), then Martin Luther King, Jr.'s observation that we are all substantially alike "underneath the skin" would not be true. And if that were the case, then the problems associated with achieving racial integration in educational and work place settings would be much more complex and difficult than the civil rights and racial integration advocates are so far willing to admit or acknowledge.

Note that a lack of sexual assertiveness in which the merest hint of extramari-tal involvement becomes reduced to some sort of betrayal of "all that is right" may constitute the present principal Caucasian defense against Negro and His-panic attempts to encroach upon the traditional white male power bases. This is particularly the case when an individual "offender" has made it clear though his own actions that he has no interest in protecting the insecurities associated with the perhaps slipping white male grasp upon the levers of American power.

Genetic predisposition to fight or not possibly negatively correlated with IQ
Date: 2/16/99 12:10:35 PM Eastern Standard Time
to: the editors (The American Prospect, The Nation, The New Yorker)
from: Andréas Daniel Fogg
Letter from Somerville February 13, 1999

Behavior potentially controlled by a gene or set of genes influencing the predispo-sition to either stand and fight or instead either flee, withdraw or otherwise avoid violent conflict, that the predisposition to fight, whether purely a learned charac-teristic or both learned and influenced by some genetically inherited characteris-tics, that this predisposition to resort to violence instead of either retreat, (flight)

or compromise or simply avoidance may be negatively correlated with the ability to think creatively either reflectively, morally, sociologically or technologically.
In other words, he or she who has a short fuse, who can be easily pushed to violence is less likely to exercise their intelligence in stressful situations and hence is less likely to be capable of high levels of achievement in either academic, work or indeed any context.

And yet, those who are determined to avoid loss of face in any competitive interaction may see contests in which intelligence is a crucial factor as settings in which the display of aggression may be legitimately allowed to influence the question as to who may have achieved superiority. That is, it may often be the case that when two men converse, the larger one may simply seek to appropriate the ideas expressed by the smaller, saying in effect, "that's what I was saying all along." In effect when this occurs, it occurs in the context of threatened violence and it is tantamount to intellectual theft. The likelihood of intellectual theft occurring in casual conversation is in fact extremely great, the temptation to steal ideas is enormous, even for those of smaller stature. Hence the rationale of the writer, who writes in the vague hope that since his ideas or the ideas that he has appropriated and/or modified from others may, since they are distributed under his name in a printed format, result in his receiving at least some of the credit for their formulation on the one hand, and, on the other hand, that, because the ideas are presented passively by the disseminator, that is, they are read or not read, depending upon the inclination of the reader, rather than orally or aggressively as in the case of the spoken rhetorical word, be less likely to result in his persecution or punishment by representatives of the powers that be who might take offense in the event that some of his comments are deemed critical or offensive. Consider what would have been Jesus' fate if his comments had been published in written format rather than uttered aloud and as a result be subject to the vagaries of collective memory and its likely distortions.

February 14, 1999

Speculative:
Of "civil society" "NGOs" and "Corporate Welfare"

David Rieff and Michael Clough address the topic of what functions so called civil society fulfills in this week's The Nation. And, I just received a letter from Ann McBride and Common Cause describing the extent of Corporate Welfare. A question arises, are Corporate Welfare benefits subject to affirmative actions quotas or merely guidelines? I suspect the answer is guidelines. Clough ends his piece with the invocation that people should learn to "provide their own protection."

And, Rieff points out that technically speaking the NRA (National Rifle Association) should be considered an NGO but it isn't presumably because it is considered politically incorrect by those who define what an NGO is. Perhaps, no doubt, the sources of funding for the NRA are qualitatively different from the sources of funding of the more typical NGOs. Also, the typical NGO member seems to be politically and personally very different from my impression of the typical NRA member. The feminists seem to be the ones most seriously opposed to the ownership and mastery of firearms. Yet in assuming this position, justified on the grounds that having guns around poses a danger to children and others, they tend to ignore the central point of the NRA which amounts to the idea that having a gun or having access to a gun and having the skill to use it effectively allows smaller people to argue with larger people. As the larger man says in the movie, I think Homicide, if you didn't have a gun with you, we wouldn't be having this conversation at all. Of course some large people are amenable to hearing reasoned, superior argumentation from smaller people, but many simply are not. Some of these larger persons are or will be in prison, others are recipients and controllers of corporate welfare. It is almost as if the enlightened NGO members, who, it is my impression sometimes behave in entitled ways that are likely explained by the probable fact that their expenses are all taken care of by some unknown but suspected central corporate donor, have been politically neutralized as a result of having been put on the dole. Hence, they are allowed to be as moral as they wish amongst themselves, all the while congratulating themselves on their economic entitlement, so long as they do not either express their views in a rabble rousing manner in the media and so long as they don't interfere too much with the linked system of corporate welfare which Common Cause estimates at 625 billion dollars over the next five years. So they protest rhetorically but not so loudly as to upset the golden goose so to speak.

The onus of racism reexamined;

Traditionally the blame for racism has been placed squarely upon Caucasians. White racism, traditionally, has been defined as the problem facing American society. Little or no attention has been paid to its' opposite number namely Black racism. Indeed, if those who defined the nature of the civil rights struggle are heeded clearly, one would come to believe that Black racism is either inconsequential or non-existent, in any event not a phenomenon that society should in any sense pay any mind to. Yet in most long standing emotional problems or conflicts, whether individual or collective in nature, there are usually (at least) two sides to the story. And unless both sides are examined it is unlikely that the problem or conflict will be resolved. In the case of racial prejudice in America the blame for the sentiment has been placed squarely on the Whites, non of the blame has been placed on the Blacks. This situation may not be entirely fair. Note that while Whites are often unwilling to interact with Blacks it is also often the case that Blacks are just as unwilling to interact with Whites even with Whites who are willing to interact with them. The mental health establishment is quick to accuse whites of laboring under the burden of delusions of grandeur, yet, it would seem, it is loath to similarly label Blacks. The putative justification for this apparent pro Black prejudice probably lies in the fact that it is believed that Blacks need to sustain all of the self esteem that they possibly can in order to be able to continue to strive to succeed in light of prejudicial White beliefs to the effect that Black's are inferior in educational studies and intelligence in general; and in light of the likelihood that they may give up on their studies in the event of early or continuous setbacks in which their achievements fall short of those of Whites. Non of these considerations are applied to Whites who may feel inadequate in the areas in which Black achievers typically excel more than White achievers, for example in certain sports, certain forms of music and dance. Yet many Blacks may be loath to interact with Whites in contexts in which their achievements do not measure up, or, they may simply be loath to interact with Whites at all, since the uncomfortable possibility of being shown up only may emerge in reality in the event of actual social interaction. Such acts of Black social rejection undoubtedly play a role in the encouragement of reactive feelings on the part of Whites, reactive feelings of anger at having been rejected, which feelings may have in the past, and may continue even in the present, to be transformed into White prejudice against Blacks. In any event, this slant on the situation just occurred to me and I thought that perhaps it had not occurred to others as well. Conflicts and resentments may perhaps be avoided in the future if individuals are aware of the tendency of numerous members of the other group, whichever group is the other group, to avoid all social contact on the grounds that some feared outcome or other may result from even casual passing social contact. Note that theoretically this may be the case when the groups in potential conflict are of different races or, for that matter, when they are different ethnicities, nationalities, religions or even of different socioeconomic classes.

February 15, 1999

We are sometimes sexually aroused by persons of different races, religions, nationalities, ethnicities, classes. When such arousal occurs between members of the same sex, particularly when the persons involved are males, the origins of prejudice and antipathy may become apparent. Voice contact can be made or avoided. Eye contact can be made or avoided. When all such contacts are avoided the groundwork is set for continuing hostility and interpersonal insecurity. For when such contacts are feared and avoided, the implicit message that is delivered is equivalent, in terms of the primary process, that is the emotional statement is delivered that "the other does not exist." That is the other does not exist "to the rejecter" because the avoider of eye contact literally refuses "to see" refuses "to recognize the existence" of the other. And since he refuses to recognize the other's existence, he also refuses to respect the rights and needs of the other's "sisters" in so far as they exist in the aggregate. Since the others "sisters" are not respected as part and parcel of the mutual recognition of each others existence, they may be potentially robbed or sexually abused and raped, implicitly, at least in so far as the avoider admits emotionally (to himself). Hence when the other out group member refuses to make eye contact with you, let alone speak with you, he reserves the right to himself to play fast and loose regardless of the consequences, with the female (and, for that matter, the male) members of your racial, national, religious, ethnic or socioeconomic group. Hence the refusal to make such relatively inconsequential contact is often seen as threatening to the other who seeks such contact; threatening since it is seen as an indication that the others' intentions toward himself, the members of his representative group and the women who are part of his representative group, that his intentions may well not be peaceful and benign but rather are likely to be hostile.

Consider too the fact that in cities, it is generally recommended to members of the middle class, incoming from the affluent suburbs, for example, to avoid eye (and social) contact with "strangers." This recommendation seems to be based on the often accurate presumption that, when eye contact is initiated by a member of someone assumed to be poor, that such contact is initiated solely for the purpose of accomplishing a semi peaceful albeit implicitly threatening solicitation of monies. Thus the following sort of interaction it is hoped will be avoided: "Hi buddy, how you doing? Can you spare ten or twenty bucks?" The implicit threat behind such an interaction involves the imputation that if the individual accosted refuses to part with the requested sum, that he will no longer be the accoster's "buddy" and may well become the object of an assault. So the sort of interaction that is not suspect to such an interpretation occurs when contact is sought by someone who, it is presumed, is neither poorer, nor assumed to be poorer. In American cities when such an encounter is sought, it is often usually not understood at all, or understood as preparatory to a sexual solicitation on the part of the more economically secure individual. Since this interpretation is typically imposed by the poorer individual, who often is unable to think of himself as anything more than a sexual object since he suffers from poor self esteem, he is likely to avoid all contact or in the event that contact is allowed, the poorer individual may attempt to convert what might have been a perfectly innocent friendly mutually reinforcing social contact, into a "professional sexual transaction" that is, to turn it into a transaction involving sex for money, that is an act of solicited sexual prostitution.

Stateless nations and cultures, an international priority (re Kosovo, Turkey, Iraq..)
Date: 2/19/99 12:50:08 PM Eastern Standard Time
to: the editors (The American Prospect, The Nation, The New Yorker)
from: Andréas Daniel Fogg
Letter from Somerville February 18, 1999

The recent developments in the Kurds' quest for either a state or more recognition for their potential nationhood suggest possible grounds for a reformulation of the problem. That is, a possible solution to the Kurds grievances, short of carving up adjacent state territory, may involve the establishment of national Kurd institutions which would serve the needs of Kurd peoples from locations in other states. For example, one could envisage Kurd radio and television stations which would be allowed indeed encouraged to service interested populations. Likewise, one could imagine a Kurd oriented large pro bono legal services corporation which would serve the needs of needy Kurds who seem to be suffering from anti-Kurd based persecution. Problems that such a legal services corporation could legitimately address might and should include cases in which the population concerned is being unconscionably economically exploited, that is being paid economically, sociologically harmful, low wages. That is, the argument could be made, presumably in a formal international court, but also in the informal court of educated wealthy public opinion, to the effect that increasingly lower sweatshop like wages are, in and of themselves, harmful to the overall economies of the nations involved and indeed to the world economy as a whole.

Similarly such an organization could coordinate the funding and establishment of one or more universities and/or university departments which are focused upon the development of Kurdish history and culture.

And, in fact this paradigm, for dealing with unrequited aspirations for statehood perhaps should be extended to apply to other demographically significant threatened national or cultural or religious groups (including those currently found in Kosovo).

Fiction re Trojan horses and implicit popular political models
Date: 2/28/99 1:31:55 AM Eastern Standard Time
to: the editors (The American Prospect, The Nation, The New Yorker)
from: Andréas Daniel Fogg
Letter from Somerville February 22, 1999

Now it should be clear that this, what I am about to begin writing, is fiction, that is, there is no resemblance between the people that I am writing about and any real people, but clearly I think that there could be such people with characteristics such as I hope to clearly sketch for you, the reader's edification, which means generally, hopefully, improvement or perhaps simply education. Anyway, it seems to me that since the end of the cold war, which for those of you who don't remember it, consisted in a colossal nuclear and conventional arms race and a competition in the area of spreading national influence amongst the nations of the developing world which needed help and generally a hair raising, nerve racking state of international tension such as might be expected in a situation where the threats of being willing to go to nuclear war were being taken seriously by statesmen and citizens in both major power blocks and indeed throughout much of the rest of the world. Indeed, so seriously were the Communists taken by many ordinary Americans, and indeed so seriously was the ideology taken, that it is the author's contention, even today, more than nine years since the Soviet hegemony over eastern Europe ended, that a significant number of Americans continue to labor under the delusion that the public version of the denouement of the cold war is in fact a lie, an illusion, a propagandistic smoke screen which hides the truth from the people, the truth being it is believed or perhaps in some cases hoped, that in fact the Communists actually won, that in fact they are presently controlling the US economy. Note that this belief is consistent with the belief that the Communist ideology namely from each according to his ability, to each according to his need also is being used as a distributional rationale, a putative justification for who gets what and why, to whit, that those who succeed have successfully managed to gain entry to the American Communist Party. This implicit view has been expressed if no where else, on the usually somewhat innocuous Fox cartoon program, The Simpson's. However, it should also be noted that holders of this belief, a belief, by the way, which in and of itself yields the bottom line of hope to all, regardless of their abilities, works, proclivities towards either work or temporal or moral responsibility, likely find it's possession extremely comforting since in a sense it holds out the promise of limitless financial success for all, regardless of the merits of their work, if any. Hence when relatively uneducated, relatively poor individuals are offered one or more credit cards and told in no uncertain terms that they can run up charges of several thousand dollars and be required to pay off only a minimal monthly balance of say ten or fifteen dollars, the logical conclusion that quite likely comes into their minds is in fact likely to be the idea that you see, the Communists, the friends of the working people, really did win. Here they give us these credit cards and we can buy enormous amounts of stuff and only have to pay off a little bit at a time. And after awhile we may have to declare bankruptcy, but we'll worry about that later. And besides, the laws of bankruptcy are actually pretty lenient.

Maybe, then, they think, the Soviets or their agents have actually taken over, AH HAH!! So that means that we should do all we can to help the powers that be since they actually are the "good guy" communists. The Republicans, after all were the ones who actually made peace with the Communists, weren't they? And the Republicans are the ones who support American investment in China, along with the middle of the road Democrats, including the President, right. And both political parties pretty much support globalization meaning the exporting of American jobs to lower wage earning population bases. Just today we hear that Levi Strauss is closing eleven North American plants. laying off five thousand nine hundred workers. It would be interesting if someone were to do an actual study of how many of these laid off workers are rehired at significantly lower wages. I would like to see some simple unequivocal numbers. The author worked for a number of years for just slightly above the minimum wage, working for two bosses who took advantage of, what at that time was poor self esteem, to tell him that he was lucky to be earning even that much. The author knows what it is like to feel like a failure and to be earning very little money. In such a situation, it makes sense to put one's faith in a magic card which will eventually supply, it is hoped, all one's needs, including one's needs for a whole lot more socioeconomic status.

And then when after months of waiting for the hoped for rewards to accrue, and they don't, or the credit card becomes worthless, what then? Perhaps they turn to the militias or terrorism, or perhaps they push drugs or rob banks, or maybe they turn violently against others, either family, friends or strangers. They had elevated their expectations partly in response to the generalized promises of the television media, far beyond the legitimate reach of their truncated, often diminishing incomes. These are elevated almost always delusional expectations, one warehouse worker is "holding out" for a popular attractive female TV star. How many other children of the suburbs, living at home with mom and dad, rent free, are living in worlds determined by hyper inflated delusional expectations? And how many moms and or dads are encouraging these delusions?

February 24, 1999

The catch phrase during the Joseph McCarthy period of communist witch hunting involved the accusation that so and so is or was "a card carrying communist." Now most of us are clearly card carriers, as well. The implicit question in the popular mind then is, what real privileges exactly does the possession of such "cards" yield in actuality?

Consider the fictional case in which a fictional mother, who is also a covert somewhat famous novelist, refuses to allow any substantive political or sociological theoretical discussions at the dinner table. The question is "why," "why" does she suppress such discussion? Is it because she selfishly wishes to write her own impression of these ideas later in the privacy of her secret authorial retreat? Does she realize the dampening effect she has upon the intellectual activity of her family?

Is this impulse to restrict intellectual discussion perhaps characteristic of a society which has been transfixed by its passive posture before the so called media mavens, the so called media pundits who we are trained to accept as the arbiters of what is intellectually and socially appropriate? Is the perhaps authorial mother merely transmitting the societal phobia against expressing individual ideas out loud? Probably.

February 26, 1999
North Peak Lodge
Sunday River
Newry, Maine

It would appear that informed, "educated" causal importations (that is, as is, it is imported that anger and sexual arousal "cause" high blood pressure, or, an increasing money supply caused by printing and redistributing income (and money) may counteract deflationary tendencies) constitute a sort of intellectual capital, that is, such ideas, particularly in a scientific age, literally constitute economic values in and of themselves. Indeed this has always been the case, though not recognized as clearly as at present. In the pre-enlightenment past causal ideas often needed to be connected to divinely inspired religious teachings in order for them to achieve social recognition and in order for their bearers to receive economic rewards. Today ideas need to be recognized as important by some societal source of authority, before the public institutions will be willing to show credence and respect. But in the interim, those who are willing to share their "intellectual capital" with others who may eventually grant public recognition may have a competitive edge over those who let their ideas sit in drawers unread by others, sometimes for years at a time. (Such private "selfish" writers, however, have an advantage over those who merely verbalize their thoughts, and these are ahead of those who think but don't even speak their ideas out loud.)

Barker Lodge
Sunday River

As in, consider "the import" of what I am saying. Also, perhaps a better word is "imputation" instead of importation which derives from turning a noun, "the import," into a verb "to import" and hence "importation."

Men whose only sure route to "life after death" may involve the creation of long lasting "important" intellectual capital, may sometimes harbor misogynistic attitudes towards women in part when they don't respect the value of intellectual activity, in part because the women have a relative certainty of achieving some sort of immortality i.e. through having children, which contribution by a man is more suspect i.e. some other man may be the father; and the man may develop a phobia about participating in sexual activity out of a belief that the possibility of literal long life if not relative immortality may be removed in the event that the man acquiesces in the creation of one or more substitute versions of himself. The logic being, the creation of a younger version of the self results eventually in a diminution of the actual need for the ego, hence absent the real need for the self, the process of aging accelerates or is merely less retarded.

But this logic can be reversed by the point that being involved in a mutually satisfying non abusive relationship with a woman may constitute actually, being of more use to God or the forces of Heaven and Earth (Nature) than may be involved in sanctimonious holier than thou so called abstinent virtue.

North Peak Lodge again

Physical reinforcement and the generation of intellectual capital;

Usually it makes sense for friends or a couple, one or more of whom are involved in generating intellectual capital, to talk "around" or "around about" problems that are of mutual interest and importance. If the problems are addressed head on, in conversation, that constitutes a sort of tacit collaboration. When we are talking about a sexually involved couple, of course, there is the danger that the sexual relation may come to be at risk; if the woman, for example, uses sexual favors to influence, guide and control the work. Usually a man will not wish to place his relationship with his wife or girlfriend at risk when he attempts to generate intellectual capital. If the work must meet her approval before it is shared she becomes in a sense a sort of final censor. If she doesn't understand your work (many women are not actually as smart as they like to think) the question she will worry about the most is, "are you getting paid enough?" If so, she probably will not make a fuss about your wasting your time. But if you aren't getting paid and she doesn't understand your work, or thinks she understands it and thinks that it is wrong, bad or harmful, then you may have to choose between such work and her, always a painful choice.

Subway (restaurant)
? Norway, Maine

In fact, a consort, a spouse, deserves some of the credit and some of the blame for their partner's accomplishments.

Back in Somerville, MA

Striped clothing and the assertion of self importance

Consider the possible unconscious implications associated with some individuals who wear striped shirts. It sometimes appears that by wearing striped shirts, that they are unconsciously "pulling rank" that is asserting through symbolic behavior that they "have status" have "rank" more rank than those who do not assert such through such a choice of apparel. You don't notice this phenomenon unless you are on the lookout for it, but people who wear striped shirts, sweaters or blouses, I have noticed, seem unconsciously to want to initiate verbal contact themselves, rather than by allowing or encouraging others to speak to them first.

Subj: alcohol influenced ruminations on Don DeLillo's play Valparaiso
Date: 3/6/99 9:05:14 PM Eastern Standard Time
to: the editors (The American Prospect, The Nation, The New Yorker)
from: Andréas Daniel Fogg
Letter from Somerville March 1, 1999

We expect, nay demand the truth from the media, as if we have a right to it. Meanwhile, the assumption that the rules of the game, namely that we get to watch the TV media programming in return for our willingness to be interrupted by numerous disjunctive yet rationally meaningful appeals which helpfully inform us as to what courses of action are appropriate, allow us to escape from the numerous private sources of shame which we all fear. That is, if we could only spend our way out of these persistent feelings of inadequacy, yes that's it, then everything would be just fine, we wouldn't have to rebel against anything or anyone, we wouldn't have to risk the angst of showing disrespect for any of these personable personalities who regularly assure us that they are watching us, "we'll see you tomorrow" they blithely assure, so we are being seen after all, we do exist, thank God and the wonderful people in the networks who deserve every penny of the exorbitant wages they receive, by God we wonder if anybody cares and sure enough they assure us that they do. It's so wonderful, and if Medicare premiums go up, so what, those are the people who deserve to be rolling in clover, they after all, have a handle on the problem of sin, not having to worry about it since none of us really can touch them anyway, and if you can't touch someone, you can't sin with them, right, so bravo for their wonderful purity, and their cheerfulness and never mind that we are poor and that the reason they are so damned cheerful is that we are letting them get away with grand theft. And who cares about all the bribes they offer the politicians to make sure that they will continue to get away with grand theft (made possible through relatively low high end taxes and relatively disproportionately minimal or nonexistent broadcast licensing fees), because after all, we like having our thoughts interrupted and we like buying on credit and living as if there were no tomorrow, who cares about bankruptcy, they probably aren't my kids anyway.

Artificial insemination, the double bind between science and humanistic religion;

Which are you for, the naive mass media inquisitor demands, are you for enlightened science or for the unenlightened Dark Age fundamentalist religion? It's either you're for Darwin and evolution or for the Gospel and/or Genesis. You have no other choices. Surely you will not hear about other choices from any of those so called wise persons who inhabit TV land. In fact you won't hear about those choices from the TV wise persons, for to hear about those choices would suggest the possibility that they are not the only possibilities, that perhaps Darwin did not have all the answers, but that there might be other alternatives to Darwin, other that is than the answers of Genesis. Perhaps, after all, human development occurs in a different manner than does genetic evolution. Humans after all are capable of a sophisticated something known as learning, learning on levels of sophistication relatively unknown to what are euphemistically known as the less sophisticated primates and species. And if that were the case, then we could perhaps break the seemingly ironclad connection between science, Darwin and the imperative desirability of availing ourselves of the supposedly superior seeds of strangers, which imperative currently seems to subvert the previously operant justification for the traditional nuclear family, namely to foster the creation of biological children who are genetically related to both mother and father. But I think that the need is to confront the question in public, to debate it, to air it, rather than, as the liberal feminists have sought to do, declare it resolved. That is, to dramatize the debate in art; who is happier, he who brings up his own children, or he who brings up someone else's children. Are there any drawbacks in bringing up a son, for example, who closely resembles his father? Do they tend to crowd each other to much? Are they too much alike for comfort, perhaps? If the son is clearly not of the father's seed, is the connection between father and son never established, or can it never be established? Is there any shame which accrues to the mother if she admits that her child is the result of a sperm (or egg) donation, if so, does shame attach to the child, what views do traditional religions hold in this regard, is there room for anything short of total intolerance? Meanwhile, the time needed for training for highly sought occupational positions increases, thereby pushing the age at which males (and some females) marry back and back, thereby reducing the likelihood that they will be capable of successfully conceiving children and increasing the likelihood that the spouse, in despair of conceiving, will resort to either infidelity or a sperm or egg bank.

March 2, 1999

A question that needs then to be asked is, "is not TV watching causing a sort of masochistic collective gratification?" What might the sources of pain consist in? Pain could come from implied invidious comparisons i.e. from the perception that ego falls short of the income necessary to consume in conformance with the implied, suggested, advertised models of conspicuous consumption (at levels which suggest that the consumer is "a winner"). Then the entire programming scheme, with a few notable exceptions, mostly cartoons, seems to consist in deliberately planned statements and images which are designed to condition the viewer to feel the need to spend their monies in targeted acts of consumption. The mechanism that is appealed to, it seems, is the individual's need to conform to the mass pattern, to avoid appearing to be an outsider or a loser. And the continual disruptions of consciousness that are caused by the interrupting advertisements have the effect of discouraging any independent thought patterns that the viewer might per chance develop.

Digression: possible programming format for developing computer based learning for dollars programs;

The learner would read a piece of randomly selected writing, and then answer a series of short questions about its content. These questions could consist in true or false, and/or multiple choice, and/or short answer questions, the answers to which the program would seemingly be able to evaluate effectively. When the learner had passed a specific level of difficulty enough times, receiving in the process some symbolically significant monetary rewards, they would be able to advance to a higher level, with the possibility to earn larger monetary rewards. At some point they might be encouraged to submit answers which involved paragraphs of writing, or even pages or chapters of writing, but such encouragement would only be likely to occur at the higher levels of achievement, or perhaps at the earlier levels, in conjunction with continuing short answer, multiple choice, true false testing.

Clearly such a program would have to be voluntary, particularly for those who had graduated from college and then either gone to graduate school and/or dropped out.

There would clearly be a danger that such programmed, rewarded learning could be used to condition and propagandize the learners. However, such dangers might be counterbalanced by clear statements to the effect that responsible dissenting views, if adequately defended, are likely to be at the least tolerated and perhaps actually rewarded.

March 4, 1999

Media license fee assessments;

It would appear that TV or radio station licensing fees should be based upon gross revenues acquired by said station during the preceding year that is sales revenues accrued before any salaries are paid out. Then the government could assess a reasonable percentage of this gross as a sort of amalgam of a "tax-fee." The rationale for imposing such a burden on a media station is based on the notion that any meaningful fee or tax should be based upon the overall revenues accruing to the management of the station that is the revenues coming in before management is able to so generously reward itself for its efforts. Hence if a meaningful fee tax were assessed, the public coffers would be more appropriately and proportionately enriched, and the sometimes seemingly obscene salaries that media figures currently seem to manage to attract because of the extremely competitive market would be reduced as a result of the fact that the overall revenues available to the station managers and owners would be reduced. The rationale for reducing the profitability of media broadcasting stations is based on the idea that, in the first place, the air waves belong to the public, that is, that private media broadcasting stations utilize the public airwaves with the permission of the government which is supposed to be serving in the interests of the public at large. Hence if the government is giving these broadcasting licenses away without receiving anything like their true market compensation value, then the government is doing the public a grave disservice. This is particularly the case when you stop and consider the fact that the economy's needed advertising functions are being accomplished at the cost of driving the American population to the point of distraction and as some would have it, disorientation. Indeed it might be argued that one of the reasons that the media hold so much prestige within the society has something to do with the great privilege and wealth correctly imputed to those who manage, own and produce the offerings of the medium, since at present it is tacitly understood that since they are so fabulously well rewarded, that therefore the material that they present must be terribly important. Perhaps as a result, the average American watches something like six hours of television in each twenty-four hour period. Time that might be spent with books, newspapers, computers, spouse, children, extended family or friends is instead spent before the television in the vague hope that amidst the titillation and advertisements the true path to happiness and success might become apparent.

It should be pointed out in this regard that the government licenses broadcasters so that they will be able to serve and to some extent fulfill the real needs of the public; and, that the public and the mass market do not exist primarily so as to be able to serve the needs of the broadcasters. This point often seems to be overlooked.

March 6, 1999

The effect on wages and the so called stock market "bubble;"

The point about gross corporate taxes being assessed before wages and managerial compensation are subtracted from the taxable gross is probably worth being considered. This is particularly the case in regard to corporations who make the bulk of their income from serving local, immovable markets. Such corporations include media oriented corporations whose audience is roughly commensurate with the national tax base. Hence, if a corporation which owns NBC, ABC or

CBS were to be taxed at a higher rate, say the gross was assessed for tax purposes before wages and managerial compensation were subtracted, such a corporation would be unable to move it's operations outside the country since its' primary market lies within the country. And if it attempted to retaliate by moving some other division's productivity to a country with lower wage rates, it is probable that such a move could be met with successful monetarily punitive antitrust actions.

The consequences of such a suggested change in tax assessment, (presuming that such a move would indeed constitute a change) might include a downward pressure on wage levels in general, or, more likely, these pressures would be exerted in the form of lower salaries and compensation packages at the higher end of the compensation scale, that is, the salaries of CEOs and Executive Vice Presidents would be likely to diminish across the board. Such an outcome in general seems preferable, from the point of view of the overall health of the economy and the society, since wages at the low end of the scale are more severely needed than those at the high end, the latter which seem to be utilized primarily as vehicles for investment in either luxury items or esteem enhancing investment in what often is a stock market characterized by high levels of investment in stocks yielding relatively low levels of profitability. Since the primary mechanism for increasing such levels of profitability is to sustain and increase rates of low end wage increases, it makes sense for at least a good part of the suggested wage cutback to be assessed against the compensation packages of higher, already comfortable, executive level management.

The effects of an archetypical "winner take all" sort of reward scheme on society's moral fabric;

When a society allows itself to fall into a pattern in which a relatively small proportion of earners, say one or two per cent of the earners, are considered to be "winners," that is, in a position to afford the ideal levels of consumption which are supposed to be so desirable as to constitute "proof of success" as defined by the television media, and, sixty or seventy per cent of the earners feel sufficiently deprived consumption wise as a result of being in positions where they receive low, stagnant incomes which cause them to feel continually deprived, then that sixty or seventy per cent is likely to begin to consider, in significant numbers, the possibility of violating traditional moral standards in the vague hope that as a result, they will be able to receive higher earnings. The logic is imbued in the folk wisdom that, contrary to the teachings of the Protestant Ethic, "only the wicked succeed."

This being the case, it is suggested that if Conservative politicians sincerely wish to "restore the nation's moral fabric," that they can begin to do so by advancing policies which will cause lower level wages to rise to the point where more wives and spouses can afford to work less and spend more time with their families such that the first consideration is less likely to be "what can I do to pick up a quick extra fifty bucks?"

Ruminations on status and income distribution
Date: 3/19/99 10:38:12 AM Eastern Standard Time
to: the editors (The American Prospect, The Nation, The New Yorker)
from: Andréas Daniel Fogg
Letter from Somerville March 7, 1999

Institutionally endorsed mechanisms for conferring status;
　　Starting in high school and college, American society tends to confer status on those who excel in athletics, tending to neglect intellectual or academic achievers. While it is true that good students make the Honor Roll or the Dean's List, they don't get to wear (and do not receive) special sweaters with special letters (or even long or short sleeved tee shirts as tokens of recognition). In fact they pretty much have to keep the news of their achievements to themselves. I don't think the membership of the Honor Roll or Dean's list is or was usually made public, certainly not verbally, out loud. Hence the athletes get all of the public recognition and celebrity; someone who is or was, merely a very good student, tends to be relatively ignored i.e. receiving less or no status recognition. In adult society short of appearing on television, in general, the only mechanism that the society endorses for conferring status involves paying salaries and bonuses, which sums allow for the utilization of conspicuous consumption. Occasionally there are rewards or awards conferred within companies and universities which purport to recognize achievements, but in general the pattern from secondary and higher education persists, that is, athletic accomplishments are rewarded, intellectual accomplishments are glossed over.
　　Now it may be the case that intellectual achievers do not necessarily wish to receive widespread public recognition, many of them may actually experience such public acknowledgments as embarrassing. Such individuals may also be loath to engage in competitive displays in which the goal is to outspend and show up competitors for positions in the socioeconomic pecking order. But for many in the society attempting to appear to be more successful than others is what life

is all about. Hence there is the perceived need for those at the high end of the income distribution to distinguish themselves from their peers and competitors by earning ever higher salaries and accumulating ever larger piles of wealth.

March 8, 1999
Gate House Lodge
Sugarbush South
Mad River Valley, Vermont

So the challenge seems to be, how can society allow people the right to express their need to declare, attempt to assert "more status" short of a highly dis-equilibriated scheme of income distribution? If there were other mechanisms by which qualified individuals could effectively assert status, if and when they wished to do so, then the need for the few to claim a lion's share of the rewards might be less pronounced.

Tir Na Nog Irish Pub
Somerville, MA

The ageless femme fatale, evidence, she, supposed descendant of Sinclair Lewis and/or Upton Sinclair, has a symbolic presence at Sugarbush. What does this mean? Who is she? Don't know. Don't care. Don't know if she is good or bad.

The northern Vermont women seem to wear their souls inside out, on their sleeves, so to speak, as if there were no competition going on. Perhaps they are naive. At any rate it is quite charming.

Ethan Allen demanded of the British at Fort Ticonderoga, "Open up in the name of the great Jehovah and the Continental Congress!" Notice that he didn't appeal to Jesus Christ.

It would be interesting to make a list of famous Vermonters. Vermont is known as the home of Ethan Allen, just as Connecticut was the home of Nathan Hale, and nobody else in particular comes to mind.

Mind you now, I have been drinking and should not be held entirely accountable for what I am writing. And when it is transcribed, you should consider it to be drunken ramblings, for which the author may hopefully be forgiven.

March 14, 1999

Socialism seems to presuppose the lack of any need to utilize income differentials as mechanisms for distributing differential levels of status, indeed, socialism seems to presume that there is in fact, no particular need for differential levels of status whatsoever. Such a presumption, i.e. the desirability of income equality and indeed of general status equality, of total social egalitarianism, is probably quite naive. It is questionable whether society would be capable of making any sorts of complex decisions whatsoever in the event that the ideal of equality, currently and since the inception of the nation, given lip service in the United States, were ever literally and comprehensively implemented. Even in the Soviet Union, before its dissolution and in China, before the market reforms, Communists were "more equal" than ordinary citizens, and, it is my impression, that some "elite and entitled Communists" were more highly economically rewarded than others.

Raising the minimum wage vs. imposing higher corporate taxes on broadcasters and possibly on other corporations as well;

Raising the minimum wage further entails the disadvantage of squeezing the profits available to small businesses in particular, but also the profits of larger corporations as well. Such profitability squeezes become increasingly hazardous in deflationary situations. On the other hand, raising corporate taxes on gross, pre salaried income is likely to have the result of lowering the higher end incomes of the so called corporate elite, incomes which have appeared to many as exorbitant, and in the event that such tax revenues are redistributed to benefit lower end earners' substantial standard of living through increased EITC(earned income tax credit) reverse tax support or through increased level of support for day care salaries and general availability, or increased Medicaid support, then the aim of increasing the standard of living of the bottom forty and fifty percent of earners might be accomplished with less damage to the smaller scale business institutions which provide so much of the actual employment in the society. This might particularly be the case if any increased levels of EITC support were channeled directly into regular pay checks on a weekly or biweekly basis. Hence, if it were determined that a given level of income deserved such and such a level of EITC support, then the IRS could fund such support, divided by fifty two, twenty six or twenty four, depending upon the length of the utilized pay period, so that the support could be utilized as a matter of course throughout the year; hence the temptation to squander a larger sum at the end of the year would be avoided.

March 15, 1999
North Peak Lodge
Sunday River
Newry, Maine

It's been snowing heavily all day, a sort of heavyish, slightly wetish snow, not terribly easy to ski in, but it could be heavier and wetter. The roads are reportedly bad between here and Boston, so I've decided to miss tonight's symposium on Ibsen's play, The Master Builder, at the American Repertory Theater in Cambridge.

Meanwhile, I'm running out of ideas that I feel the need to write about. There is this idea associated perhaps with Jesus but also at times with Judaic teachings, "Render unto Caesar that which is Caesar's!" Clearly when Ethan Allen demanded the surrender of King George's Fort Ticonderoga "in the name of the great Jehovah and the Continental Congress" he was not rendering unto Caesar (in this case George) that which (was) Caesar's. Neither were any of the other American Revolutionaries. Neither was Judah Maccabbee, neither Bar Kochba. Perhaps our anger and resentment at the powers that be is of such a magnitude that it must be suppressed and transformed into a sort of awe inspired reverence coupled with an adolescent style sort of hero worship. Hence we tend to let the so called great i.e. the CEOs and multibillionaire and some of the political leaders—particularly when they are personally wealthy, particularly if they have inherited great wealth, we tend to forgive them their wealth and power, as if to say "hey! They deserve it or the family deserves it." Something there is that feels guilty about taxing that great wealth, as if to do so might be tantamount to admitting to jealousy or envy or even feelings of aggression that cannot be recognized for fear that such feelings might be acted upon and severely punished. The thought seems to be that to even admit the existence of the gripe, of the perception of a grievance, of the perception of a "wrong," to admit such a perception might qualify the aggrieved party for membership on a rich men's "list of enemies" whose number might be destined for persecution, discrimination or worse. Hence the assumption that those who have much deserve no less and probably more tends to persist even in cases where the cards seem to have been "stacked" flagrantly and unjustifiably in their favor.

In this way, the so called power elite tends to perpetuate itself. In some ways their morality is more refined and such refinement is seemingly a requisite for those seeking to hold and pass on great wealth. That is, such individuals cannot be great indiscriminate womanizers, for to be such, or to wish to be such, is to put oneself in a position where one's energies and resources, both emotional and financial, are likely to be diluted to the point where they can no longer sustain any sort of concentrated efforts. Hence the Don Juan sort of character, the profligate womanizer, while he may have inherited great wealth, or perhaps merely (inherited or earned) intellectual privileges, if he too flagrantly womanizes, he is likely to lose the respect of his constituents and/or colleagues. Of course in situations where his power base is sufficiently strong and his policies sufficiently wise, he may be able to get away with quite a bit.

The holder or "inheritor" of intellectual privilege or status is likely to be in a different position than the inheritor of great wealth. Contrast, for example, Presidents Clinton and Kennedy. Kennedy was not resented as a self-made smart guy, as Clinton seems to be.

Part Three: Spring

Am foreign/economic policy: an anti-missile system; Israel, Palestinian statehood
Date: 3/21/99 2:42:47 PM Eastern Standard Time
to: the editors (The American Prospect, The Nation, The New Yorker)
from: Andréas Daniel Fogg
Letter from Somerville March 20, 1999

That developing an antimissile system without an accompanying conciliatory, nurturing economic foreign policy would encourage higher levels of unnecessary international tension and a greater danger of nuclear or biological miscalculated disaster;

It is probably important for whoever is representing the United States internationally, in the State Department particularly, to be ever aware of America's correspondents' needs to maintain and save face both in the eyes of their own citizens and the eyes of the citizens of the world. This is the case since receiving significant amounts of foreign aid alone itself may constitute a perceived if tacit loss of face i.e, "you are offering us this…, what do you think? That we are not capable of taking care of ourselves?" On the other hand, the absence of sufficient aid or investment may result in fact in unfolding developments involving either economic recession or depression involving one or another of the two great dangers, inflation or deflation, as well as the possibility of famine or perhaps flooding (or predatory war)..

National military assertiveness a "phase" of socioeconomic development or evolution;

It would appear that a period of militaristic assertiveness, jingoism, if you will, tends to be found in the evolutionary development of most nation states. This may well be true in the case of the People's Republic of China. They have already, indeed, demonstrated certain belligerent characteristics in regard to the state of Tibet, the issue of Taiwan continues to be unresolved, and they continue to imprison those who seek to institutionalize political dissent. It certainly appears that the Chinese have "great power" aspirations that continue to take totalitarian forms. And, while the United States cannot claim to always have had "clean hands" our policies since the end of the cold war it seems, do not include unprovoked violations of other nations' rights and territories in anything like the magnitude associated with the Chinese actions toward Tibet and those threatened toward Taiwan. (editor's note: written in 1999).

Differential levels of wealth in China, Russia, and the Third World in general versus levels of wealth found in the United States and Europe;

Suffice it to observe that generalized standards of living in Europe and the US are vastly higher, throughout most of the income distribution, than those found throughout the income distribution in China, Russia and the rest of the Third World (documentation would be helpful). Hence, it ought to be a policy of the US government at the least, to act economically in such a way as to increase the magnitude and improve the stability of the currencies of these poorer countries. Such an aim may be accomplished through regular investments in the banks and stock exchanges of those countries, investments from both the private sector and the IMF and World Bank whose actions are significantly influenced by the opinions of supporting governments; a principal one of which is the United States. It would appear that the danger of nuclear or biological acts of aggression directed at the so called "have" nations at the behest of disaffected elements within the "have-not" nations could be limited or vastly reduced through a coordinated policy of unobtrusive aid and investment on the part of the US government through both the Federal Reserve, the State and Commerce Departments, as well as the international economic organizations (the IMF and World Bank, principally) which seek to address international economic problems in the interests of the "developed economies." In the absence of such supportive economic policies, the danger is that a foreign policy characterized largely by defensive military investments of questionable effectiveness is likely to result on the one hand in an enormous waste of fiscal resources and on the other hand, in a failure to effectively defuse such resentment based economic tensions as seem to almost inevitably follow from widely publicized discrepancies in the standards of living associated with rival and competitive nation states.

Note that such increases in US generated quantities of foreign aid and investment presupposes increased levels of funding and liquidity within US government coffers. Such increases in liquidity could come from increased utilization of tax revenues or, more likely, through increased sales of US government treasury notes. Note too, that when such notes are exchanged for newly minted specie, newly minted currency, that the price of such treasury notes offered for sale is likely to go down and the interest offered in exchange, the yield, is likely to go up. How much such notes will yield in any given instance depends of course upon the strength of the demand for US Treasury notes, notes which are denominated in US dollars. In general when dollar liquidity is increased deliberately in order to fund aid or investment in the poorer nations of the world, the result is likely to be higher US interest rates. Such higher rates are likely, in turn, to pull, for a time, significant numbers of dollars out of the US stock markets. Hence the tradeoff associated with increased levels of US funding for aid and investment in the poorer nations of the world is predictably lower levels of profitability in the US stock markets. (editor's note: too many if's here). On the other hand, such increased levels of investment in poorer nations' economies are also likely to result in increased levels of US exports and final purchase sales to those countries, hence in improved balance of trade statistics and in increased levels of corporate profits. Finally, increasing standards of living in the poorer states of the world is likely to coincide with a diminished felt need on the part of the would be strong men leaders of the poorer nations to scapegoat and attack either the US, the Europeans or indeed peoples of "other" states or of other "other peoples" of relatively indigenous, local minority ethnicities.

Note that interpersonal male to male solidarity is often achieved, particularly during periods of perceived poverty or perceived feelings of personal, collective inadequacy, through the mechanism of scapegoating and vilifying members of minorities who are perceived as different and therefore "other," and who collectively refuse to acknowledge the superiority of the members of the majority group. In such circumstances of collective insecurity (characterized by feelings of personal inadequacy), many individuals may come to acquire satisfactory, acceptable, "successful" self images as a result of their own identification with members of their own ethnic or racial or national group whose successes are depicted throughout the society in the available mass communication media outlets (television, radio, newspapers, cinema, the internet). Such vicarious feelings of success may, in the absence of any real opportunities for achievement and recognition, or in the absence of the will to attempt to seize such opportunities as may in fact exist, such vicarious feelings of success may sustain large numbers of relatively ordinary, unpretentious and unambitious citizens and allow them to live their lives content with what, statistically speaking, constitutes "ordinary" levels of success and ordinary standards of living. It is terribly important for the well being of any given society, that most of its members be content with their lot in life, with their standard of living. As noted, when large numbers of citizens do not feel content with their lot in life and despite their best efforts are unable to achieve acceptable levels of success either in their own eyes or in the eyes of their wives, children and extended families, this, theoretically speaking, is when scapegoating and vilification of "other" minority groups, either within or outside the society, occurs.

Capitalism, scapegoating the Jews and Yom Kippur and Passover;

Since the Roman Catholic Church decided that in the main only Jews should be allowed to loan money "at prevailing interest rates," Jews became the western world's original and largely only capitalists. This unique status was one source of anti-Semitism, unquestionably. However, Jews played into this role, in many cases. For example, during Yom Kippur, the holiest day of the Jewish year, congregants ask God to forgive them for any promises that they made to him during the previous year, but which they were unable to fulfill. The obligations incurred between fellow human beings, whether Jew, Christian, Muslim or any other creed, are not dealt with during Yom Kippur. And while it is true that perhaps the essence of Judaism can be summed up in a version of the Golden Rule, "do not unto others as you would not have them do unto you!" The examination and implementation of this rule in practice and in terms of the political and economic challenges of the present day is usually conspicuously absent from the prayers, sermons and congregational discussions of the typically pious Jews who regularly attend these and other religious services. Hence, the typical activities associated with being religiously Jewish tend to focus on the Jews' obligations toward God and to neglect his obligations toward both other Jews who are less fortunate than themselves and more importantly upon the reciprocal relations between the Jews and the other members of society. (editor's note: there are significant exceptions to this rule, even on Yom Kippur). The question, what obligations have Jews incurred over the past year toward non-Jews and to what extent are these reciprocal obligations being fulfilled or neglected tends to be avoided in contexts in which the community gathers together as a whole. Doom when it has come to the Jews in the past in the "Diaspora" has usually taken the form of acts of vengeance performed upon and against the community by aggravated and aggrieved non-Jews. This was the case in all of the Russian pogroms and during the Spanish Inquisition, during the famous Dreyfus episode, and during the Nazi Holocaust. Yet during Yom Kippur, when religious Jews believe that literally their fates, whether they will live through the next year or not, will be decided by God, injustices performed by congregants against each other and against non-Jews get little or no attention. Instead the focus is upon attempting to acquire God's forgiveness for failures to meet his requirements. And when and if doom comes in the form of anti-Semitic attacks, the rationale of the religious is, "well, we must not have obtained God's forgiveness."

Hence among the religious Jews there is little or no focus upon the structural weaknesses of the socioeconomic system neither upon the weaknesses, or possibilities for improvement of the still capitalistic economic system. This appears to continue to be the case among religious Jews both in Israel (the Haredim) as well in the other nations of the world. Hence these religious Jews allow their fate to be determined not so much by their own actions vis a vis the other peoples of the world as by the result of the Papal Catholic decision, centuries old, to cast the Jews as the capitalist lenders of the world. And while this decision has acquired a less decisive character since the inception of the Protestant Reformation, since which Protestants have also been allowed to profitably lend monies, the difficulties associated with Capitalism in extremely difficult situations still tend to get blamed upon the Jews, since as the Catholics might put it, although there continues to be much antagonism towards the Protestants, "at least they believe that Jesus Christ was God's only son and the true Messiah," never mind that the world is far from being saved.

So in the opinion of the writer, the religious Jews and the secular Jews would be a lot better off if they realized that the implications of the Passover story are that participants should continually be reexamining the acceptability of the quality of life of their neighbors, whether these neighbors are Jewish, Christian, Muslim, Hindu, Buddhist, atheist or whatever. And in terms of responsibility, the questions" how are we as Jews responsible, are we in some way guilty of performing modes of exploitation of others such that God and society, whether formally or informally, whether legally or illegally, might find us guilty?" need to be asked. And if we have been guilty of the unacceptable exploitation of others, then shouldn't we do something about it??

How Israel might counter the "phased strategy;"

That it has been observed that significant numbers of Palestinians even within the Palestinian "peace camp" harbor some positive feelings and thoughts for the so called "phased strategy" wherein the Palestinians attempt to make peace with the Israeli, obtain some territory and then later, when they are stronger, attempt to drive the Israelis out of the area. The question is, what is likely to be the wisest Israeli response to such a strategy? The course of action advocated by the Likud party, under the leadership of Benjamin Netanyahu at this point seems to be one of total denial and rejection of the Palestinian Authorities peaceful gestures. There will be no Palestinian State, no land in or around Jerusalem will be ceded to the Palestinians for their use as a state capitol. Instead, Netanyahu threatens to attack the fledgling state in the event that it dares to assert statehood. Of course, if a declaration of statehood were postponed until after the Israeli elections scheduled for May 17th then Arafat might be able to deal with an entirely different face of the Jewish State. But in the event that Statehood is declared on May 4th, as planned, and in the event that fighting and terrorism occurs, there is the real danger that the results of the election might be tipped in favor of reelecting Likud and Netanyahu. Possibly the reverse could occur. But in general avoiding the frivolous loss of lives should be a priority. By declaring statehood before the Israeli elections Arafat might well be stepping into an Israeli rejectionist trap, a trap which could well entirely scuttle the prospects for peace between Arabs and Jews in the region for some time to come.

A more likely successful strategy for the Jews would likely entail allowing Palestinian statehood, providing economic assistance as well as investment and policy oriented advice while all the while maintaining social and diplomatic engagement on levels that permit communication but are not felt to be intrusive and burdensome by the Palestinians.

The Stranger revisited;

In a newspaper story dated March 19th it was revealed that a fourteen year old apparently Jewish Israeli boy was stabbed in the chest in Arab East Jerusalem. He suffered injuries, was treated and recounted that the reason he had been attacked was that he had rejected "indecent proposals." This story sounds something like Camus' novel, The Stranger. In that novel, if I remember correctly some sort of emotional and/or sexual tensions exist between the protagonist and "a stranger." These tensions are never confronted, never recognized for what they are and instead the result is a violent attack. It appears to me that considerable quantities of the antipathy between Palestinian and Jewish men could be dealt with far short of violent confrontation if these tensions were dealt with with humor and friendliness rather than with outright denial and rejection and a sort of compulsive need for avoidance.

Resolution of Kosovo hostilities, growth of money supply, wages in Vermont
Date: 3/26/99 11:44:57 AM Eastern Standard Time
to: the editors (The American Prospect, The Nation, The New Yorker)
from: Andréas Daniel Fogg
Letter from Somerville March 22, 1999

Economic situation in Vermont;

I ran into an old buddy in northwestern Maine, last night who used to drive a big, I guess, eighteen wheeler and now works in a quarry. He joked that Vermont was "all communist." The wages he said, were significantly lower than in Maine and New Hampshire and there is a vast gap between the incomes of the retired rich and the young; houses are extremely expensive relative to Maine and New Hampshire, he said, and the opportunities for the young to earn a decent living are inferior to those found in New Hampshire and Maine. How these traits lead to the conclusion that the state "is communist" is unclear.

Interest rates and the money supply;

Note that in general, as more treasury notes are offered for sale, the price tends to sink and the yield and interest rates tend to rise. And, of course, when treasury notes are sold, both the principal and the interest must eventually be paid back. Hence when treasury notes are sold, the federal debt increases by the total amount of the principal sold plus the interest due, all, of course, over the life of the note. On the other hand, if the principal and interest are paid back with newly treasury minted currency, then that projected debt is simply retired without incurring any depletion of Federal tax revenues. The danger, of course, in retiring Federal debt with newly printed currencies, is that such an act, which involves, obviously, increasing the amount of currency in circulation, may trigger inflation. However, in the presence of strong enough demand for US currency, it may well not be the case that inflation will result. Such strong demand would theoretically be caused as a result of deflationary conditions which might tend to be corrected in the event that newly created funds were applied in such a manner as to counteract the deflationary effect.

A possible resolution of the hostilities in Kosovo;

Propose a modification of the composition of the proposed occupying, peace-keeping force such that it would include Russians and some soldiers from eastern Europe. Then attempt to get UN Security Council approval of this new peace-keeping plan, which upon Serbian acceptance would involve the cessation of NATO generated hostile activities.

The rationale behind this suggestion involves the recognition that the Russians are unhappy for two reasons, one, because they failed to sway the West from using force, and two, because they failed to sway the Serbs to comply with the West's requests. The Serbs see the request for an imposed NATO force as a violation of their own sovereignty. Including traditional Russian allied troops in the occupying troops' number might well ease the Serbian anxiety about allowing such an occupying force on its territory.

Otherwise and/or further mediation suggested;

Otherwise, the suggestion is that mediational hearings be held on the possibility of restoring "autonomy" to the Kosovar people in Kosovo. Such hearings would presumably directly deal with the question as to what difficulties the Serbs have experienced in the past with Kosovar autonomy and how such difficulties could be dealt with, while at the same time, substantially restoring said autonomy.

Additional observations and comments
Date: 3/29/99 7:19:11 AM Eastern Standard Time
to: the editors (The American Prospect, The Nation, The New Yorker)
from: Andréas Daniel Fogg
Letter from Somerville March 28, 1999

March 28, 1999
South Ridge Lodge
Sunday River
Newry, Maine

The snow is wet granular and I'm dressed far too warmly, it's much warmer than I anticipated; so I turned in my lift ticket after two runs.

Something about Kosovo. It almost appears as if one of the objectives of this attack, coming approximately on the fiftieth anniversary of the founding of NATO is to demonstrate the practical dimensions of our present relationship with Russia, NATO's original antagonist. Meanwhile, the ostensible justification for the attack, "to save the Kosovars from Serbian aggression," is not being fulfilled, in fact the attacks on the Kosovars are increasing and appear to be designed to accomplish an "ethnic cleansing" if not genocide. It is perhaps worth remembering that there exists a long-standing enmity between the Serb and Kosovar peoples, an enmity that far antedates the government of Slobodan Milosevic. It is likely that this long-standing historic enmity, an enmity which is likely so pervasive that it plays a determining role in the continuing formation of the national characters of the two peoples, is motivating and has been motivating the violence on both sides. It is just that at present, the Serbs are winning decisively. It is possible that more bombing will bring the Serbs to accept the current NATO peace terms (but dubious), but much more likely, if they (the Serbs) are allowed to save face in some crucial way, For instance, if the peacekeeping force included significant numbers of their Russian allies, the Serbs would be much less likely to see its' acceptance as the total abnegation of their national sovereignty.

Somerville, MA

I suspect that it is hardly a coincidence that the First Lady is currently visiting Tunisia and Morocco. This supposed support for the Muslim Kosovars no doubt is intended to prove to the Muslim Arabs, and the world, that the US is capable of acting in the interests of Islamic peoples. And if this is indeed a related objective of the current campaign then this goal might be most effectively accomplished if the Serb violence against the Kosovars were ended quickly through the introduction of a ground force that is truly neutral including disinterested allies of both parties i.e. Russians serving as allies of the Serbs and Islamic forces from other parts of the world, possibly including Russia or states that were formerly part of the Soviet Union. Remember that Serbia, Kosovo and the former Yugoslavia are not and never have been members of NATO. Some western NATO troops might be included if their presence were deemed acceptable by the Serb government and the KLA. Although in the event that the KLA requested western NATO troops, to balance against the Russian troops, presumably a deal could be worked out, as could the need to develop joint Russian NATO patrols. Remember, before NATO and Clinton decided to freeze the Russians out of this operation, Russia and the US were enjoying substantively good relations. Perhaps these can be restored and further deterioration averted.

Note the principal thesis, that the ethnic cleansing is occurring as much as a result of the chaos caused by the NATO attacks, which allow for a lawless, anarchic environment in which rogue Serb elements have become free to implement their national historic goal, a goal that is centuries old, to drive the Muslims out of Kosovo, as it is being caused by a deliberate, conscious decision on the part of the government to drive the Kosovars out. However, the government may well have decided not to attempt to control such rogue elements as are apparently currently burning homes and threatening and probably implementing murderous violence. If this is the case, then the Milosevic regime may seek to blame the Kosovar refugee exodus upon the anarchic conditions created by the NATO attacks. And such a claim may indeed be partly justified. One can imagine certain Serb elements that would, upon being told that they had one or two wishes to see fulfilled in the next 48 hours, after which time they would be killed, would wish to see first of all, as many Muslims either dead or driven out of Kosovo as possible. Increasing the comprehensiveness of the NATO attacks may be tantamount, under the present anarchic conditions, to imposing such conditions and options upon significant numbers of rogue Serb elements.

China in the WTO and the unconvertible Yuan, prejudice against Kosovar Muslims
Date: 3/30/99 1:19:59 AM Eastern Standard Time
to: the editors (The American Prospect, The Nation, The New Yorker)
from: Andréas Daniel Fogg
Letter from Somerville March 29, 1999

The non floating Yuan;
   Is it advisable to admit China into the WTO so long as they refuse their currency to have generalized convertibility status? That is, if the Chinese refuse to make the Yuan convertible into dollars or Euros or Rubles, should they be given an equal status in the WTO with other states which do allow their currencies to be convertible? If the Yuan remains insulated from international currency fluctuations, would this "insulation" allow a China with membership in the WTO to behave like a rogue elephant against whom justified economic retaliatory sanctions, should the need for such arise, could not be directed?

Reflections on antipathy between some Muslims and Judaeo-Christians, and examination of perceptions of sexual potency and self esteem in secular, religious and multicultural contexts;
   This, it is suggested, is fictional material, the author was friends with a relatively secular Muslim for a number of years, but the reflections discussed have only a peripheral relation to that friendship. It appears that some Muslims prefer to think of women, with whom they are romantically even maritally involved, as if they were like brother and sister. Hence there is an assumption among some of the Islamic that they, the Muslims, are allowed to religiously womanize, to seek numerous female partners, since they have a "correct" attitude toward women. Therefore they may assume that non-Muslims are primarily interested in phallically ravishing their women partners. This seemed to be the assumption of the author's former Muslim friend. That is, he seemed to assume that the only objective that the author could have, when speaking to attractive women, was to

become carnally involved. Presumably this presumption was a projective presumption, that is, the Muslim friend harbored such fantasies about women, but because he was a Muslim, thought that his fantasies were acceptable, but because the author was not a Muslim, he, the Muslim, sought to discourage even prohibit such interactions on the part of his friend, perhaps by implicitly threatening violence. Hence his statement to the effect that the author had a "small member" and therefore should refrain from speaking with a certain attractive Polish woman. This statement was apparently based upon a misinterpretation of the effects of a medication that the author has been taking, a side effect of which seems to involve the inhibition of casual anomalous sexual potency, that is potency which is not provoked by continuous or relatively regular and anticipatable social and perhaps physical contact. Hence, casual, impersonal sexual relations with prostitutes or women with whom the author had not formed some sort of a relationship, seem to be out of the question. And since so many women are so busy, and unwilling to spend the social time necessary to form an actual relationship, the author appears in practice to be impotent. But he harbors a grudge against this particular Muslim, his former friend, for attempting to keep him from talking to one particular woman. It may be the case that when Muslims are a sub population of a multicultural at least partially secular culture or society, as in Kosovo, Israel, Bosnia, to some extent the United States, Britain and elsewhere, that resentments of the sort described above may contribute to the formation of a sort of generalized resentment against the polygamistic Islamicists. If this is the case, if this sort of latent thinking lies beneath existing antipathies between Serbs and Muslims or between Jews and Palestinians, then recognizing such thought patterns in cultural and artistic expressions, plays, movies, television, might go a long way toward sensitizing at least leaders of the cultural groups (those who set norms) such that courses of conduct that do not involve affronting the sensibilities of differing religious and ethnic groups within multicultural societies might emerge into consciousness and social practice.

Note that in secular society, many women tend to see themselves as so liberated from traditional moral strictures that they actually, in practice behave psychologically as if they were extremely wealthy prostitutes that are withholding their loyalty and time from commitment to any single man. Such women may in fact also refrain from bestowing their sexual favors upon any men, for health reasons and out of a desire to pay lip service to their traditional moral religious backgrounds. Remember, we are speaking of the effects of the interaction between religious mores and secular moral or amoral imperatives.

'What all this has to do with the possibility of obtaining peace in Kosovo is not clear, unless, that is, Slobodan Milosevic could some how be convinced at this late date that the ethnic cleansing that is going on apparently presently against the Muslim Kosovars is wrong if not a crime against humanity and a vast overreaction to any affronts that the Kosovars could conceivably have committed against Serbs in the past.

Fictional speculations about imputed meanings associated with death, Kosovo
Date: 4/3/99 12:38:22 PM Eastern Standard Time
To: the editors (The American Prospect, The Nation, The New Yorker)
from: Andréas Daniel Fogg
Letter from Somerville April 2, 1999
Fiction:

Consider a fictional story; a young man, the narrator, goes skiing in Northern Vermont when he is a junior high school student. One of the boys that had gone on the trip is killed in a tractor accident, the following spring. The next fall the narrator enrolls in the first year of high school and becomes friends, spontaneously, with a young man who has the same phonetic last name as that of his friends' friend who had been killed in the tractor accident. The narrator and his new friend remain close friends throughout their high school experience. The question is what if any meaning can be inferred from these coincidences? Incidentally, the narrator until recently had successfully repressed the entire coincidental nexus, having changed the name of the deceased in his memory to "Zack."

Clearly, there is no necessary inference. The coincidence can be dismissed as having been caused by the narrator's subconscious wish to continue his relationship with his friend (and his friend's friend) from the area in New England from which he had moved after the completion of the seventh grade. However, a more insidious inference is possible, an inference which might serve to symbolically justify death. This inference, the sort of inference which might tacitly encourage warfare and it's accompanying loss of life, runs along the following lines. The "soul" of the boy who died in the tractor accident "flew" from New England to the Chicago area and inhabited the narrator's new friend, impelling him toward becoming the narrator's friend. This sort of interpretation would serve to justify killings in ethnic cleansings, warfare itself and of course genocide. It could also be used to justify negligent homicide and even murder. It is the sort of characteristic thinking that one might associate with what are somewhat euphemistically called "Fascist" political movements.

April 3, 1999

Notes: Perhaps the most outrageous violation of international and national law, of human rights and common decency is the apparent decision on the part of the Belgrade Serbian government, to strip the fleeing Kosovars entirely of their documentary articles of identity. Thus the Serb police and border officials, it is alleged, steal the Kosovars' passports, birth certificates, property deeds as they exit Kosovo, thereby complicating and seemingly negating any possibility of their return to Kosovo without the development of a sort of legal chaos—unless, that is, the Kosovars had been able to preserve some written evidence of their ownership of their homes and indeed of their very identities. This brings up a point made by an old friend, who was a retired television news writer, to the effect that in the United States, you don't seem to have an identity unless you have a mailing address. What happens to the identities of refugees who have been deprived of homes, mailing addresses and identifying papers? Proving that they are who they say they are becomes in this case much more problematic. Therefore the Serb policy constitutes a truly profound act of violence against the very fabric of civil society. Such an affront to international society, it is suggested, definitely requires and demands some sort of international punishment. Such a punishment, it is suggested, probably should be imposed upon those responsible for implementing this policy, and it probably should involve severe prison sentences. Once all the members of the UN Security Council, including current dissidents China and Russia, are willing to accept the inherent gross wrongness and illegal and immoral character of the Serb policies vis a vis the refugees, then military steps designed to bring end the aggressive Serb policies Serbs might be implemented more effectively. In the case that Russia and China continue to obstruct decisive UN actions vis a vis Kosovo, it would appear that genuine economic pressures need to be brought to bear upon those countries. For example, the idea of continuing to bestow most favored nation trading status upon the Chinese seems pathetic and absurd. Likewise granting them entry into the WTO. In the absence of Russian cooperation in the imposition of economic sanctions against the Serbs, it would appear that the US should clearly indicate its reluctance to continue subsidizing IMF aid to that country. Indeed, it is odd that the question of imposing economic or trade sanctions as an alternative to the air war never was considered, at least not in the press. It is almost as if there were a tacit view on the part of Clinton, Blair and the NATO leaders and Slobodan Milosevic to the effect that humanity needs a large scale war.

The wisdom of bombing the Ministry of Interior Affairs is also questionable, when you stop and consider that evidence that might be used to convict Serbian human rights criminals may have been destroyed in the raids.

Re: Handling ethnic antagonisms
Date: 4/7/99 12:03:11 AM Eastern Daylight Time
Dad,

I don't know of many unqualified successes. South Africa is interesting. But recent developments leave a great deal to be desired. There the situation is further complicated by racial differences and perhaps wider cultural differences. Don't know much about the Czech situation. Lebanon is interesting, very multi cultural, but there I suspect the lesson is that when the economy deteriorates or when there is pressure caused on the economy because of migrations of poor immigrants, or as in pre Hitler Germany caused by reparations and culture shock and probably poor or unwise economic local and global engineering, then social forces can result in the generation of intra sub cultural or intra cultural antagonisms and sometimes violent attacks.

That's why I think it important for social scientists to look on society and inter societal problems from a dynamic perspective i.e. from the point of view that assumes that things are constantly subject to change, change involving reactions to cultural and mass media statements, to perceptions of relative economic deprivation, to the amount and quality of work available and to the adequacy of wages (among other factors); all of which seem to be mediated and stimulated by political appeals.

Re: Prejudice against Kosovar M...
Date: 4/7/99 12:11:48 AM Eastern Daylight Time

A question that arises is, are there any promising or successful efforts amongst either Palestinians or other Muslims whether Arab or otherwise, to reorient the Islamic religion toward more modern positions on women's rights and, I suppose, on the religious acceptability of charging interest when lending money. It is my understanding that this practice was and is prohibited by Islam. However, my understanding may be incorrect. It may be the case that the prohibition was against charging excessively high interest. If not, this is a possible example of how that religion might adapt to the needs of the modern economic capitalistic systems, i.e., by reinterpreting the Koran so that charging interest is allowed, so long as it is not deemed excessively high.

Defending democracy by deliberately offending Russia and China
Date: 4/9/99 11:17:53 AM Eastern Daylight Time
to: the editors (The American Prospect, The Nation, The New Yorker)
from: Andréas Daniel Fogg
Letter from Somerville April 5, 1999

Notes: that the Chinese system is conceptually, qualitatively different from that of Cuba. For instance, Cuba's regime has been characterized by relatively overly simplistic Marxist imperatives to immediately and totally abolish all private capital holdings. This imperative is apparently clearly not present in present day China.

Therefore although the political party in control wishes to label itself as Communist, we in the neo capitalistic west should recognize the qualitative evolution that has occurred in China, that is, it is an evolution toward a more humane and effectively wealth generating economy.

Meanwhile in the modern west, in the US in particular, government and the legal system have evolved in such a way as to increase the delegation of decision making powers to specialized regulatory agencies which function subject to broad congressional review (and executive review) but basically impose their views without much systematic public democratic discussion. Hence the number of overall functions that are handled democratically has declined. As a result the public perceives a withering away of democratic control. Among some paranoiac elements on the right this transference of power to relatively dictatorial regulatory agencies has been interpreted as the traditional archetypical "communist plot." Hence there is a temptation on the part of Democratic neo liberal political leaders to distance themselves from the former traditional Communist powers, namely China and Russia, by posturing against those powers in the military sphere of affairs. That appears to be what is happening presently in the disagreements between the US, Russia and China over what should be done about the conflict in Kosovo. None of these three powers is willing to risk the possibility that they might be perceived as anything but totally autonomous vis a vis the wishes of the others. As far as China is concerned, the question arises, if they may devalue the Yuan, and if such devaluation were to have an international impact, then wouldn't the existence of such an impact require some international convertibility? So is the Yuan floating or not? Perhaps partially?

Note that the perceived problem with capitalism, with lending money for interest, seems to be experientially that the act of charging interest tends to involve a denial of friendship, fellowship, a change in the experiential quality of so called community life.

Hence originally I am under the impression Jews were not allowed to charge each other interest. Then under Catholic Papal law, Catholics were not allowed to charge each other interest (I don't think that they were allowed to charge anyone interest) and the Pope decreed that Jews should perform the societally needed function of lending money in return for interest. Presumably the Papal rationale involved the perception that charging interest tends to disrupt the sense of communal identity and good fellowship, hence non Christians perceived as outsiders, Jews, were appointed to be the community's bankers. Communism, then, it is thought was originally designed to recover the sense of community, the longed for lack of alienation that Marx thought to have been destroyed through the evolution of Capitalism.

By this logic the true member of the community wouldn't think of charging another member of the community interest for the privilege of borrowing funds. Now that we have widespread capitalism even in China and Russia, the problem of sustaining the sense of community, of making friendship feasible and possible, in truth never actually solved by the Communist regimes, continues to rankle. To this end neo nationalistic sub cultural thinking has attempted to move in and lower the boundaries and defenses between persons, thereby, it is apparently hoped, making friendship and a feeling of community possible in both rural and urban settings. The challenge to the nationalist solution arises typically in contexts in which one or more nationalistic cultures are forced to interact. You can see such conflicts in the world's hot spots, for example in Northern Ireland, in Serbia and Kosovo, amongst Israelis and Palestinians the existence of the other group constitutes a challenge to the idealized nostalgic sense of community that arises from the perception that everyone in the country is (relatively) the same. In fact this nostalgic view of a community with a uniform national culture does not in and of itself satisfy, or if it does, then the satisfaction does not last. Within such uniform cultures soon enough differing strains and interpretations arise. Class conflicts develop. The economy cannot grow without capitalism (without some accumulation of capital, and there is no incentive to accumulate capital, or less incentive, if there is no interest available). Capitalism involves the extraction of profits from the labors of one's neighbors, whether such neighbors are of the same nationality or religion or not. Extracting such profits is not a particularly friendly act. Good fellowship tends to suffer and become rare as a result. People become unhappy. Wars result when a society agrees that some other group is "bad" and should be declared an enemy. Hating and fighting such an enemy allows the members of the society to overcome the alienation associated with personal ultra individualistic profit seeking and self advancement. Modern society is an extremely lonely self centered place. There is what I think David Riesman described as ultra individualism, which allows certain individuals to be given enormous economic credit for accomplishments that are actually possible only because of the support of others both within their organizations and are possible because of the general level of civil peace and order. Present day Capitalism tends to minimize the economic rewards associated with being a non disruptive public spirited citizen. Many such non disruptive citizens have to struggle with relatively low pay. The Democratic left tends to believe that good behavior needs to be systemically economically recognized by the society, by, for example, increasing the earned income tax credit, by, for example, subsidizing non threatening forms of education and day care. The implicit thought of the conservatives seems to be that the way to discourage population growth is to keep wages for the young at punitively low levels, to make life for the young as difficult as possible. Of course there is something to be said for mature parenthood, but how mature? The children of the upper middle class, it should be observed, may not be inclined to marry until they have achieved some sort of success on the level that they aspire to achieve. Hence one way to discourage early marriage amongst such individuals is to subvert or defer the recognition of their legitimate achievements.

April 9, 1999

The doctrine of the immortality of the soul and its implications in psychotic interpretation;

The thinking may go something like this, if you will permit an ethnomethodological like reconstruction, the ultra nationalist believes that one group, usually but not always his group is far superior to some other group against whom prejudice and hatred are felt. Hence the belief is that if a member of the hated group dies or is killed, if they are good, they may well be reborn as members of the admired, privileged group. Hence you may have Serbs killing Kosovars, telling themselves that after death the good Kosovars may be reborn as Serbs. Similarly by this logic the Nazis may have believed that by killing Jews, they were allowing the good ones, the good Jews, to be reborn as members of what they insisted on believing was the German master "race." Poor American Blacks, in despair at the lack of opportunities available to them so long as they remain uneducated, and lacking sufficient real interactive capable educated Black role models, and sufficient incentive to overcome functional illiteracy and their sense of being perpetual outsiders, whether they are quiet or aggressive, may resort to performing drive by shootings directed at other Blacks who they believe to be "good" in the perhaps inarticulate belief that upon going to "the other side" they may be reborn as a White person or middle class Black person and so have some hope of achieving success.

A rationalization for psychosis;
   It is probably important to see this sort of thinking for what it is, that is a form of a rationalization for psychosis. It is also probably important to recognize the seeming fact that the presupposition which allows for this sort of psychotic like thinking derives from prevalent religious views which assume the immortality of the soul. Clearly, however, what is likely to tip individuals or societies into death dealing psychotic states or policies is likely not merely the existence of the religious beliefs, which are probably endemic in most cultures, but rather the existence of sufficient absolute deprivation and psychological pain such as create the need to reach out from the secure bounds of a host culture in search of people with alternative traditional modes of thinking the perception of whose existence allows for considering the possibility that changes in traditional patterns of behavior and thinking are possible and may well be needed. Then, individuals operating in a psychotic state may feel compelled, out of reverence for their traditional cultural forbearers, to show some significant level of disrespect for the bearers of the alternative culture, whose existence and presence has allowed them to conceptualize and perhaps begin to realize needed cultural changes and innovations. The greater the guilt that is felt upon the realization that the traditional fathers and grandfathers may not have had all the answers, the greater the need to punish members of the outsider group. In extreme cases as has been seen, this disrespect can be transformed from verbal slights into physical attacks on property, on land and on life and limb.

Exposure to Islam, secular sexual liberation theory and "big winner" capitalism;
   For example, the exposure to polygamistic Muslims may have contributed to the development of a tacit system of monogamy which included loose affiliation with mistresses. This emphasis on mistresses seems to be associated with southern European cultures like the French, Italian and Spanish, all of which likely had

greater exposure to Muslims than for example, the English, Irish, and the Germans. Note that in the case of the Spanish and Italian cultures, which tend to be largely Roman Catholic, polygamy was not explicitly accepted, no doubt out of deference to a conception of women's rights, but a thrust of the polygamist principle, that one man might sexually associate with more than one woman, rather than visa versa, or not at all, was adopted. It is not my intention to attempt to judge this impulse, merely to note that in the present climate of heightened personal awareness, accompanied as it is by an ideology of individualism which tends to derogate the value of merely assisting and contributing to achievements, without effectively laying claim for the principal credit for the accomplishment, whatever it may have been, large numbers of men are becoming comparatively speaking economically relative non-players, lacking the economic resources to be able to compete in displays of conspicuous consumption, which displays become integral instruments in the attempt to attract the attentions of more than one attractive women. Hence with the systemic generation of relatively few male "big winners," and the implicit materialistic view of many women to the effect that wealth needs to be rewarded (with their social if not physical attentions), there arises a greater perceived need for some variation of the polygamist model.

The differing outcomes resulting from interactions with Islam in Kosovo versus in Spain or Italy or perhaps indirectly in France, may perhaps be accounted for in part by differences in doctrine between Roman Catholicism and Eastern Orthodoxy, the religion of the Serbs, as well as by the fact that the Muslims maintained a presence in Europe in Kosovo, whereas it is my impression that there has been little or none in Spain or Italy at least in the last 500 years..

Multicultural interactive strategy, Kosovo, proactive social science
Date: 4/11/99 9:48:21 PM Eastern Daylight Time
to: the editors (The American Prospect, The Nation, The New Yorker)
from: Andréas Daniel Fogg
Letter from Somerville April 10, 1999

Multicultural interactive strategy;

It would appear that a strategy for both socioeconomic advancement and achieving interpersonal happiness in multicultural societal settings probably involves an emphasis upon the formation of friendly alliances between ego and some members of other competing cultural (and/or racial, as the case may be) groups. Such alliances allow the ego to demonstrate toward other members of such an "other" cultural group, that he, ego, should not be considered entirely unsympathetic and should not be considered an enemy, that is subject to gratuitous verbal (or, in extreme cases, physical) attack. The difficulty with forming such alliances lies in the fact that peer pressure against them may often exist. Hence their maintenance should be considered something of an accomplishment, a feather in the cap so to speak. A further difficulty that arises against the formation of such alliances involves the need to overcome prejudices and preconceptions usually found amongst the members of both groups to the effect that "members of our group" are "just better" than members of the other group. Such in group views for example, seem to be prevalent among many members of American Black and White society. In general such in group "hype" is inversely related to the amount of earned self esteem held by the individual. I emphasize earned self esteem as opposed to self esteem derived from inherited wealth or social position, for examples. That is, to the extent that the individual genuinely respects himself, or herself, because of their activities and accomplishments vis a vis their work, their friends, their family, their hobbies, they are less likely to be dependent upon self esteem derived from their membership in some cultural, national, religious or racial grouping. Hence it would appear that one way to weaken intercultural antagonisms in multicultural societies is to provide relatively pressure free areas of activity or learning in which individuals are encouraged to achieve potentially esteem building accomplishments, accomplishments which may potentially down the road lead to income opportunities. Such opportunities have in the past been theoretically provided in institutions of higher learning and in public and private middle and high schools. Such opportunities could theoretically be expanded and extended to the Internet.

Sunday River Brewing Co.
Bethel, Maine

Dealing with the Kosovo situation;

There may be something to be said for giving young men and women the opportunity, given the presence of a genuine need, to live or die as heroes. That genuine need may be present today in Kosovo. In order to neutralize and defuse Russian (and Chinese) objections, Russians surely should be given the opportunity to participate in the designated peacekeeping force. Absent Serb consent, the Russians need to be confronted diplomatically and publicly, in the television media, with the evidence of the wrong that the Serbs are committing. But before all this happens, the Serbs need to be given the opportunity to themselves accept a hypothetical joint NATO/Russian peacekeeping force. Since such a force would only be withdrawn jointly and coterminously, the Kremlin would need not fear a NATO based occupation and subjugation of Kosovo (a part of Serbia). While such a force (really a police force which would be accompanied by UN and other neutral observers) is deployed, the Serb armed forces would substantially withdraw from Kosovo and a systematic mediational effort would begin to hear, evaluate and analyze both Kosovar and Serb grievances (against each other). After grievances were considered, the general normative conditions for reestablishing an autonomous Kosovo within Serbia would be enunciated. If such a structure were deemed not feasible by Kosovars, Serbs, NATO and Russian officials, then a partition plan with relocations could be formulated. Questions that need to be considered include, for example, can alleged Kosovar insults to Serb dignity possibly justify the ethnic cleansing, destruction of identities and genocide that objective observations conclusively suggest the Serbs are currently perpetrating? If not, perhaps even the Russians would admit that absent Serb concurrence to Kosovar autonomy (and resettlement, and reasonable restitution over a reasonable period of time) that a partition plan heavily favoring the Kosovars should be instituted.

Absent Russian willingness to participate as relatively objective mediators, the introduction of more irregular volunteer troops—already apparently 200 strong—to aid the Kosovo Liberation Army should be seriously considered. Introducing regular NATO ground forces into the arena, while seemingly a good idea (given the illegality of genocide under international law), would likely have the effect of strengthening right wing reactionary and neo fascist factions in the Russian government and society.

Notes: if social science is proactive, must it be utopian, if proactive, how can it be pragmatic?

April 11, 1999
North Peak Lodge
Sunday River
Newry, Maine

Can a proactive social science be pragmatic?

A proactive social science is capable of speculating about specified consequences which might theoretically be predicted (or extrapolated) as consequences flowing from the adoption of recommended courses of action. Theoretical predictions (and actions that are appropriate causes of those predicted consequences) need not be limited to macro level societal experiences that have already happened. When, however, large scale idealized changes occur, they may fail to achieve their aims. There is such a thing as bad or wrong theory, inadequate theory. When implemented theory fails, (even if it is supposedly the product of some imagined dialectic), it is labeled utopian or perhaps "dystopian" theory, in hindsight. When such moves, however, are successful, they tend to be labeled as "pragmatic and innovative," as "moving successfully into the future" as "meeting the changing and evolving needs of humanity" and so forth.

All theoretical constructions tend to be based on the use of logical mechanisms like "such and such is true (will happen) if and only if (IFF) such and such conditions are substantively present. There is also "x may follow if it is preceded by y" that is "y is a necessary but not sufficient condition if x is to occur." Then, the task is to find out all of the factors necessary to definitely cause x; all this needs to be done probably out of the public view because if initial actions are taken on a public mass scale before causal mechanisms have been understood, the character of the situation may become popularly redefined, transmogrified even reified. Hence perhaps the perceived social distance between policy regulating agencies, those social scientists whose thinking and research should inform the actions of such agencies (and the legislatures), and the public at large.

Dialectic in context, command structure of joint NATO/Russian force
Date: 4/16/99 11:28:46 AM Eastern Daylight Time
to: the editors (The American Prospect, The Nation, The New Yorker)
from: Andréas Daniel Fogg
Letter from Somerville April 13, 1999

The dialectic in theory and practice (re China, Cuba, North Korea et al.);
The so called dialectic, a tool advocated and used by Marxist regimes to the end of justifying and lending an aura of predefined finality and inevitability to their policies, may or may not be useful in processes in which thinking about policies occurs. However, when a political regime uses the or a dialectic label in order to impose consensus, that is, when political consensus is imposed in a totalitarian manner without any possibility of either public or private organized dissent, then the effectiveness of this method is likely to be severely curtailed because of the absence of any possibility of the incorporation of either genuine positive or negative feedback into the political decision making process.

April 14, 1999

Dialectic (continued);

The idea of dialectic, originally formulated by Hegel, I was taught, and adopted by Marx, involved three phases or functions or components of the so called thinking process. These included perhaps, it's been a long time, "thesis, antithesis, and synthesis." The thesis involves a basic proposition, the antithesis its opposite or contradiction or negation and synthesis is the supposedly inevitable, infallible conclusion arising from the melding of the first two components. Note that typical communist parties cloak their pronouncements and rule in a cloak of inevitability roughly analogous to "Papal Infallibility." Thus, the communist parties' conclusions, it is typically asserted, cannot be wrong. The problem with relying on an intellectual process within a totalitarian political structure which prohibits and severely punishes dissent (with imprisonment and some cases, death) lies in the fact that only if dissent is allowed is it possible to continually modify and update the original (empirical) parameters and terms and definitions of the baselines of the dialectical reasoning process. Hence a dialectical policy making process that is cut off from genuine information from the populace, cut off from empirically valid, relatively free and uncoerced feedback, such a policy making process is unlikely, is unable to fulfill even approximately, (even theoretically assuming that dialectical thinking is the answer, is the ideal form of thinking), the real needs of the population.

The structure of a joint NATO/Russian peacekeeping force (in Kosovo);

A possible formula for dividing command authority between NATO officers and Russian officers involves the utilization of a NATO officer in command of the unit, platoon, division, whatever, with an accompanying Russian officer who has the authority to veto a given command for some valid, appealable reason. Any such vetoed command would not take effect until and unless it had been passed up the chain of command to a designated group of upper echelon officers whose composition would include representatives of major NATO powers as well as Russian representation. The Russians would not have equal representation on such an appeal board, neither would they have absolute veto power, however, their opinions would be treated with respect, and in the event that their position were overruled by the larger board, they would have the right to record in writing the reasons for their dissent. Such a command board would in fact, presumably be in place in substantially this form if Russia were in fact a formal member of NATO.

Giving Russian officers such authority in the field would have the result of providing an incentive for NATO and Russian officers to develop a similar strategic point of view in the field.

Milosevic's psyche, the Yuan, Russia's (and the West's) ideological identity crisis
Date: 4/22/99 10:22:52 AM Eastern Daylight Time
to: the editors (The American Prospect, The Nation, The New Yorker)
from: Andréas Daniel Fogg
Letter from Somerville April 18, 1999

Note: Milosevic probably, in some convoluted way, holds the Kosovars responsible for his parents' suicides. A psychiatrically trained or at least oriented mediator might still be able to bring such an orientation to the Serb leader's consciousness, preparatory to dismissing it as presumably an exaggerated aspersion of imputed collective guilt.

Note: if the Chinese Yuan does not float but can be devalued vis a vis the dollar, presumably that means that the Yuan is artificially pegged at a specific value of the current value of the dollar?

Note: there is a possibility that global economic pressures are pushing the United States into a military confrontation with Serbia and potentially with Russia. Thus a large scale conventional war in Europe would provide "employment" for those who are currently unemployed in Russia and Europe. Russia may be in danger of further defaults on its' international borrowings, seemingly unable or unwilling to impose progressive taxation on its necessarily nouveau riche, this measure seeming to this writer as a necessary prerequisite to the creation of a functional middle class based economy. And, without such an economy it seems dubious that Russia will ever be able to even begin to repay the kind of debt that it is racking up. Someone said on the radio that "as far as he was concerned Russia was merely a 'paper tiger';" but it should be noted that while Russia's conventional military capabilities and economic capabilities seem unimpressive, her nuclear capabilities are not, and pressuring those in positions of weakness is more likely to lead to desperate exaggerated overreactions than would be the case in a scenario in which a stronger economy were being pressured.

A Russian ideological identity crisis;

Russia, it seems, is caught in a sort of ideological identity crisis. Desperately seeking to disassociate itself from all things Marxist, it is unable or unwilling to adopt and implement the best, valid components of Marxist theory, components which are currently incorporated into most mainstream Liberal economic theories. Thus the idea that taxation needs to be progressive is consistent with the basic Marxist theoretical thrust to the effect that there are certain dangers associated with the unchecked accumulation of capital in the hands of the wealthy. Thus liberals advocate a measure short of the total expropriation of private capital, i.e. progressive taxation. But apparently so anathema do the Russians feel towards all things Marxist, that they are unable to effectively utilize the theory of collective interconnected merit, a critique of ultra individualistic "pure laissez faire capitalism," that would effectively allow the formation of a decent standard of living for all, not merely for the ruthless and lucky few.

April 19, 1999

Russians may be beginning to assume the role of pirates;

This business of continually loaning large sums of monies to countries that are unable and/or unwilling to adopt measures that could allow them to pay off the debt becomes extremely embarrassing both for the countries doing the lending and for such a recipient. If the country doing the receiving utterly refuses to adopt any semblance of the suggested measures, yet still requests funds, it begins to change its' perceived status from mendicant to pirate. And pirates, it is thought in conventional wisdom, need to be confronted militarily. Hence the need is either to get the Russians to agree to a viable economic plan by way of which they could be able to predictably repay their western debt, or to humiliate them militarily. Attacking their ally Serbia is a way of humiliating them militarily. Putting in ground troops would be a further humiliation. However such further humiliation would entail the risk of a Russian/NATO military confrontation which could conceivably escalate into a nuclear confrontation. Hence the need to focus on not just Serbia but also upon Russia's economic problems and strategies for dealing with those problems.

Russia's psychological need for a power elite;

Sociologically speaking, it should be noted that the Russians have always been enthralled by and seemingly need, relatively great concentrations of power, whether economic or political, in the hands of the few. The Czar's powers were largely unchecked by the Dumas. The Soviet Union was relatively capitalistically speaking egalitarian, however, political power and privileges were concentrated in the hands of a relatively small elite group. Now in a capitalistic Russia there appears to be a reluctance to progressively tax their new capitalist elite minority; perhaps this reluctance is related to a psychological need for relatively unchecked authority figures?

NATO's need to prove itself in Serbia;
    Then of course there is the likelihood that (if) the Serbs are not being offered the option of accepting a joint NATO/Russian force this fact is being caused precisely because among other previously mentioned reasons, the leaders of NATO really want to take this opportunity to prove themselves to be great soldiers, to do what the Whermacht and Napoleon could not do, and, to take "the stuff" out of a younger, seemingly frivolous, upcoming younger generation.

The upcoming generation, lack of seriousness and the economy;
    But one would think that there are other less dangerous ways of squelching frivolity. For example, much of this so called frivolity is caused by the fashion industry. Consider the psychological effects of extremely skimpy bikinis, for example. When semi nudity becomes the norm, desire becomes commonplace and mundane, it ceases being special, never approaches being sacred, and, as a result marital or even cohabital bonds loose their special character, sexual partnerships come to acquire a short term status if they exist at all, the family becomes problematic. Divorce and the single life become the norm, psychological security rare, eventually mental health levels are likely to degrade and deteriorate if they have not already. These trends allow for more and more women (and men) to find their primary sources of social satisfaction and orientation in the work place rather than in the home. Large numbers of families, if they do so at all, eat supper together with the television on. This trend is clearly good for the work place; but only so long as the quality of the personal lives of the upcoming generation is not significantly dysfunctionally degraded. And, it is far from clear that a war will discourage this trend.

Death cults, significant other, class, ethnicity, systemic coping with anonymity
Date: 4/26/99 5:15:57 AM Eastern Daylight Time
to: the editors (The American Prospect, The Nation, The New Yorker)
from: Andréas Daniel Fogg
Letter from Somerville April 22, 1999

Fictional notes: Both misters Quincy and Summacanno had, in passing, made what the narrator took to be metaphorical references to "death like" experiences that they themselves had managed to somehow survive. Thus Quincy had claimed at one point, seemingly with a straight face that he had not lived beyond the age of forty. Yet he was currently by most methods of tabulation, in his seventies. Summacanno had commented when told about a woman who had survived a car crash to the effect that she "had died." Summacanno had been, the narrator assumed, trying to strengthen the rehabilitative experiences, and future personal strength, of rehabilitating mentally ill patients. That may have been Quincy's motivation in making his remark to the narrator. Note that Quincy may have made a similar remark to one of his sons who has perhaps not coincidentally suffered psychiatric difficulties himself, having been at one point diagnosed as a paranoid schizophrenic and having dropped out of a prestigious and highly selective law school. Perhaps the shooters in Littleton, Colorado, heard similar remarks from some significant adults in their lives.

The combination of such seemingly ambiguous and portentous remarks combined with the educational system's (and the larger socioeconomic system's) emphasis on rewarding athletics and largely ignoring the accomplishments of all but the "really big winners" (and sometimes even the big winners as well, after all, as it has been noted, genuine excellence and merit may be commodities which are not highly marketable in the mass, television media. This is the case because intellectual materials that require genuine thinking, thinking that may not be comprehensible to many, probably do not draw enough mass market share to justify their presentation on television. Hence, the photogenic simplifiers are the people who draw the large salaries and acquire the prestige associated with the presentation on television. The actual initiators of these ideas are often totally or relatively socially and economically ignored by the society; laboring in either totally anonymous isolation or in the relative isolation of the universities.) Both in high school and college and indeed the larger socioeconomic system itself may make for the sort of volatile mix which has caused the incubation of the lethal acts which we have seen. Indeed, the narrator heard one mental health worker, from Germany; say out loud, in the presence of recuperating mental patients, that "such and such a painter "was not famous or successful because he was not yet dead."

The use of make-up by the Littleton shooters

Note too, that there were reports that the shooters in the Littleton debacle were members of a group which characteristically wore long black trench coats to school and wore (presumably) (facial) makeup. Thus it appears that the image that they projected and intended to project apparently amounted to being in a sort of unisexual "drag." Assuming the appearance of made up women yet dressing in trench coats, which can be worn by both men and women, and can be used to conceal weapons (as in for example the first Terminator film) suggests that these boys may have been "identifying with those (women or men) experienced as aggressors" experienced as aggressors because of their ability to attract the attention of so many others largely because of their attractiveness. It is also possible that the use of makeup may have sought to emulate the practice of both male and female television "authority" figures of wearing the stuff. There may also be the possibility that these boys were expressing resentment against their sisters, i.e. that putting on makeup may have allowed them to be mistaken literally for their sisters, or for women to whom they bore a striking resemblance, thereby possibly attracting the attention of men who might have romantic interest in such "sister" figures and short circuiting that attraction, sabotaging that attraction, if you will by impersonating the sister figure and giving contradictory signals to potential suitors.

April 23, 1999

Note several anecdotes, for example, a caller on the radio program "The Connection" identifies himself only as "Terkle." This usage seems innocuous enough unless you consider the fact that in the Boston intellectual community the name Terkle is most readily associated, by the narrator at least, with the professor Sherry Terkle, who is at MIT and deals with the interface between politics, society and high tech information technology. Using surmise, which may be totally off base, one can construct a fictional scenario wherein the caller is Sherry's brother, who longs for the days of early adolescence, perhaps, wherein young men are known solely by their last name, because, if you think about it, young girls simply do not count in such groups. Hence, in such a longed for context, there is no need to distinguish the young Terkle from his sister. Terkle alone is a sufficient identifier.

The other observation that I have to offer here has to do with a young woman with whom I am acquainted, who works in a coffee house in Somerville. I have noticed recently that she apparently has a double who cuts (his) hair the same way, wears similar or indistinguishable glasses and often dresses the same way i.e. tee shirts and jeans. The double however, apparently wears some makeup, no beard is apparent; the only evidence in fact that he is a man in drag is that his head is, upon reflective examination, somewhat larger than that of the girl in the coffee house. Now clearly this "double" may not be a man in drag, she may be a woman with a larger heard. She may or may not be known to the girl, we will call her Anne, in the coffee house. As has been pointed out, large numbers of look alike persons often congregate in some of the urban areas, particularly those which are educational centers. So this is a fictional, surmised point.

Note however, that the society spends enormous amounts of time (and money) confers enormous status on adults who play adolescent games like football, baseball and basketball. The assertion is that this emphasis is not accidental but rather reflects mass societies longing for the days of adolescence wherein the relations between the sexes were either unimportant or as in high school, often adopted with a sort of gung ho unambivalent and naive totalistic enthusiasm. In contrast, you have people with PhD's driving taxi cabs for lack of employment opportunities.

April 24, 1999

Issues on the table for the weekend: the definition of a "significant other," its' implications in terms of sexual behavior, norms, gender roles, divorce and marital or cohabital stability, going back to Socrates' and Plato's Symposium. The issue of class may become confused with the problems associated with living in multicultural and multiracial societies; that is, when ethnicity or race are assumed to be equivalent to class membership, then it becomes impossible for a multicultural culture or society to hold together. On the other hand, or conversely, when examples of countervailing tendencies are widely publicized, that is, when examples of individuals originating in groups which typically are assumed to be equivalent to, for example, a lower socioeconomic class, when such individuals' success and membership in at least some of the categories which constitute upper class or upper middle, or middle class membership when such membership is widely publicized in either the press or television media, then these individuals' success gives hope to the other members of their group to the effect that "success for one of 'us' is possible." But the whole possibility of such success may also serve to attack the naive assumption of the cultural supremacist, the ultra nationalist functioning in a multicultural setting. This assumption is that members of his group are the only real people in the society, that is the only people who are worthy of notice, the only people who could possibly make a difference in what is going on. Therefore, he assumes, the only people worthy of recognition for their success are the members of his own group. When others are recognized, his sense of self esteem and/or personal security, which may well derive largely or even exclusively from his membership in his national or cultural or religious or racial group, may be either diminished or questioned. If only Italians "count" then how can it be that there is an Irish mayor of Somerville? Or, visa versa, if only Irish count, then how can there be an Italian mayor of Somerville? Or, if only Catholics count, then how can there be any successful Protestants, Muslims, Hindus or Jews?

The presentation of (the presumed injured) self as a problem to be overcome in multicultural society;

The self is presumed to suffer from an imputed status liability, whether that liability is ethnic, racial, and religious or class based seems to be less important than the fact that a liability is likely to exist for most ordinary people. Thus much of American cultural "development" over the last thirty or forty years has involved an assault on the presumed hegemony of what were derisively called "WASPS" (White Anglo-Saxon Protestants). In the nineteen sixties this was particularly the case. At first the media sought to replace the WASP hegemony with Jews, particularly Jewish liberals. During the sixties there was an alliance between liberal Jews and African American civil rights organizers. This alliance fell apart apparently when both groups realized that each appeared to be a liability to the other. Judaism, with a relatively more encouraging attitude toward sexuality than that of Catholicism (at least on the surface), fell into, it seems, a state of relative unfashionableness with the onset of AIDS, which disease suggested to many the idea that sexual abstinence before marriage constituted the safest course of conduct, this idea being in conformance with the Catholic indictment of extra marital and premarital sex as being wrong and acts of fornication which would eventually result in participants going "to Hell" (correct me if I'm wrong, please.) So that now, to a statistically uninformed viewer, Catholic identities are quite acceptable in the media; whereas Jewish surnames seem, unless the individual is someone "really special" to be unfashionable or even shunned. But nevertheless the challenge both in the media and in public settings in which conversation can be overheard seems to be to successfully present ideas of some intellectual challenging content without incurring the also presumed damaging label of "pointy headed intellectual whom nobody likes." This challenge also involves the idea of challenging the normative turf of any of the supposedly aggrieved identity groups whose primary purpose in most cases seems to involve the defense of their memberships right to call itself normal and to be immune from apparently any public or private criticism or discrimination. These identity groups include first and foremost the homosexuals both male and female, then those racial and ethnic groups which seek to blame their relatively poor socioeconomic performance on the larger society's presumed illegitimate attempt to discriminate against them, these groups in American society today are predominately the African Americans and the Hispanics, which are the most vociferous in their protests, but also, more quietly, the Native Americans more commonly known as the American Indians. Then there are the Jews and the Muslims who both lobby to avoid negative depictions of themselves in the media and to avoid job and public discrimination and harassment as well. To the unsystematic observer, as I have indicated, Catholics seem to have acquired mainstream respectability, largely because of the AIDS problem. Whether Catholics will continue to enjoy the popularity that they currently enjoy outside of the Boston area when and if the AIDS epidemic is cured remains to be seen.

So the narrator personally has a problem with the presentation of his own self in public. Or in more ordinary language, he is quite shy. The point I am trying to make, however, is that the challenge for art and the media involves finding words and scenarios to present relatively ordinary people presenting themselves to other ordinary people in markedly civilized yet satisfying ways. This seems to be what American society has lost. We seem to have elevated marginal behavior to the status of being the de facto norm. That is, non-marginal behavior is presumed to be both uninteresting and unsatisfying and from the point of view of marketability, unsaleable in either book store or box office. This tacit hypothesized market decision, having it is suggested been made by television and movie moguls and by book publishers probably reflects a sort of anomic state of being that is partly being caused by economic forces associated with globalization and partly results from the toleration of poor sloppy intellectual thinking going unchallenged in the media. Thus our collective definitions of self and appropriate behavior are in most cases not subjected to any sort of rigorous thinking but rather seem to be reduced to the easiest simplest terms possibly understood by "most ordinary not particularly reflective people." Thus the "significant other" is someone with whom one spends the most time and energy and such a person is without question one's sexual partner. That's obvious to the ordinary person. To the ordinary person that's the "way things are supposed to be." Furthermore, the entire scheme of identity politics, particularly when it involves the assertion of homosexual rights is based upon the assumption that "one should be involved in sexual relations with virtually anyone who is important (to you)". Now by my remembered reading of Plato's Symposium, this was the principle that Socrates died protesting against. Namely that sex and thinking should not be regularly, promiscuously mixed.

It is important to keep in mind that in the world in which Socrates lived women were second class citizens and most men were presumed to be bisexual. Socrates was presenting the argument that sexual arousal was likely to have a deleterious effect on the quality of intellectual thinking. This insight is it seems to the narrator crucial to the evolution of western thinking and technological development. And the entire normative development of the second half of the twentieth century has involved the propagation of the countervailing view contained in the so called sexual liberation movement. That view is in a nutshell that everyone is entitled to their fair dose of regular sexual bliss and that any views, norms or values that serve to detract from the individuals rights to such bliss must back off and be rendered harmless and ineffectual, assume in short the status of archaic "blue laws." Thus society cowers before the homosexual's right to proclaim himself or herself normal and OK and not a threat to anyone least of all themselves. Meanwhile the idea of dispassionate thinking seems to have fallen into disrepute largely surrendered to the practice of playing with computers. This habit, however, ignores the fact that computers' thoughts are no better than the thoughts of those who enter the data and increasingly the ideas and pictures themselves. These people are decidedly unfashionable since they embody the idea of lonely sometimes sexually independent often frustrating and potentially futile quite possibly economically uncompensated, brain wracking work. And it is asserted that when such thinkers communicate with each other that sexual as opposed to merely physical contact is likely to be avoided as involving unnecessary confusion and the assumption of unnecessary interpersonal vulnerability. Since this vulnerability is incurred each time two people "lie down together," it is suggested that in fact cohabital status is in fact inimical to the active continuation of a vital intellectually dynamic "significant other relationship." Clearly while a man and a woman may choose each other in part based upon some intellectual affinities and mutual orientational respect, it may be the case, it is argued, that the purpose of a cohabital relationship may not necessarily include an intellectual collaboration. Certainly if a cohabital relationship, particularly a heterosexual cohabital relationship, seeks to prohibit the formation of significant other relationships of a non sexual nature with individuals who are not part of the spousal dyad, then such a heterosexual bond, while perhaps orgasmically enormously satisfying, is likely to be experienced as socially and intellectually prohibitively burdensome. Indeed the individual's need to be free of his or her lover's control when denied can result in their giving up on heterosexuality (or any sexuality) in general. In fact this confused alienation is precisely what the narrator sees as fueling the current spate of marital and spousal breakups and the current popularity of homosexuality.

Consider the spousal romantic imperative, for example, "if you love me then you want me to be with your friends, you want to share everything with me." Placing such an authenticity requirement upon a sexual relationship whether heterosexual or homosexual involves the required surrender of the individual's entire self into a new organism that is the romantic dyad and while it is true that two heads are better than one when one of the heads is female that is likely to be the one that is calling all of the shots. Hence the sincere male lover who places absolute and complete priority upon fidelity and devotion to his woman effectively gives up his right to think for himself. This right can be retained only so long as he is potentially willing to sacrifice the pleasure that the woman offers in the event that his thinking no longer meets her approval. To this end he may go to extraordinary lengths in order to retain his intellectual independence. For example, he may literally conceal his work from his spouse or wife in order to avoid the possibility that he will lose her as a sexual partner in the event that she disapproves of his work. When and if such hidden work occurs the sexual partner cannot by any stretch of the imagination be considered to be any longer the only "significant other." They can of course be considered a or the "sexually significant other." But that is the point that I am trying to make namely that a sexually significant other while quite important and desirable may often not be able to be an intellectually significant other.

April 25, 1999

Note that occasionally fictional persons who the narrator rightly or wrongly assumes to be important pseudonymous writers sometimes have the habit of showing either a lack of interest or an actual attitude of disrespect or distaste for what the narrator assumes to be their own published work. Such a posture toward one's own work, when displayed before one's children and/or spouse or friends may have the effect of removing or distancing said works importance vis a vis the writer's relations with either their spouse and/or their children or friends. This attitude of disinterest also has the merit of allowing the published work to sink or swim on its own, without its author personally advancing its' fortunes in any particular way, other, that is, than through the act of having written the material and having allowed it to be published.

Department of Feminist Tripe: Ms.Graff (spelling?), a lesbian feminist from Harvard suggested on the radio program, The Connection, that children whose mothers have had sex with more than one man during the possible period of conception, such children are healthier than the "children of only one father." This is a (lesbian) assault on the legitimacy of the notion of possessive romantic love. Ms. Graff should perhaps be burned in effigy by members of the pro family faction. (I'm working on my third glass of beer here, which goes to prove the psychological difficulty involved in criticizing members of the Harvard establishment.) But instead it is insisted that all views be accepted or at least tolerated. Outrage is considered taboo. Note that homosexuals consider heteros deviant and heteros consider homos deviant and nobody is allowed to ridicule anybody so as a result almost everybody feels deviant or in other words somewhat ashamed to express themselves, present themselves in public.

A fictional hypothetical society;

Note a fictional hypothetical society in which job security although not necessarily a rising standard of living requires a membership card. One of the criteria for membership is a minimal level of income. The other criteria are not known, never known, and only guessed at. However, members come from across the political spectrum. Membership is a little like being registered, if registered you count, you are known, you have an identity. If you are not a member, you do not count, you are not distinguishable from relatively anonymous, relatively "faceless" members of the anonymous mass society.

Contrary to popular belief, membership does not entitle you to unlimited income. That is merely a popular fantasy no doubt inspired by the fact that the membership credit card has no spending limit. Gaining membership can be quite iffy.

An alternative heterosexual relatively stable interaction schema;

An alternative heterosexual stable "moral" model: this is fictional. The father seeks out conversations with other men. These seem to give him pleasure. His wife does not interfere with these conversations but makes her presence felt by remaining on the periphery of the interactions. Hence for the most part "deviant" sexual activity between the father and his male friends is precluded by the presence of the wife, if not the inclinations of the father toward platonic non sexual interactions (with other male friends). Both the father and his friends are in most cases sufficiently heterosexually inclined to respect the wife's right to intervene at her discretion. So she keeps them straight yet they are sufficiently interested in what each other has to say so that a sort of male/male non sexual bond forms as a result of their discussions. Furthermore, since one is an academic social scientist and the other either the same or an aspirant to being the same, some actual intellectual progress may result from their conversations. But the wife by no stretch of the imagination considers that she has the "right" to sleep with her husband's friends. Such a "right" or actually quasi imperative (because according to Ms. Graph, the result will be a healthier child) is a (new) Feminist conceit, born perhaps out of economic and status resentment and a misanthropic wish to subvert lasting heterosexual bonds and change society's normative view of female/female sexual unions i.e. from deviant to normal and even desirable.

Paying pro athletes exorbitantly high wages disparages "adult" occupations
Date: 5/11/99 2:39:31 AM Eastern Daylight Time
to: the editors (The American Prospect, The Nation, The New Yorker)
from: Andréas Daniel Fogg
Letter from Somerville April 29, 1999

When society values or confers enormous status on occupations which functionally speaking are little more than glorifications of childhood and adolescent concerns, preoccupations and practices, it should not be surprised when the children of that society withhold their respect from (even actively display disrespect for) adults involved in lower paying yet clearly, functionally speaking, more useful occupations. Hence a problem is found in the disparity between the valuation that the mass market, as currently regulated, places upon professional sports and the valuation placed upon more specialized although less highly lauded occupations.

May 2, 1999

(See clarification at bottom of the paragraph)
I read somewhere that under the rule of Tito, Serbs were not allowed to return to Kosovo. So presumably at some point in recent history, like during the 1970s, some group, it presumably must have been the Albanian Kosovars who have since come to occupy ninety percent of the province, drove Serbs out. It is relevant to the quest toward finding a viable peaceful settlement to the Kosovo conflict to know the accurate historical facts concerning this incident or series of incidents. Similarly, it is important to know the facts as they are recounted and justified by both parties to the dispute. Clearly, if there were a series of Kosovar attacks which caused an exodus of Serbs in the 1970s, such a fact would begin to explain some of the Serbian justification for the ethnic cleansing that currently certainly seems

to be going on. And if an ethnic cleansing of the Serbs by the Kosovars had occurred, then its existence would seem to be relevant if one were disposed to partition the province as a mechanism towards resolving the conflict. That is, under such a circumstance one would not feel compelled to partition the land under a formula by which the Kosovars would receive ninety per cent and the Serbs ten per cent.

CLARIFICATION: the article, in the Political Science Quarterly, by Sanya Popovic, suggests that it was the Nazis who drove the Serbs out of Kosovo during WWII and that Tito, in 1945, in the interests of establishing a general peace, prohibited Serbs, who had apparently been expelled from Kosovo by said Nazis, from returning to Kosovo. Note that Tito was a Croat and a Communist who had presumably fought against the Croatian Ustasi Nazis but also presumably against the anti Nazi but royalist Serbian Cetniks. So that the Serb drive to return to Kosovo is old, but not as old as has been suggested, merely dating back most recently to the 1940s. I have recently read somewhere, but cannot remember where, cannot find the reference that some Albanian Muslims from Kosovo fought against the Serbs in Kosovo organized as a force allied to the Nazis. If this indeed was the case and Tito prohibited the Serbs from returning to Kosovo after the war, then I and others are correct that the Serbian grievance against the Albanian Kosovars dates back most recently merely to the Second World War.

May 6, 1999

Organ Donation;

It is true, I suppose, that there should be no legal market for the organs of the dead. However, prohibiting a legal market may lay the groundwork for a black market in this area; indeed, a (NPR) report suggests that such a market exists in Egypt. However, it is absurd to expect people, often themselves economically deprived, to "out of the goodness of their hearts" agree to make their organs available "to those who need them" in the event of their deaths. A reasonable way out is for the government to agree to pay a standard fee to the estate of deceased donors. While such a practice would not eliminate the appeal and likelihood of a black market in organs, it would at any rate, serve to dignify the posture of potential donors. Why poor deprived individuals should be confronted with the dilemma of whether or not to make their organs available gratis is frankly beyond me. And the fact that I and others have been forced to make such a decision, retrospectively, enrages me. However, it should be noted, that I am working on my third bottle of beer.

Historical parameter for conflict resolution in Kosovo;

If it is indeed the case that Kosovars participated in the Nazi genocide against the Serbs, and it appears that it was the case, then any attempts to incorporate history into a psychiatrically oriented peace making effort should include gestures to bring to consciousness not just Serbian violations against the lives and property of the Kosovars, but also the extent both real and estimated of the Kosovar/Nazi genocide (as well as estimated property seizures) against the Serbs.

May 8, 1999

Professor Sanya Popovic e-mailed me to the effect that there were two SS divisions, one in Bosnia Herzegovina and the other in Kosovo, during the Second World War. They were respectively the Handzar SS and the Skanderbeg SS. What exactly they did to the Serbs at that time is the subject of contentious partisan debate, since estimates of the overall number of Serbs killed by the Nazi range from 20,000 to I think, 800,000, according to the article by Sanya Popovic. And when the Nazis killed people, they had a habit of appropriating whatever property possible.

Organ donation reconsidered; a female psychiatrist who is under the illusion that I am under her care points out that if estates were paid for the organs of the deceased who had agreed to be donors, then there would be a motivation for members of the family to conspire to commit homicide against the potential donor. I am interested in this problem (since it has been mentioned on NPR and referred to on a Fox science fiction television program, not to mention Robin Cook's novel) because I believe that its' appearance is a symptom, and an obviously horrific symptom, of the potential for a breakdown of civil society. Indeed it is of far more concern than for example, whether more people are bowling alone than in the past. The report on NPR claimed that in Egypt, the poor were occasionally killed "so that the medically needy rich could 'have' the organs." I seem to remember hearing of something similar happening in Brazil. In such circumstances the idea that we live in a classless society, often perpetrated by the American media (presumably in order to allow for unified appeals to 'everyone') appears as the true absurdity that it clearly is. Indeed the existence or potential existence of such normative breakdowns should serve as a motivation to attempt to reduce the differential distribution of wealth. Part of the difficulty involved in achieving such an end lies in the quality of normative culture associated with the American if not other national working and poorer classes. Part and parcel of such cultural normative orientations involves what Erik Erikson would probably have called a systemic underlying high level of basic mistrustfulness. Thus the typical working class individual would not think of sending his hard earned dollars to someone that he was not long time friends with (and maybe not even then). Such an action would be characteristic of a "sucker." Such a distrustful worker would hypothetically project his own likely action in such a circumstance onto to the potential recipient, that is he would likely abscond with the money, so why wouldn't the investment broker? So, the typical worker does not invest, instead he spends in order to maintain "face" in the community, even to the point where he goes into debt. Of course there are exceptions to this observed rule. Such exceptions typically manage to rise to higher socioeconomic positions.

A fictional vignette: The narrator, having fallen head over heels in love in a consummated summer romance, returns to college and discovers that his anticipated occupational success has not materialized and that further, the summer romance has ended, the woman having decided to marry someone else. The narrator is devastated, but maintains the illusion that the beloved woman will eventually rejoin him. In fact at one point he is unwilling to respond to what appears to be a sexual overture from a different woman who has the same first name as the woman who had rejected him. Then, heartbroken and teary-eyed, he goes bowling alone. And, a seeming miracle occurs. The narrator, who hadn't bowled using big pins for years and then had often been unable to score higher than one hundred fifty (out of a possible 300 perfect score), starts bowling all strikes. He scores first; I think 225, then 280, then two or three games of perfect 300s, twelve strikes in a row. He can't believe this is happening to him. He realizes that he may be dreaming and so saves the score card as proof that it really happened. However, for years it never occurs to him that the whole incident may have been an extremely realistic dream. He never looks for the scorecard.

The narrator knows a young man who claims not to value money. "I sometimes burn it," he says. Why this attitude? We return to the legal position on not compensating organ donors. Society says, "We need organ donors" but because people might be encouraged to either commit suicide or murder in order to receive compensation, if compensation were made available, therefore we offer no compensation to organ donors or to their families or estates. Therefore organ donors are placed in the difficult psychological position of explicitly denying that their bodies and for that matter therefore their deaths seem to have any monetary value. This implicit symbolic statement clearly is absurd and contradictory and therefore organ donors are likely to be quite assertive when it comes to justifying their existences and the value of their work products. This tends to be the case since they likely feel it necessary to contradict the symbolic statement that they feel they have been forced to make in order to ensure that society will have at least one organ donor. If such individuals find themselves in desperate financial and occupational straits, for example, if they are recovering psychiatric patients, they likely are searching for some gimmick which will allow them to escape the social and occupational stigma associated with those who are or have been labeled, rightly or wrongly, mentally ill. Alternatively, those who are merely young with little or no working experience and little or no money may also find themselves in such a bind, expecting to land a prestigious high paying job but being forced instead to settle for a relatively low paying low status job—and then eventually be forced to be grateful that they are earning as much as they currently receive. Such individuals in effect may be settling for jobs that involve downward socioeconomic mobility. Indeed this is the case when a young person finds that he or she can neither match not surpass the level of accomplishments of their parent or parents. The temptation for such individuals is to think of themselves, to label themselves, as "failures" simply because they have been unable to match the achievements of their parents.

May 11, 1999

Organ donation reconsidered again; anyway, given that a black market in body parts were illegal, and that murder is illegal, what assurance is there that the state's deliberate decision to avoid compensating organ donors would serve to prohibit an admittedly illegal black market. That is, there is likely to be a black market, financed by the very rich who are in need of a donor regardless of whether the state provides a financial incentive for donation or not. The state's ability to deter a black market in body parts is more likely to be related to the sanctions arrayed as potential punishment for indulging in the practice and to the relative supply of available donated organs. That is, if there is a relatively plentiful supply, the need to create and sustain a black market would seem to decrease. In this regard the psychological status of a potential donor would seem to be relevant. Just as it would seem to be inadvisable to sell life insurance to an individual who had been diagnosed mentally ill and who harbored acute self destructive feelings, similarly, it would seem to be inadvisable to allow such a suicidal person to become a pledged organ donor whose estate was in line to receive some market oriented estimation of the value of his corpse.

But all these speculations are quite macabre, and I apologize for boring and perhaps offending the reader. In fact I am of half a mind to simply erase all reference to the subject from this piece. However, the subject may turn out to be of some interest and even importance. Afterall, when the rich become much much richer than the poor, they are likely to at the same time begin to think of themselves as somehow much much more important than the poor. If this discrepancy in accumulated wealth were to result in a diminished respect for human life itself, such a result would be truly horrific and a far more dramatic bit of evidence that civil society was breaking down than merely an increased number of persons found to be bowling alone. And, when you think about it, are we really sure that there isn't even today, a black market in body parts? Again, I apologize for likely offending the reader. And there is the further question of how the state might determine if potential donors were in fact suicidal, since psychiatric therapeutic relationships are theoretically private and inviolate. Perhaps potential organ donors should be required to submit to an interview with a Red Cross nurse or an accredited social worker, in which they would be asked if they were under the care of a psychiatrist or psychologist and whether at any time in the last three years, for example, they had harbored strong or moderately strong self destructive thoughts. Or, perhaps psychotherapists should be required to notify the state organ donation control administration, if such a bureau exists, of the fact that such and such an individual is a psychiatric patient who should not be given any financial incentive in connection with his or her death. I confess that all this is beyond me and that in fact I am more likely frightening myself more than I am frightening the reader. Again, I am sorry if I have rained on your parade. The only reason I will send this along is because I am accustomed to sharing virtually everything remotely serious that I have written down. Somewhere in these ruminations there may be some valuable thoughts.

Administration's imbalanced approach to Kosovo problem
Date: 5/22/99 12:28:49 PM Eastern Daylight Time
to: the editors (The American Prospect, The Nation, The New Yorker)
from: Andréas Daniel Fogg
Letter from Somerville May 15, 1999

It appears to the writer that the NATO terms for a settlement in Kosovo are too severe and based on a one-sided view of the situation namely, that the Serbian position is all bad and totally unjustifiably, indefensible, whereas the Albanian Kosovars are all innocent lamb like victims. Notice that in America we hear nothing of the activities or history of the Kosovo Liberation Army (KLA). As far as the press is concerned in the US, the KLA does not really substantially exist; it is not a factor in considering what the requirements for a peaceful solution should be. Thus any suggestions that the KLA might not allow itself to be substantially disarmed in fact are dismissed. The unbending requirement is that all Serb forces must be totally withdrawn, leaving the 200,000 Serbs in the province without any military protection other than their own armament and the international force. Notice that there is no requirement for the KLA to withdraw. It is suggested that this formula is unfair and designed to perpetuate NATO's ability to exercise its air war muscles. "It's not much of a war, but it's the only war we've got" used to be the mantra of the war loving hawks during the Vietnam War. Perhaps the same could be said of those who are committed as a matter of principle, to the so called revitalization and rejuvenation of the American military. This commitment, however, is somewhat hypocritical since it explicitly avoids the "risky" use of ground troops; not that I am advocating ground troops, merely instead suggesting that the Administration is not really interested in negotiating a fair end to this conflict.

Emotional manipulation utilized as a correlative of "leadership";

The skilled manipulator can, using affection as a carrot and criticism and the possibility of rejection as a "stick" manage to control either his friends and/or his subordinates, coworkers (and occasionally, persons for whom he works i.e. superiors). For example, consider the case of a fictional old friend (this old friend is in fact, the younger Murdock son discussed earlier, he who in his youth had had a great fondness for bright red shirts, son of a noted psychoanalyst, who had become a successful or at least accredited psychoanalyst), who had always managed to achieve, on the surface of things, more success than the narrator; that is, he went to a more prestigious college, got a prestigious advanced degree from a prestigious university, has a more prestigious job than the narrator, yet they have been friends since childhood. Note, that despite all of the friend's accomplishments, the narrator has never really acknowledged (the friends) "superiority" or greater importance, except in the area of athletics, (and physical height), where the friend clearly has been a more successful competitor. Now, the friend comes to town, from out of state for an in-law family party, phones the narrator up and says that the narrator can drive for about an hour and he, the old friend, will allow the narrator to accompany him while he rents a tuxedo. No mention is made of sitting down for even coffee let alone a meal. The narrator suspects that he is being effectively slighted i.e. the Harvard grad doesn't have time for his old friend who doesn't even have an Ivy League degree, perhaps he will be offered the "opportunity and privilege to carry the distinguished Harvard grad's tux?" Yet if he rejects the offer or suggests that unless some actual visiting time is offered that he will be unable to make the meeting, he will, he knows, be jeopardizing the "old" friendship. So he feels terrible. And in fact he almost gets into an auto accident the night before he is supposed to hear from his old friend. In the event, the friend, perhaps realizing that the narrator will not accept the bait involving an acceptance of imputed deprecation, offers to meet in University Square. But the next day he backs out of even this leaving the narrator feeling somewhat sad but also somewhat angry.

Emotional leverage, "people skills," and management;

It would appear that in the so called service jobs, supervisory skills tend to involve what are loosely called by some "people skills." Which means, I suspect, not having or wanting to have such myself, so far, that the supervisor or manager is adept at using emotional affection and indebtedness as motivational tools which enable him or her to induce subordinates to work and work hard? In other words, the successful supervisor or manager uses the threat of emotional punishment and/or temporary or relatively permanent rejection as weapons with which he drives his subordinates toward the successful completion on a regular basis, of their occupational responsibilities.

May 16, 1999

The New Republic on violence in the media;

In what appears to be an informative and valuable article Gregg Easterbrook, in the May 17, 1999 TNR claims that the seeming spate of school based mass killings has been stimulated by the depiction of violent acts in movies and television. The article is valuable because it refers to a number of recent films which depict violence often against jocks and especially against women. Easterbrook's claim is that the young are often allowed to see such films and that because their characters are relatively unformed, individuals with borderline like psychiatric problems tend occasionally to emulate the films. Indeed, his implicit claim is that only a relatively few such emulations constitute a breach in the sense of security associated with a stable civil society.

Fictional discussion of societies' need to depict violence against attractive women;

Consider a fictional character who claims to never have attended college but nevertheless persists in wearing sweatshirts which depict long past Harvard football perfect season scorecard results. Such an individual, if he hasn't gone to college is quite a success, having risen to the level of successful, secure lower level supervisorship. However, if as it is suspected, he is in fact a Harvard graduate, his achievement as a successful lower managerial supervisor is at best unremarkable and at worst slightly pathetic. This individual has recounted to the narrator words to the effect that he resents women in the work place because they use their feminine attractiveness to get ahead of men.

Suppose what we are looking at in all of this supposedly legitimately artistic Hollywood violence against women and, it should be noted, against heterosexuality itself, is a reaction against the feminist move into the work place; a reaction which implicitly endorses misogynistic feelings and at best male/male bonding and at worst explicit homosexual bonds, behaviors and alliances which serve to allow men to resist the feminist assault on their (our) previously sacrosanct lock on the higher end of the economic ladder.

Here's a thought; that the requirement that society's norm makers need to fulfill is that heterosexuality continue to be linked to economic motivations. That is, women need to continue to act as if their expressions of sexual preference, their selection of a partner or of partners, should reflect an economic dimension. Note that the inception of feminist sexual liberation theory and the widespread dissemination of contraceptive devices both tend to allow for behaviors which embody the disconnection between economic realities and the choice of sexual objects. Hence, it is suggested, we have the attempt to terrorize the population against relatively frivolous, usually heterosexual, sexual choices and behaviors. However, frivolous homosexual behaviors while carrying a risk of contracting and/or spreading HIV are less threatening to the basic family structure than are promiscuous heterosexual behaviors which tend to be more satisfying and therefore compelling and therefore capable of disrupting an economically based functional marital alliance.

Inflation and the oil cartels;

The recent increase in the Consumer Price Index and for that matter, the Producer Price Index, seem to be largely the result of the recent decisions by the oil producing corporations to effectively raise the price of oil and gasoline by cutting back production levels. Since this is the case, the inflation that has been noted is unlikely to be effected positively by raising interest rates. That is the relationship between the money supply and the inflation is less direct than the relationship between the policies and the greed of the oil producers and the inflation. Therefore, a more effective means of dealing with this hopefully temporary economic downturn is to attempt to influence the oil producers to reverse their decision and restore production to its previous level. This could it seems, be accomplished most obviously through either or both of two courses of action. One, threaten the oil producers with antitrust litigation. The recent merger between Mobil and Exxon, for example, can only serve to limit the effect of competition on cartel induced decisions to raise prices by limiting production. Two, make it clear to the oil corporations that half way measures to lower production and raise prices will be responded to by the US government and perhaps by other governments acting in consultation as well, with measures to encourage the utilization of renewable environmentally benign energy sources and perhaps with higher taxes on greenhouse generating i.e. carbon based fuels as well. In fact, it could be pointed out that such higher taxes on carbon based combustible fuels are environmentally desirable, and may therefore be forthcoming anyway. Further it perhaps should be pointed out that the oil companies are at risk of being painted as environmental, global criminals, firstly, and that the sorts of price rises that are occurring will not, in the absence of readily available environmentally benign alternatives make much of a difference in the global warming equation. Therefore the oil companies are risking triggering a global recession simply in order to obtain a larger slice of the consumers pie and that if they don't stop and restore production, and that even if they do restore production levels, they may be in for a government and insurance based public relations assault on their moral respectability, their supposed good intentions and indeed their very need to exist.

May 17, 1999

Feminism's impact on norms and mores again;

Note that with the inception of feminist thought women, in perhaps vastly larger numbers than previously was the case, have discovered the existence and functions of the clitoris and as a result have been able to sexually empower themselves, that is, they have been able in enormous numbers to teach themselves to become 'orgasmic' or capable of having orgasms. Previously, it may be fair to say, this talent had been confined to prostitutes and a statistically small number of sexually active women. The other women regarded sex as a matter of duty, of doing the right thing, the expected thing, something that was merely designed so that they could produce children. With the inception of this capability women's functions relative to men in the work place and society in general have qualitatively changed. The appeal of an orgasmic woman, when it is directed at a particular man becomes a sort of all compelling appeal. Responding to such an appeal becomes emotionally and physically and psychologically an all consuming experience. Some men, the narrator included, end up feeling sometimes as if in a sense they are literally becoming, psychologically speaking, the woman who is currently in the process of either psychologically or actually seducing them. Whether this sort of transformation is inevitable is questionable. Whether its presence should be considered strength or a personal weakness is also a question. The narrator, who considers his primary function to be that of a writer, and a socially unrecognized and substantially unrewarded writer at that, thinks that his own personality seems to have been suppressed, or perhaps degraded or perhaps 'burned out' long ago. In other words, the narrator sees his self as a sort of entity that requires minimal maintenance and support, merely enough emotional sustenance so that he is capable of finding important ideas to which he can then intellectually respond. The narrator actually does not particularly 'like himself,' in fact he much prefers virtually any attractive woman who is willing to give him a or some vicarious or real, physical sexual stimulation. That is, he would rather visualize himself as such a woman, prepatory to making love to a ghost which impersonates the woman who has occupied his imagination. However, becoming the woman or a woman who 'would' wish to seduce him psychologically is socially a non starter. That is, what happens to social interaction when a man and his current fantasy partner must interact in the real world with others, whether friends or when meeting new people. Does the woman step aside, or does the man step aside? To step aside seems to involve assuming a sort of second class status. Then, there is the question whether if the man has become the woman, has the woman become (the man)?

It clearly does not do to attempt to interact socially in the real world if you are a man, if you are unabashedly impersonating a woman. Perhaps what is needed is for the narrator to practice actually being a man. Yet the system does not seem to reward, certainly has not rewarded in the past, his efforts in this direction. Indeed, there is some question as to whether the system rewards maleness at all, other than in the movies and sports. The men who seem to have 'made it' in the socioeconomic system seem to have cultivated a sort of quasi effeteness. They are careful in their presentations of self, never to get too angry, never to get too assertive, and never to appear too masterful, too powerful. All those strong typically male characteristics seem to need to be muted, if the presentation of self is to succeed.

Socioeconomic functions of height, speculations education
Date: 5/24/99 12:06:45 PM Eastern Daylight Time

to: the editors (The American Prospect, The Nation, The New Yorker)
from: Andréas Daniel Fogg
Letter from Somerville May 22, 1999

Topics to be discussed: current background on the functions of height in Ameri-can society, speculations on behavioral enhancements of height, as opposed to genetic enhancements of height; negative effects involved in directly rewarding tall people as over and against equally or more qualified shorter people.

In the late seventies there was a popular hit song either called, or with the refrain, "short people got no reason to live." Our society is supposed to be a dem-ocratic meritocracy wherein merit is supposed to be more important than intimi-datory potential in determining who receives the greater rewards. If in fact taller people are regularly being recognized as achievers because they are taller, rather than because they are more deserving, then, it would appear that there may be something wrong or less than ideal about our society's reward structuring mecha-nisms.

I have a friend at work who fairly regularly mentions that Bill Russell, the former Celtic professional basketball star center, started out his career measuring six foot nine, but then somehow grew to be six foot eleven. My friend leaves it to his listeners to surmise what specific intervening events spurred Russell, then pre-sumably in his mid or early twenties, to grow the additional two inches. I men-tioned the subject of Bill Russell's height to a middle aged single male bar tender friend of mine, a guy of about say five foot seven inches height, with something of a beer gut and he gave me a cold star saying "Bill who?" It is interesting to speculate what young men might do in an attempt to somehow "get taller," par-ticularly if being tall is seen as a prerequisite to substantial success.

I broached this question to a friend, a friend who likes to engage in specula-tion, even speculative speculation on such matters, and he, who was at the time moderately intoxicated suggested that a good percentage of those who spurt up to great heights during adolescence and in their twenties actually do so after they have been somewhat painfully anally sodomized either by brother, cousin, rela-tive, "friend" or possibly, an unknown stranger. His theory is that this painful experience leads them to literally stretch out their bodies because, because of the pain, they have more reason to want to deter any potential future sexual aggres-sion against themselves. However, my friend goes on to suggest that many of these extraordinarily tall young men actually have become effectively tall male eunuchs, genetically speaking. That is, he theorizes, during the sodomy essential parts of the male reproductive apparatus i.e. presumably the prostate gland may have been ruptured making such tall men essentially reproductively sterile. He backs up this astonishing and, to the narrator, dubious conclusion by pointing out the fact that in many cases, the children of these very tall men bear little or no resemblance to their fathers. This view, he holds, if spread and given credence, would in effect amount to a "short person's revenge" against all those tall folks who have in the past been rewarded in many cases simply because they were taller and so more frightening to those giving the grades, writing the checks and making the promotions.

And, on the evolutionary level, if there is any connection at all between acquired learning and genetically passed on characteristics, then in fact, if my inebriated friend is right, society may be creating an evolutionary genetically dysfunctional situation if it tends to reward tall individuals who have become incapable of personally engendering their own children.

Of course you have to realize that the political correctness people have played a large role in the struggle to disconnect the link between learning and genetic inheritance. They did this in the attempt allegedly to remove pressure to achieve from the children of the rich and learned, and also in the attempt to assure the children of relatively low level achievers and earners that they had an equal chance of achieving success as did the children of the middle and upper middle classes. That is, the asserted disconnect between learning, acquired characteristics and genetic inheritance appears to be based more on perceived social need rather than upon informed biogenetic data based theorizing. The point I am attempting to make here is that this disconnect, while functional on equalitarian grounds, likely has the drawback associated with it suggested by my slightly inebriated friend, namely, that those who actually carry say genes of a cognitively superior ilk have no particular motivation to pass such genes along, indeed, they may be currently being encouraged to effectively disempower themselves genetically speaking, in response to a media based campaign of suggestion which if followed, they hope will lead them to grow taller and acquire the ability to "cement" strong male bonds which in turn will allow them to maintain positions of leadership in the society, acquire larger pay checks, attract (and protect) attractive women. In short, my friend suggests, getting taller will allow them to achieve all of their goals except, that is, to have their own children, or indeed to have any children. And if, as often seems to be the case, their occupational positions are based more on their ability to inspire fear than upon their actual qualifications, then it becomes apparent why some high school students are increasingly resorting to the utilization of firearms in an attempt to inspire some fear and gain some respect on their own.

Of course, it's important to note that for the last ten or fifteen years, (I'm not sure exactly when it was) height enhancement drugs sufficiently expensive so that they would only be available to the children of the middle and upper middle classes have been on the market. At the approximate time when these drugs came on the market it was remarked, probably on National Public Radio, that they would be sufficiently expensive to the extent that they would be inaccessible to members of the working and unemployed classes. If my time frame is correct, then many of the tall bright optimistic, entitled ("we deserve success and economic privilege") young stars of today's college brood owe their impressive physical stature to this drug. Would that their intellectual stature remotely approximated this physical stature.

May 23, 1999

A strategy to resolve the Kosovo situation;

If it is given that you accept the need for NATO to moderate the terms that it is extending towards the Serbs, then the question arises, how might NATO and particularly the Clinton Administration be persuaded to accept such a moderated set of requirements as the basis for a potential settlement?

Possibly, if the World Court quietly, privately, informed the Clinton Administration to the effect that unless the terms were moderated with dispatch, the World Court or the Hague would feel compelled to announce to the world words to the effect that an inquiry into the possibility that NATO was guilty of crimes against humanity as a result of the manner in which it has intervened in Yugoslavia's current civil war would be launched. The possibility that President Clinton, Prime Minister Blair and others might be publicly charged with war crimes if they did not drop their insistence, and indeed the charade, that NATO is on the side of the angels and the Serbs the reincarnation of the Nazis, might likely result in a timely realistic realignment of NATO requirements for a settlement. This strategic recommendation is based upon an extension of the principles behind Pugwash, during WWII (which I know of only by hearsay) and the recent Oslo negotiations between relatively low profile but influential and well educated Israelis and Palestinians.

The heritability of a genetically based intelligence potential is suggested;

If intelligence is genetically inheritable at all, and my somewhat outdated reading of DNA and RNA theory suggests that it is, then it is likely heritable in the form of intelligence potential, that is, how smart or wise the individual could become under relatively ideal learning conditions. Actual intelligence level, it is suggested, varies genetically and depending on the quality of past and anticipated interactions with significant other persons, that is depending on whether the individual anticipates that he or she will be rewarded for future learning achievements or whether in contrast, he or she will be ridiculed, rejected or even verbally or physically attacked. In this respect the quality of teaching is important. It is, it is suggested, the rare teacher who does not become somewhat put off by a student whose achievements surpass their own. In fact such high level of achievement usually results in the student being passed on to the next level, if there is a next level. Hence success often results in the termination of the teacher student relationship; a fact which in the event that that relationship also includes an element of friendship can in and of itself constitute a source of learning inhibition or resistance.

Does society really want to encourage widespread learning?

The question needs to be raised, does society really want to encourage widespread learning beyond, for example, the supposed needs of what are presently construed as "the service economy?" The answer we are currently getting is a sort of defiant "no!" Certainly those who would encourage liberal arts learning for its own sake tend to be unwilling or unable to produce the political muscle necessary to effectively reward a significant number of those achievers in the societal job market. The typical joke going the rounds is that computer science majors, hard science majors, business majors and some others do all right after graduation. Liberal Arts majors on the other hand end up working at barely minimal wages in fast food joints, asking, "Do you want fries with that (burger)?" If a broad based humanistic education is desirable for more than those who have inherited money, then the society may need to expand the quantity of financial resources that are currently being allocated for the support of (more) adequately funded job tracks. And this is a real question. For example, those elites who have inherited large quantities of wealth may in fact be resistant to the widespread dissemination amongst the masses of higher liberal arts learning. Some of such elite persons may find their own supposed mastery of society being increasingly challenged as a result of such widespread learning and, as a result may resist its spread by resisting politically its funding. The challenge, as I have attempted to point out, involves moving from a socioeconomic calculus based solely upon a scheme of necessities associated with the consumption of already clearly perceived, needed goods and services, to a socioeconomic calculus based upon a scheme of necessities that would hypothetically be associated with a society that had achieved its basic consumption needs and more and then went on to use its wealth to encourage as many of its members as possible to improve the cultural quality of their lives. Such a scheme of affluent necessities would involve the elevation of individually hand made artifacts over less expensive machine made products. Individually produced plays would likely come to be valued economically over and above mass produced movies and television. Such a valuation might be facilitated by further utilization of interactive meetings between cast members, directors and members of theatrical audiences. Afterall, having the opportunity to speak with actors who have just completed the depiction of real emotional events in one's immediate presence might be just the draw to insure the revitalization of the live theater (not to mention the revitalization of sociability itself and society's sense of reality and accountability).

Economic reconstruction in Kosovo, punishment for underage gun carrying
Date: 6/6/99 8:21:18 PM Eastern Daylight Time
to: the editors (The American Prospect, The Nation, The New Yorker)
from: Andréas Daniel Fogg
Letter from Somerville June 1, 1999

Further fictional developments to the Murdock story;
    Did the (younger) Murdock daughter, the youngest child, commit suicide and if so, was she replaced by some mysterious agency that is replaced by a near double?
    The Murdock daughter had had quite large breasts, yet the current woman perhaps playing the role of the Murdock daughter, has small barely obtrusive breasts. This fact raises the question as to whether the woman currently playing the role of the Murdock daughter is not someone else; and if this is so, then where is the actual original Murdock daughter? Is she even alive, and if not, then what happened to her? The narrator cannot even remember what color her eyes used to be. All this has been suggested by an encounter the narrator had with a woman who resembles the daughter, a woman who had blue eyes, like the current occupant of the role but who was wearing perhaps a long raccoon skin coat on an evening in which the temperature was easily in the mid to upper eighties Fahrenheit. So what was the world telling the narrator through the appearance of this apparently discombobulated woman?

June 3, 1999

A characteristic of mass American, North American, US culture involves the imputed assumption that a normal red blooded person, should not, as a matter of course, experience any particular fear or anxiety about getting involved sexually with a new partner. The idea that getting involved sexually might have significant if not irreparably harmful consequences is an idea that mass culture is unable and unwilling to absorb. This is the case because 'the actor' in mass culture is presumed to be an individual from the at best lower middle classes, an actor who is so most pronouncedly on the make that is he is eager to assert his normalcy, his 'heterosexuality' and to this end the culture is willing to reward him for any symbolically significant steps that he might make towards declaring an affinity for the female sex. The idea that such an individual might be finicky, might take his time, might pause to consider the options, might be willing to forgo going all the way on the first date, if offered the opportunity, all these options are dismissed by the mass culture as evidence of biologically based sexual deviance. The idea that consenting to form a sexual union is in fact a weighty important decision, one that should not be entered into frivolously, is anathema to American culture and to American norms.

And yet there are vast numbers of American males who do not personally conform to this pattern, that is there are vast numbers of American males whose background is middle class, upper middle class or better, that is there are vast numbers of American males who really should think twice before they get involved sexually with a woman as to the appropriateness of such a union and as to the prognosis for the success of any potential output of such a union. Such second thoughts should clearly not be stigmatized by the omnipresent other, who holds a place of honor in all our psyches, as evidence of deviancy. Rather, they should be recognized by the cultural spokespersons, whomever such may be personified as, as legitimate necessary components of reality. Otherwise, there is no middle ground between the supposedly all powerful female of the adolescents' imagination and the unrecognized and utterly repressed male adolescent of the supposedly normal heterosexual's imagination.

Economic reconstruction of Kosovo and adjacent states a priority;

Clearly such reconstructive, supportive moves' adequacy will play a large role in determining the ultimate success of the international peacekeeping force's efforts.

Economic supporting moves should probably include IMF and Federal Reserve moves to prop up the Serbian currency as well as some sort of combination of direct aid in real goods and services as well as some moves to integrate Serbia and Kosovo into the scheme of priorities associated with the international globalized economy.

June 5, 1999

Punishments for underage persons caught carrying firearms advocated;

It is suggested that one way to deal with the problems being caused by the phenomenon of youths being allowed to carry firearms is to institute mandatory forms of punishment against any such youths caught carrying firearms before they are actually used. Such forms of punishment could include prescribed amounts of public service to be performed at below minimal wages, or no wages, like for example, a designated number of hours to be spent picking up trash along public highways, shoveling snow in winter, plus a certain amount of mandatory psychological therapy. Such public service work would needs be done perhaps, while wearing articles of clothing which clearly identify the offender as being an underage gun carrier. Perhaps wearing such clothing would be mandatory after the second or third offense, but shown to those convicted of a first offense.

The guidelines for psychotherapy would needs, it is suggested, include an emphasis upon the psychological needs that are satisfied by carrying a gun, first identifying those needs and then exploring with the individual modes of behavior which might be substituted for the gun carrying mechanism. For example, the question could be raised, is the individual who seeks protection by carrying a gun not in some way perhaps unconsciously, provoking the possibility of aggression against his person. The therapist would need to raise the question with the client "are you behaving in some fashion unbeknownst to yourself in an emotionally provocative manner which in fact is causing others to pick on you?"

The dangers associated with widespread possession and carrying of firearms also need to be pointed out to both clients and the school age population at large. That is, the point needs to be made that the transmission of wisdom and knowledge from the older generation represented by parents, teachers and in some cases clergy to the younger generation of middle and secondary school students is being severely impaired by incidences in which disturbed underage shooters terrorize and kill teachers, classmates and psychologically damage the sense of security of the entire society. It should perhaps be added that the stance of certain factions within the psychiatric community are partly to blame for the enhanced levels of personal insecurity currently apparently being experienced by the marginal youths who are being most extensively and most apparently effected. That is, it is probably fair to assert that the amount of helpless anxiety and anger felt by those few shooters who are actually manifesting the problem is actually being experienced, albeit less acutely, by statistically far larger numbers of students.

The question being raised is "is the current orientation of the American Psychiatric Association currently reducing or perhaps increasing such levels of anxiety?" Clearly middle school through college (years) and in many cases beyond are the years when many individuals experience and are expected to experience "identity crises" of either a sexual or in some cases a political and/or ideological nature. The psychiatrists and psychologists, likely in an attempt to ease the stresses and difficulties associated with such crises have, it appears, been attempting to literally redefine them away. That is, when Erikson originally coined the term identity crisis, the word crisis was appropriate because at that time, I believe, psychiatry defined sexual deviancy that is homosexuality, as literally a disease, a mental illness. So the rationale of the gay psychiatric theorists was to eliminate the crisis character of what was going on by attempting to normalize the "other" pole of the sexual confusing series of events. Never mind said the liberated psychiatrists, that much of western religion stigmatizes homosexuality as a sinful abomination, the classical Greeks thought homosexuality was normal and much of enlightened western learning and culture is derived from classical Greek tradition. In fact it is revealing how much western and American architecture includes buildings whose columns betray a reverence for Greek culture. Those who study and perhaps emulate this classical culture, however, tend to be relatively highly educated and in the past at least to have been located sociologically in middle, upper middle and upper socioeconomic classes. It may be wise, however, to note that classical Greek culture and Roman culture, which was heavily influenced by the Greek, including sexually normatively, it is suggested, all failed to survive in an embodied form the passage of the centuries, whereas the great monotheistic religions which took a different normative orientation have continued to survive.

Class characteristics of mass cultural heroes
Date: 6/14/99 12:15:08 PM Eastern Daylight Time
to: the editors (The American Prospect, The Nation, The New Yorker)
from: Andréas Daniel Fogg
Letter from Somerville June 6, 1999

Topics: the archetypical American mass cultural cinematic hero has no real socioeconomic status of his own (he may be a teenager or college student, living off of parental support, or he may be a blue collar worker or for that matter a white col-

lar worker located in the middle or lower middle class, when such a lower middle class individual fantasizes about what his life would be like if he attained an upper middle class level of income, or if such an individual actually attains an upper middle class level of income, without however for example, acquiring an adequate liberal arts college orientation, then such an individual represents a reorientation of class definition, such that educational attainments cease to be correlated with class designation, that designation having devolved into a description solely defined by wealth, having lost the designated meanings which according to Weber had in the past included status level of occupation as well as quality and status of one's educational background), tends to be a latent homosexual in the process of actively denying all non hostile impulses toward other men. Such men tend to be heavily reliant on possessing one or more firearms. Such possessions give them the capability to actually or potentially, if only in fantasy, triumph over other male romantic rivals by committing lethal aggression against them. The possibility that they may not wish to annihilate any and all or even some romantic rivals or as they fantasize, potential rapists, such a possibility is cognitively inadmissible, that is, it is denied or repressed.
(editor's note:???)

June 9, 1999

NATO/UN bombing of civilians;

Professor Stanley Hoffman, apparently speaking on the radio program 'The Connection,' points out that there is a lack of ethicality associated with the NATO air campaign in Kosovo and Serbia i.e. he suggests that bombing with its gratuitous but apparently necessary damage against civilians is unethical particularly because NATO is unwilling to risk the lives of ground troops. But it is important to note the fact that if ground troops were in fact to be committed, that there would still be a need for an air war, with bombing and just as likely a chance for damage to civilians, in fact, if NATO committed ground forces and failed to pursue a campaign for air superiority, the Serbs would be likely to extract a price in NATO military lives as a result of this humanitarian based refusal to use this technological edge. In fact if NATO merely pursued a defensive air campaign, using fighter attack air craft for example to deter Serbian bombing, the length of the campaign would likely be extended as a result of the lack of damage that would have been imposed on the Serbian war machine if bombing were undertaken. And the result of this extended campaign would involve more extensive NATO and American military casualties. Clearly, Professor Hoffman has a point that air war generated civilian casualties are an abomination, a terrible and horrendous fact. But since the development of the airplane, starting most significantly in WWII, air campaigns against civilians have been accepted military strategic policy. To suggest that such casualties would be more morally acceptable if the lives of ground troops were at risk, however, seems dubious. The civilians are just as clearly regrettably dead or wounded. The argument then, it would seem should be couched as follows, that the campaign itself is unnecessary and wrong and that it should be stopped. However, Professor Hoffman does not make this argument since he fairly clearly does not believe it to be the case.

June 12, 1999

Suggested compromise between NATO and Russia;

That NATO/UN peacekeeping units include representatives of NATO forces and in each case a or several Russian military officers and support troops; that these Russian officers would be given a veto over NATO/UN officers commands, but that these vetoes, when issued, would be immediately forwarded to a panel of military law justices, functioning as a sort of international on the scene military court, which court would include representatives appointed by each of the permanent members of the UN Security Council.

Topics: cultural and normative conflict in American society between the religious working class, the religious middle class, often merchants, the so called upper classes, which consist most particularly of those who have inherited great wealth from their parents and grandparents and who are most usually not also self made men or women, and the irreligious which category includes most prominently the professional and technologically trained as well as those who have made a profession out of the process of higher education. Note in this regard, that someone who had inherited moderate wealth, like say for example, Bill Gates, and then managed to convert that inherited advantage into a vast fortune based upon his own technological expertise, such an individual it is suggested, predicted, is not likely to be part of a religious conservative sort of political orientation. Contrast William F. Buckley, who it is assumed inherited significant wealth, yet whose expertise seems primarily based upon his facility at advocating politically and ethically based conservative thinking, rather than upon other non-conservative oriented skills. The evidence as to the nature of Bill Gates political orientation derives from reading occasionally Microsoft's magazine, SLATE, which appears on first glance at least, to assume an independent left of center sort of political orientation. Thus, it is predicted that those who have merely inherited great wealth are more likely to be politically conservative, less likely to be supportive of mobility facilitating educational funding for the masses, than are those who are genuinely proud of their accomplishments and earnings, regarding them as just rewards for genuinely deserving work.

Comments about the Chinese;

The Chinese civilization was quite advanced several, many centuries ago. The Chinese invented gun powder and the letters that the Japanese call 'Kanji' which form the pictogram sort of multi symbolic 'alphabet' that the Japanese have supplemented with two smaller phonetic alphabets (hiragana and katakana) more akin to those used in the West. I do not think that the Chinese have, even to this day adopted a phonetic like alphabet, but I could be wrong about this. The Chinese regularly, as a matter of course eat for dinner 'man's best friend.' They do this and yet persist in calling non Chinese, including Americans and Europeans and Japanese and probably Vietnamese and Kampucheans and Russians indeed every one who is not Chinese, 'barbarians.' As a boy the family's noble 'duck hound' a standard albeit flawed French poodle, used to wait for me when I returned from school. When she saw me, I could see, from a distance that her ears would perk up as she rose and rushed to meet me, seemingly deliriously happy. I want to put down on record, that I do not respect the Chinese practice of eating dogs. IN Fact I regard that practice as being in fact barbaric, as is the practice of deliberately suppressing the Tibetan religion and culture, which I don't particularly endorse but which I would defend on the grounds that it is relatively harmless, so long as individuals are allowed to freely reject it in favor of more modern scientifically verifiable orientations such as are offered, for example, in part by those Chinese teachers who perhaps share with me an appreciation and reverence for, you will forgive an important childhood memory, the ordinary hound.

Reflections on 'the monarchy' wherever it may be found;

King Abdullah has recently acceded to the Jordanian throne. I have felt for some time that the best way for the monarchical system to be incorporated into a democratic nation state system has been exemplified by the British constitutional monarchy. Lately, since the scandals associated with the royal family brought on by the activities of Princess Diana, the late and former Princess of Wales, I have been forced to reconsider what the role and function of royalty in a functioning democratic nation state should be. Clearly these comments might be relevant to the Jordanian situation, if the new King Abdullah were interested in considering instigating a change from a monarchical state away also from a Muslim theocracy, toward a secular democratic state such as are found throughout much of the so called developed world. In such a line of thought it occurs to the narrator that a royal family, with its royal wealth, could whether in Britain or Jordan, endeavor to fund in the name of the Royal Family various and varied research efforts whose results could be made available to both those in the universities and the worlds of business and religion and to the public as well, perhaps in a less technical, less complex format. Funding and perhaps participating in the implementation of such research efforts, whether they be medical, technological, purely scientific or social scientific would indeed provide royal families with a more positive and constructive orientation than they perhaps hold at present.

The function of higher education;

It is suggested that given the existence and widespread distribution of pre-printed articles, that the seemingly simple nature and purpose of higher educational writing, thinking and research may have become more complicated and multifaceted than it had been in the past. That is, it may be the case, that widespread publication of scientific or so called objective theoretical thinking about pressing social problems may suffer a delay since one of the functions of education has become not simply to place as many of the so called 'right answers' into as many mouths and minds as possible, but rather, once such right answers have been apprehended by say one or two thinkers or thinking researchers, the question that appears to come to the fore is "how many others will also independently arrive at similar conclusions, given a generous quantity of prompting from their professors?" Clearly, if some such innovative writings are published and made available, it will become relatively impossible to determine whether or who is capable of arriving at similar conclusions on their own. Hence, one of the functions of higher education may have become not simply the dissemination of what have become accepted answers, but also, as one of my high school teachers was fond of saying, 'the separating of the wheat from the chaff,' so to speak.

The evolution of the Chinese political system;

It should be noted that in regard to the US voting system, the narrator has felt for some time that the problem with the use of literacy tests as criteria for who gets to vote, has been that such tests were being used deliberately as a means of racial discrimination. That is, if it were required that prospective voters be able to read an average difficulty newspaper story in the United States and if the evaluation of this skill were not racially tinted, then such a test would seem to be a reasonable component of an enlightened democratic fair system of government.

Similarly, if the Chinese were to allow voting based upon the passage of some meaningful literacy and educational test, then I would regard such a move away from one party hegemony toward a mass cultural democratic eventually multi party, multi polar political system as a crucial positive sociological evolutionary step.

to: the editors (The American Prospect, The Nation, The New Yorker)
from: Andréas Daniel Fogg
Letter from Somerville June 20, 1999

That a weakness of the Clinton administration involves their psychological need to, through the flagrant and perhaps stylistically gratuitous use of power, demonstrate their ability to temporarily dominate the course of events, and the American people, without feeling any particular need or responsibility to build a democratic consensus. This was apparent in the handling of the Administration's health care plan which was developed without feedback from either the press or the American people by a small group headed by Hillary Rodham Clinton and Ira Magaziner. And it was evident in the manner in which the NATO decision to bomb Kosovo and Serbia was never convincingly and thoroughly justified in the press to the American polity. For instance, evidence that Serb ethnic cleansing had been going on before the bombing began was not effectively, convincingly documented in the media.

When politicians become the equivalent of corporate managers and supervisors, that is when government assumes the guise of the corporate organizational model, the need to build and rely upon democratic consensus by definition disappears, and the result is likely to involve either the actual or potential abuse of power. Such abuses of power can occur amidst strong economic growth. Such growth in the United States has clearly been gratifying, particularly to those (a relative statistical minority) who have most benefited from it. However when political leaders feel no particular need to build a democratic consensus the result is likely eventually to lead to widespread resentment and discontent; however such discontent may not be clearly or effectively articulated. Such discontent may well have played a role in motivating the Republican attempt to throw the President out of office. However, since conservative Republicans tend to be in love with the trappings of power, yet to be also disposed toward the view that that gov't is best which governs least, disposed to spend billions on defense, yet indisposed under many circumstances to use such military force (often not in defense of merely human rights, i.e. economic interests of the US also need to be at stake, indeed an economic interest alone may be sufficient grounds for convincing "conservatives" to intervene either covertly or militarily in the affairs of other nations, see for example, the role of the US in the overthrow of the socialist Allende regime in Chile, in which perceived and actual threats to the hegemony and even existence of private economic interests and indeed actual private economic ownership itself were used as justifications by the resurgent right wing military regime to commit what are currently being construed as violations of human rights, which violations were actually apparently supported by covert American aid.)

Laissez-faire ideology, class origins and (sic) humani
Date: 6/20/99 9:20:10 PM Eastern Daylight Time
File: CORREC~1.TXT (3524 bytes)
DL Time (28800 bps): < 1 minute

to: the editors (The American Prospect, The Nation, The New Yorker)
from: Andréas Daniel Fogg
Letter from Somerville June 16, 1999

Laissez-faire economic ideology may be correlated with the social ideology roughly defined as "pure tolerance" or cultural relativism. This point came home in a recent discussion of my last piece which referred to the Chinese culturally validated practice of eating dogs. The narrator's point, subsumed under the catch phrase "if everything is permitted, then nothing is possible" is that to assume a stance which denies the possibility of international or intercultural criticism is in effect to assume a posture which accepts in practice virtually all variations in behavior, including the benumbed acceptance of sweatshop like wages and working conditions—in the name of tolerance. The point is that when normative confusion gives way to anomic normlessness then society becomes transfixed and potentially paralyzed by the fear of what is in mainstream culture defined as unacceptable deviations.

Globalization, "liberal" tolerance, laissez-faire ideology and the continuing acceptance of "the lowest bid wage;"

Social Realism in movies and TV as an end in itself, as a stimulus instigating violent real world imitation, the political end may involve instigating a reaction in favor of the disarming of the US i.e. extreme degrees of gun control paving the way for the imposition of a totalitarian state.

June 19, 1999

Hypothesized correlation between an extremely skewed distribution of income and wealth (toward the high end) and relative incidence of violent acts against self and others amongst adolescents and young adults;

It is pointed out in a recent Economic Policy Institute "snap shot" that as of 1997 the top five per cent of US wealth holders held 61.4 per cent of the wealth, the top one per cent of the population held 39.1 per cent of the aggregate wealth, the top ten per cent of the US wealth holders held 72.8 per cent of the aggregate US wealth, and the top 20 per cent of the distribution held 84.3 per cent of the aggregate US wealth. That leaves 15.7 per cent of the total nationally owned wealth in the hands of the bottom 80 per cent of the population. The bottom 20 per cent of the population as an aggregate is actually in debt, does not own any actual wealth. Hence it may be fair to conclude that ours is a country whose economy is set up to generate a relatively small number of "big winners" and a relatively large number of citizens whose holdings are proportionately and symbolically speaking and in terms of the ability to generate relatively more conspicuous consumption, much much less.

It was pointed out on "The Connection" radio program last week, pointed out by a screen writer and novelist who specializes in producing graphically violent materials, that the Canadians, who are exposed to roughly equivalent levels of violent US cinematic culture as are Americans, do not have the same problem with the abuse of firearms as we seem to have in the US The individual, whose name escapes me, did not cite any evidence or source of data to support his observation, however, if it is in fact accurate, it may perhaps be partially explained by an hypothesized relatively more egalitarian and fair distribution of wealth in Canada than is currently found in the US. That is, when the achievement of relative, proportionate economic success seems to be relatively rarer and more difficult, when the phobias associated with achieving success, computer phobia, for example, also deter innovative learning experiences which might facilitate even a modicum of such success, then an implicit ideology embracing death as a means of perhaps placating "the fates" or "the Gods" for example, may begin to find credence. You saw, this, or the narrator saw this, for example, in the film "The Dead Poets Society" in which it seemed to be covertly, soto voce, imputed that one man's greatness was made possible as a result of another youth's suicide. If one places any significance in random instances of synchronicity, than such seems to be implied in the "correlation" between the death of Marlowe and the rise of Shakespeare depicted albeit ambiguously in the film, "Shakespeare in Love." Of course, scientifically speaking, single instantiations cannot constitute a correlation. Yet the individual in search of some magic formula to explain and achieve success grasps at straws, even if they imply acts of evil and immorality. How else might one explain the incidents of human sacrifice connected with pre monotheistic religions?

June 20, 1999

The case of the downsized, laid off machinist;

This fictional individual, we will call him "Whitey Gerard" as the caption implies, had been a machinist until computerization hit the firm he worked for, whereupon he was downsized and found himself working in the same warehouse as the narrator. To help pay the rent and to support his much younger attractive wife he often worked sixty or seventy hours a week at the warehouse and then waited tables at a local restaurant on the weekends. This individual, who seemingly had been working from paycheck to paycheck, plans to buy a house. Recently it was revealed that he had managed to find a bank, he claims the "Family Bank" which would allow him to avoid paying closing costs and, he claims, he is only putting five thousand dollars down on the ninety-thousand dollar price tag because "he wants to" pay off an eighty-five thousand dollar mortgage, he could, he claims pay for the house outright. Now all this may be possible but the narrator strongly suspects that Whitey's credit card company has been withholding his balance due statements in hopes of luring him into going into debt based upon the erroneous supposition that he has unlimited credit that he will not have to pay back. Indeed the narrator was recently subjected to this stratagem by the issuers of one of his credit cards. However, he, being skeptical, phoned the customer service number to inquire as to whether his actual balance had been forgiven, it had not and so he requested that a replacement statement be mailed to his residence.

Part Four: Summer

Hermaphrodites and normality amongst women, evolution and liberalism
Date: 7/3/99 9:56:00 AM Eastern Daylight Time
to: the editors: (The American Prospect, The Nation, The New Yorker)
from: Andréas Daniel Fogg
Letter from Somerville June 27, 1999

Far out comments on female sexuality (I probably have gone way too far this time and I apologize);

Notes: the shame and fear felt by the so called female "hermaphrodite" is contingent upon the possibility that she may be "discovered" to be "also male." That there may be a larger number of women who fit this category than had previously been thought. Reference to a book that came out in the early 1980's that purported to discover both the existence of the so called "G spot" and also the fact that a significant number of women "ejaculate" when they have orgasms. Speculation to the effect such women may seem to be hermaphroditic because of their possession of perhaps relatively larger clitorii (than other women), that when they become sexually excited such an enlarged clitoris may be mistaken by those who have not seen them naked for a penis, thereby leading to the hypothesis that such women are in fact really men functioning in drag. That such an eventuality may result in such women tending to avoid allowing themselves to be sexually excited by men, since such excitement may result in their being "found out" to be something that men have heretofore been unable to account for and therefore subject to ridicule and perhaps rejection i.e. "so and so is really 'a man'." As a result such women may nurture pretend sexual relationships with men, limiting their authentic arousal to women partners who will be neither shocked nor threatened by any protuberance in the genital area.

June 25, 1999

154

Corporate structure's influence on incidence of critical opinion formation by corporate employees and corporate management dependent on conformity to perceived views of the "higher corporate 'line',"

June 28, 1999

Initial reactions to Melvin Konner's article in the current TAP on liberalism and evolutionary theory;

The point about children in families in which the allegedly natural father is really a step father being subject to abuse is particularly apropos to the current status of the American middle class family. Note that Erving Goffman suggested in the preface to his book, Frame Analysis, that the middle and upper middle class family was or had become typically a fabrication or rather a biological fabrication such that all or most of the children were not biologically related, that is they either were adopted, artificially (or "immaculately") inseminated or engendered by males other than the socially designated father. To the extent that Goffman was correct in this observation, and to the extent that Konner's observation to the effect that such children statistically cross nationally tend to be subject to intra familial attacks and or abuse, presumably by the 'father' but also theoretically potentially by other aggressive physically threatening aggressive characters within the family structure, then the fact of such abuse may well constitute a statistically significant source of the personal difficulties of many of the children and young adults in the US and elsewhere where such a turn of events is continuing to take place. That is, such personal difficulties may be traced to the perception within the family that such and such a child has been labeled as illegitimate or an outsider who is as a result designated as a legitimate target for either physical and/or verbal abuse or ridicule. Such attacks can of course result in the warping of such designated victims personalities to the extent that they may begin to suffer more or less acute psychiatric symptoms. Such victims need to be able to either receive or give themselves personal permission to fight back and resist and above all refute such often even in older life verbal slurs and attacks as may occur. Note that such attacks can include not merely the imputation of being illegitimate (and also too small or weak to deter such accusations through the possibility of physical intimidation) but also more general attacks such as accusations that the individual has no sexual morals and cannot be trusted with women.

Further reactions to Konner;

That normative evolutionary value in humans may be equivalent to what the sociologist Robert K. Merton termed either eufunctional or dysfunctional institutional characteristics. That normative evolutionary value in humans may also be evaluated in what Yehudi Cohen, an anthropologist, termed "adaptational value." These points become apparent in the manner in which members of a culture treat themselves, address themselves vis a vis the ethnocentric dimension which is roughly equivalent in human historical terms to the nationalistic dimension. Thus the question as to whether members of a culture are capable of directing humor at themselves becomes crucial. Ultra nationalistic individuals, ultra ethnocentric individuals tend to be unable or unwilling to direct any sort of satiric humor at themselves; this is the case no doubt because so much of their egos are tied up in pushing their own value as members of the preferred national or cultural or subcultural group. Thus the current situation in the US today is such that humor is in retreat because egos are so weak that any media centered humor which detracts from the straightforward case that such and such a group is wonderful tends to be attacked as discriminatory. But members of a group who are able and willing to gently but firmly direct humor at members of their own group or at their group as a whole have the adaptational advantage of earning the trust potentially of other non group member individuals. Thus Jews or Blacks or Gays who direct humor at their own group tend to be regarded by outsiders as not totally predisposed toward forming friendships and alliances merely with members of their own group and hence such individuals become empowered to significantly economically and socially ally with out-group members. Such out-group alliances of course tend to deter ethnocentric, xenophobic motivated attacks upon members of their own group which may occur in the event that such out-group alliances are not present.

Exception;

Eddie Murphy often seems to direct humor against his own racial/cultural group (African-Americans).

On the other hand, yesterday I saw on television a program dedicated to "Black" music which claimed that all of American music was "Black Music." Bing Crosby, Benny Goodman, George Gershwin, John Philip Sousa, Irving Berlin, Aaron Copeland who wrote "Appalachian Spring" and "Fanfare for the Common Man" Burt Bacharach and Henry Mancini among many others would not have been particularly amused if they had seen and heard this statement. This sort of group aggrandizing overstatement is tantamount to a declaration of cultural/nationalistic or, in this case, racial superiority. Such statements do not help the cause of multicultural and multiracial harmony, instead exacerbating and even creating more unnecessary and unneeded tensions.

In fact, it could be argued that over inflating the group generated self esteem of members of a disadvantaged and resented struggling minority increases the difficulties members of that group encounter when they attempt to interact and work cooperatively and harmoniously with members of society's more economically successful, generally more work oriented groups. It is also worth noticing the potential that such racially jingoistic publicly uttered statements have to inspire resentment against the members of the group which has thereby sought to elevate it's position on the societal pecking order (to the point where the other groups are not merely lowered in the order but even removed from the standings all together). Thus the lack of support for somehow finding a way to lower the costs of HIV drugs in Africa should in part be traced to observed behaviors, often perceived as aggressive, of African-American men vis a vis their presumed superiority as men over and against the ordinary working non African American working man. Such aggressive behaviors come into play typically in situations in which the possibility of initiating interactions with socially unfamiliar women either are acted upon or passed up. The manifestation of such behaviors usually amount to the utilization of a sort of sullen glare directed at the male who dares to importune interaction with the unknown female. The more attractive the female, the more intense the glare. Such glares may also be manifested by so called white males as well. For example Catholics seem to manifest a sort of holier than thou sort of attitude in this regard, assuming perhaps that because they are working class believing Catholic, they should be allowed to flirt with the women, because they would not think of getting actually sexually involved—because they are Catholic, but you, who are not Catholic, maybe even Jewish or Black or Protestant, cannot be trusted to avoid getting sexually involved with this attractive woman. The assumption of this view whether it is held by white Catholics or African American men, or for that matter very religious Jews as well, is that no woman could possibly in her right mind actually want to have genital sexual relations with any man, certainly not someone who does not understand the basic reality that for women, sex is inevitably painful.

July 1, 1999

Whitey Gerard update;

When Whitey lost his job as a machinist, he had been the owner of a house valued at about one hundred thousand. He had paid off about twenty-thousand dollars of the principal over the course of about five years (while paying about seventy-thousand dollars of mortgage interest to the bank). When he lost his job, he couldn't pay either the first or the second mortgages so the bank foreclosed and he lost his house. Now he and his wife have three kids....

July 1, 1999

Could it be that many men fight wars, in part, to avoid having to argue with and often lose arguments to, women? Consider the ignominiousness of losing an argument to a woman. We don't often think of its pitiful character. The abject humiliation is rendered all the more acute by the fact that she holds the key to the bedroom.

Arousal and HADD hypothesized to be negatively correlated with cognition
Date: 7/11/99 2:19:36 PM Eastern Daylight Time
to: the editors (The American Prospect, The Nation, The New Yorker)
from: Andréas Daniel Fogg
Letter from Somerville July 6, 1999

It is suggested that generally, statistically speaking, cognition about abstract objective impersonal subjects, such as high school and college and graduate academic work, impersonal corporate policy oriented thinking, thinking related to electronic data processing are all likely to be impaired as a result of the presence of anything more intense than mild sexual interest. Actual passionate arousal, such as might motivate an individual to actually to initiate or respond to orgiastic oriented behavior during working hours in or near the workplace, is likely to be so distracting as to seriously undermine that individual's, and the individuals that he or she personally affects, ability to do quality work. Such an effect is predicted since the individual's focus is likely to become shifted from the work, such as it is, to his or her personal goal of achieving sexual release and/or stimulation. Hence a culture, and for that matter, theoretically, an hypothesized genetic configuration which prioritizes orgiastic relief over and above the relatively asexual orientation presumed to be more conducive to work related achievement, such a culture and hypothesized genetic configuration, while seeming in the short run quite pleasant and attractive, is likely to achieve lower less successful results for its members both in higher education and in the work place.

Such a hypothesized connection appears to be relevant to the process and formation and continual reformulation of norms and mores in multicultural and sexually and racially integrated democratic contexts.

Dildoes as evidence of hermaphroditism;

Many men say that they believe that women who are socially and economically threatening "have penises." It is unclear how many of such accused women reinforce such beliefs by utilizing plastic dildo like devices on the one hand for regular vaginal and perhaps clitoral stimulation, and, on the other hand, when such devices are allowed or encouraged to protrude outside the vagina, as evidence of such feared male genitalia.

A potential archetype;

Consider a fictional case of a somewhat large young man who has not gone to college but who has managed to teach himself how to use a computer, developing quite a high level of expertise. This young man, on the one hand playfully claims to be sixty years old, makes ambiguous statements which suggest that he is if not homosexual, probably also bisexual. These ambiguous statements also suggest but do not state explicitly that only individuals who involve themselves in some sort of homosexual acts will be allowed to advance their positions in the corporation. This young man has managed to advance to the position of supervisor despite the fact or perhaps because of the fact that he is not that particularly intelligent. That is he has parlayed the computer expertise and his seeming willingness to allow himself to be utilized as a sexual object into a promotion to supervisor. The fact that he is not anywhere nearly as intelligent as the warehouse manager constitutes an advantage since he is clearly not overqualified to serve as supervisor and he is not sufficiently educated to constitute an intellectual threat to the actual manager, or for that matter, higher management. Yet his apparent tendency toward gratuitous arousability, to have erections or partial erections during meetings constitutes a sort of implicit threat to the other associates, since all sorts of petty problems and faults can be found with their work and general attitudes, should this supervisor come to feel that he is not being shown enough respect. And such problems and faults can be used to justify meager or non existent wage increases or, for that matter, what the corporation calls euphemistically, "termination" that is getting fired.

July 7, 1999

Notes; fictional vignette, the female general manager who dated a novelty shop owner and whose tenure included coincidentally the appearance amongst employees of pornographic, photographic materials depicting persons with both large female like breasts as well as well hung male genitalia.

Note incidences in which poor people of color, having achieved good educations, befriend, seduce and ultimately marry "white" wealthy women, using such alliances to serve their own socioeconomic mobility, after which it is achieved, they sometimes obtain a divorce, sometimes remarrying a woman whose coloring is closer to their own. Wealthy white women (and for that matter men) perhaps need to take note of this phenomenon, not that they can't take care of themselves, of course.

July 11, 1999

It might in fact be interesting to examine statistically the rate of divorce for so called interracial couples, examining as well the effect of socioeconomic level of each partner's family of origin.

Reactions to the "Can Goldilocks Survive" article,

In this article, which can be found in the April '99 EPN archives, it is suggested that the presence of a budget surplus in and of itself constitutes evidence of a private sector deficit. One of the characteristics of a public sector deficit is that given sufficient international demand for the relevant national currency, the public sector deficit can be paid for by the national treasury department by simply increasing the money supply, that is, by simply printing currency to pay the debt. No one in the private sector has this capability. Therefore it would appear that a public sector deficit can be utilized as a mechanism for grossly increasing both a national and the international supply of currency and as well potentially the quantity of gross economic demand. It should be noted that a country can only get away with this strategy if and only if there is sufficient continued demand internationally for its currency. If the market is far stronger for dollars than it is for euros, then the dollar is likely to be the currency selected by the international market as the mechanism whereby international demand can be increased. If the demand for the dollar were to suddenly diminish in favor for example of the euro or the pound or the yen, then one of those currencies would begin to potentially serve as a mechanism whereby the international economic demand function, particularly in poor developing countries, could be increased. The mechanism for increasing demand, as previously mentioned, involves the purchase by the main currency's central bank, or its agents, of currencies which are attempting to multiply their own volumes, that is which are attempting to increase their own money supplies by printing money. The investment by the central bank's agents in such growing currencies has the effect of countering the resultant devaluation, thereby countering the tendency for the international debt load of the effected country, the tendency of the debt load to be increased as a result of the devaluation. So that one of the factors which will determine whether the dollar continues to enjoy strong demand will involve the relative satisfaction that developing countries experience vis a vis the manner in which the Fed holds their i.e. the developing country's debt. If the Fed behaves in an arbitrary disrespectful manner toward the interests of said developing country and others, those countries are likely to put their heads together and create a better market for euros, pounds or yen for example. However, the dollar continues to have an edge internationally over those other currencies perhaps in large part because the US seems to continue to enjoy a combination of low unemployment and higher growth relative to its rivals.

Romance, reading and photorealism; reflections upon reading Don DeLillo's White Noise;

There is a tendency when you are alone with your wife, spouse girlfriend or, for that matter, date, to avoid reading. Why is this the case? For one thing, to read while in bed with a partner is often seen as being rude. The partner wants you to pay attention to her, not to some perhaps musty author. For another reason, reading encourages the development of emotional independence and independent potentially critical thought, critical thought which might encourage the reader to make political waves, perhaps to make political trouble, perhaps to say things critical of the powers that be, the authorities, the TV and movie programmers, who, the romantic woman prefers arbitrarily declare and define reality for the normal compliant citizen. Such citizens, of course, do not make trouble, in the US they often do not even vote, and if the truth be known, they often do not have much of a sex drive. Actually, many women, contrary to popular myth, prefer men with little or no sex drive. Such men are in general, easier to control. And a primary objective of today's empowered woman is to achieve and maintain control over her man or men. Her sexual needs she can satisfy either with other women or with sex toys. What she wants is a man who looks independent, has plenty of money, but doesn't have any real sexual needs that she must regularly satisfy, and a man who definitely will not embarrass her by forcing her to react to any difficult or awkward opinions, certainly nothing that cannot be found on the television or in the movies.

Women want, on the one hand, someone perceived as a protector. Hence the ideal couple involves a man who is considerably larger than the woman. Yet this need for a male role involving physical dominance today runs into conflict with the goal of the empowered woman to not be physically or economically or sexually dominated. That is, an empowered woman explicitly does not want to find herself in a powerless role, even perhaps during actual sexual interactions.

And reading has the effect, as noted, of encouraging individualistic potentially dangerous thinking. As it is said, "What if everybody actually read books and thought about things? Why, there would be chaos!" The modern social order, it is thought, depends on mass media mediated social control. Look at what happened during the sixties when much of a whole generation decided to challenge the establishment's war and think for themselves. Of course, just because large numbers of people sometimes make mistakes is not sufficient reason to require that all individuals not begin to read and think about the future course of American and global societal development. And just because a few individuals actually begin to think does not mean that everybody will begin to think. Neither is it written that just because you are thinking that you are required to spill your opinions indiscriminately before everyone and anyone. Note further that the notion of social realism, originally part and parcel of the cinematic and television industries, has, as a result of the development of special effects expertise and computer generated contrived yet seemingly realistic imagery, ceased to be part of the media's raison d'être. That is, while belief that what is depicted is true lingers in a sort of vague vestigial manner, in truth, so called normal people do not believe anything that they see or hear in either the movies or television presentations. In fact this lack of belief in the reality of what we see in the media allows us to proceed about our daily work and lives in a relatively apolitical largely self oriented manner. That is, we try deliberately not to think about the larger questions such as where is society heading, what are the social and demographic trends, how is the wealth being distributed; rather, we worry, am "I" being offended? Indeed, "is anyone being offended?" So long as no one is being offended by the media, we think, then everyone must be OK. We can always pretend that we are secretly some sort of CEO who is merely hiding his wealth deigning to associate with the so called "little people."

Possible roots of hyperactive attention deficit disorder;

It may also be worth considering as to whether cognition itself may serve as a mechanism which causes or contributes to erotic arousal. If this is sometimes the case, for some individuals, and if arousal in some contexts is experienced as either awkward, embarrassing, uncomfortable or inappropriate, then such a mechanism would serve to effectively discourage learning from occurring in public situations such as are typically found in high schools and colleges. Such an hypothesized connection might also begin to explain some of the causes of hyperactive attention deficit disorder, since the imputed result of learning might likely involve the instigation of sexual tension (even in prepubertal children) as well as tension, impatience and anger when children's ability to learn and express themselves extends beyond the teacher's willingness, competence and capability to advance the learning curricula.

Hence one possible cure for perhaps increasingly prevalent hyperactive attention deficit disorder may involve on the one hand more frequent scheduled exercise classes, and, on the other hand, increased implementation of accelerated learning curricula.

From pictographs to phonetic alphabets, societal evolution
Date: 7/27/99 2:20:39 AM Eastern Daylight Time
to: the editors (The American Prospect, The Nation. The New Yorker)
from: Andréas Daniel Fogg
Letter from Somerville July 11, 1999

Social evolution, societal complexity and linguistic development from pictographs or hieroglyphs to phonetic expressions; Pre modern imperial China and Ancient Egypt it is hypothesized, are utilized as examples of ethnocentric civilizations that reached high levels of authoritarian based economic and political development utilizing written languages based solely upon hieroglyphs or pictographic linguistic representations, that is based hypothetically upon the use of pictographic writing without an accompanying phonetic alphabet. It is hypothesized that these civilizations' ethnocentric pride, in the past, made it impossible for them to allow their writing systems to evolve in such a way as to incorporate phonetic alphabets, so that with the passage of time other cultures and nations which were able either to invent or learn phonetic alphabets which included a capability of expressing present past and future time (tenses), were able to evolve more so than the original leaders, hypothesized as Egypt and China, in the areas of technology, economics and normative and political organization. It is suggested that the presence of phonetic writing likely made the study of history and the principles of law relatively more easily accessible to more members of the polity. As a result, it is hypothesized, learning and the principles of justice, fairness and decency, upon which the development of civilization as we know it are based, were able to proliferate beyond an elite group of clerics who had the time to learn the relatively more complex system of pictographs, to include relatively ordinary working people, who as a result acquired an expertise in both law and history and culture itself which empowered them to seek to establish and maintain relatively democratic institutions which included a more equitable distribution of wealth and power than had been found in the civilizations which had relied solely upon pictographic written languages. Noam Chomsky, if you haven't thought of this already, then, well, it is suggested that considerations of the so called "deep structure" pale into insignificance compared to the differences between pictographic and phonetic writing systems.

July 19, 1999

Counteracting the declining global wage spiral, rehashing the argument;

John Kenneth Galbraith, in The New Industrial State, if I remember correctly, argued that oligopolistically tacitly organized corporations were secretly conspiring to conjointly raise prices. Perhaps one way to counter the internationally declining wage (price) spiral is for the multinational corporations to tacitly agree on the need to maintain a "floor" beneath which wages will not be allowed to drop. But before such a consensus could be adopted, its case would need to be formulated and convincingly presented. The case, as I tentatively see it, involves the theoretical demonstration that if wages were raised by all corporations operating in a given competitive sector, so that no one competitor's profits were immediately hurt as a result of having raised their wages, that the resulting increase in the magnitude of the national and international wage pools would in fact have the effect, at least in the aggregate, of increasing profits to the point where the aggregate effect would as likely as not, involve greater profits and net income than would have been accrued if the collective consensual wage increase had not occurred.

Teletubbies;

In New York City in the sixties, it used to be possible to see street people hanging around, if I remember correctly, begging, with signs hanging from their shoulders that claimed that "the CIA had implanted radios in their stomachs." If kids continue to be exposed to this Telletubby programming, significant numbers of them are likely to develop this delusion in adolescence or young adulthood, that is, this sort of a delusion, which is likely categorized somewhere in the psychiatric scheme of character flaws and symptoms of mental illness, is likely to significantly increase as a result of the continued transmission of the Telletubby programs, which I have only heard about, never seen. Now someone who has experienced psychiatric difficulties and has also managed to effectively learn to cope with them is likely to be a stronger more productive member of society than is perhaps someone whose boat has never, so to speak, been rocked. (Certainly, at least, than they themselves were before the difficulties ensued.) It is however, important to remember, that psychiatric care takes quite a bit of time and is also quite expensive. And while middle and upper middle and upper class parents often feel willing and eager and able to absorb such costs, the working class parents usually don't or can't so that working class individuals whose children are suffering such symptoms usually need to appeal to the generosity of the tax payers to pay for the aid their children may need. Most of the HMO medical insurance plans that I have seen currently include very minimal psychiatric coverage.

July 25, 1999

Chinese language and the sense of time;

I am informed by word of mouth, rather than by publication, that Chinese incorporates time into its statements without utilizing verbal tenses. Thus time is indicated through the use of words like today, tomorrow and yesterday. Thus "I go to the library today…I go to the library yesterday….I go to the library tomorrow" are characteristic English language approximations. Whether such a mechanism for expressing time is less functional than mechanisms found in other languages which utilize verbal tenses is unclear. What remains clear, however, is that it appears to be more difficult to learn to read and write a language which includes a thousand or more different pictographic symbols than it is to learn a purely phonetic language. Arguably, in a phonetic language, words can be learned and identified through listening and participating in spoken conversational contexts. Hence the sound of the word makes it possible to recognize its written expression. That at least is the argument presented.

Will raising wages through corporate collusion result in generally increased profits?

The argument is that increasing the size and depth of the wage pool, rather than merely increasing the earnings found at the high end of the economic earnings spectrum, will result in, in general, strengthened economic demand, that is more spending, more purchases, more sales tax revenues, and since one person's earnings are likely to be spent again shortly on some other purchase, a generalized incremental growth of the GDP is likely to result. Further, one cause of the deflationary wage price spiral effect is precisely inadequate demand sector strength. That is a principle cause of the deflationary effect, as for example see today's NYTimes on deflation in China, is too few dollars available for the aim of purchasing too many goods and services. In China personal economic insecurity is contributing to this effect through the people's widespread impulse to save their money rather than spend it. Perhaps this thriftiness is caused by high levels of unemployment. The Times story places the mainland People's Republic of China's unemployment overall rate at ten per cent in the cities and up to thirty percent in the rural areas. Hence citizens likely worry about losing their jobs to someone who is willing to work for less. This example thus indicates that merely increasing disposable income alone will not necessarily counteract the deflationary trend. Hence, another point may involve the need to make available goods or services which appeal to the genuine needs of the populace. The Times story cites TV sets backed up and not selling. Well, maybe the Chinese people are not as enamored of television as are other peoples. If this is the case, I say, fine. Ultra consumerism is, it seems to the narrator, ultimately an exercise in frustration. It is after all important to remember that every dollar spent in the tabulation of a nation's GDP is not of equal worth. It may be more important and valuable for a people to exercise than it is for them to be seduced into becoming couch potatoes in front of the television set.

July 27, 1999

At the risk of meddling in China's internal affairs, and with apologies to the Chinese, it is suggested that perhaps if the regime sought to cultivate more economic activity within the national borders, instead of encouraging ever lower wages in attempts to earn western currency, that through encouraging through local tax incentives intranational economic activity, as opposed to merely export oriented activity, the unemployment rate might be significantly reduced, the level of economic insecurity reduced and as a result the demand sector might be strengthened and the deflationary trend reduced or even reversed.

The definition and measurement of productivity
Date: 8/7/99 1:19:06 PM Eastern Daylight Time
to: the editors (The American Prospect, The Nation, The New Yorker)
from: Andréas Daniel Fogg
Letter from Somerville July 30, 1999

An alternative definition of productive value;

We have currently what is thought of as 'market defined' value. This often amounts to in practice, what the chief holders of capital wish to allocate towards any given line of activity or production. So ostensibly, some members of the corporate elite put their heads together and wonder, 'how much status and prestige do we think that, for example, a slightly above average artist should be able to achieve? How much do we think such an individual should be allowed to earn?' It is argued that rarely is the question posed, 'what is the value to society of maintaining a group of 'art teacher practitioners' whose merit falls individually somewhat below that of the great masters?'

In answering such a question, the peripheral point is i.e. "what needs to happen if society is to continue to maintain or extend its support for widespread participation in the arts?"

For one thing it needs to be demonstrated that participation in the arts keeps participants at the very least 'out of prison' and hopefully, 'out of trouble' as well. It is questionable whether, however, America's middle class is currently willing to fund more widespread participation in the arts and in thoughtful educational activities in general. At present, the focus seems to be almost exclusively on 'how much machine manufactured stuff' is produced and is able to be made available. As of yet there does not appear to have been any particular widespread disenchantment with the hegemonic valuation of such material goods. Yet such disenchantment could conceivably occur. Such disenchantment could conceivably be encouraged through artistic expressions of such sentiments in literature and in the (mechanistic) visual medias.

August 3, 1999

Currently if an item is labeled 'made by humans' it is considered less valuable than if it had been made by machines. Eventually 'perfect' machine made goods will become so ubiquitous, common and even inexpensive that items made by humans may begin to be considered to be more valuable. Such a perhaps paradigmatic shift might be encouraged through fictional expressions in which characters express going through a process of infatuation with machine made goods, followed by a period of disillusionment at the recognition that increasingly the actual need for human effort is being continually reduced as a result of technological evolution.

August 5, 1999

Any significant increase in the relative value of total wages, that is any increase in the relative value of the wage pool would likely necessarily be accompanied by an illusory decrease in the value of goods and services produced per dollar value of wages paid out. Such would likely be the case nationally, unless the wage increases nationally were directly offset by increases in national productivity. Again, the manner in which national productivity is measured is critical in determining whether wage increases are in fact being offset by productivity gains. And, then, when productivity is measured against an international index i.e. how much has international productivity increased, and when international productivity of machine made goods is at a 'glut' level, as I am under the impression it is, then the question of national productivity increase recedes into relative irrelevance relative to a scheme which would measure productivity in terms of usefulness and value of the current distribution and allocation of human activity.

Gender roles, harassment, passivity and being an object, gun registration
Date: 8/26/99 1:01:38 AM Eastern Daylight Time
to: the editors (The American Prospect, The Nation, The New Yorker)
from: Andréas Daniel Fogg
Letter from Somerville August 10, 1999

Notes: definitions of appropriate male behavior vary often but not only according to class. For example, appropriate male behavior, appropriate that is for initiating physical or sexual physical contact often varies depending on socioeconomic class. However, such definitions of appropriateness may also vary by race and class. And of course such variations always have exceptions. For example, one definition of appropriateness involves a sort of male centered (as in ego centered) definition of appropriate actions. By this definition, it is appropriate for men and young men to initiate physical contact with women. That is men are the subjects, women the objects of sexual activity. Such men often ask each other the euphemistic question "can you still 'get it up'?" Such definitions of appropriateness are most often held, it appears to the author, by relatively poor American Caucasians that is by working class Caucasians and by virtually all African American men. To such men, allowing oneself to be the object of women's' physically sexually initiating actions constitutes an acceptance of the by definition passive and inferior feminine role. Hence their perhaps disdain for those middle class and upper class men who allow and even expect their spouses or girl friends to clearly indicate either through eye contact and/or physical touch that they themselves actually want sexual contact and interaction. Such economically secure men may in fact be dependent upon such gestures if they are in many cases able to be sexually potent.

The problem is that in economically secure society, a man initiating sexual contact absent clear signals from his woman partner constitutes harassment or worse. Yet amongst the working class, the ability and willingness to "successfully" initiate sexual contact constitutes a measure of self esteem and personal status. Hence when socially and physically but not necessarily economically secure men make overtures to 'stranger' women, they are at once admired by the working class and at the same time they may be disqualifying themselves, absent the artificial 'aid' of affirmative action policies, from authentic membership in the economically secure classes.

August 24, 1999

To register guns or not;

Apparently, according to Newsweek, Wayne LaPierre, of the National Rifle Association, and presumably Charlton Heston as well, oppose mandatory registration of either hand guns or rifles and I suppose of automatic and semi automatic weapons as well. LaPierre is reported as having said that if guns were required to be registered legally, then a lot of NRA members who were duck hunters, would let their weapons fall out of their boats into the lake, in other words, many NRA members would prefer to lose their weapons rather than to register them. Now it would appear that the difference between having a registered and unregistered weapon lies in the law's ability to trace responsibility for a given gun's usage. The ability to trace a gun's user increases when both gun and spent cartridge or cartridges, which are unique or extremely unique, are both registered. That is, without registration, it is relatively easier to use a gun, to kill or maim relatively untraceably, that is to use a gun and avoid responsibility for said usage. Of course, someone other than the gun's owner could have used said gun, however determining such evidence is what trials are all about. Registering guns and cartridges would add presently unavailable data to the criminal adjudicative process. It would also place a premium on gun owners safely and securely locking away their weapons. In other words unregistered guns facilitate users' ability to either threaten or perform illegal threatening in fact terroristic acts. The ability to threaten such acts of course increases the relative implicit coercive power of the unregistered gun owner. Such power can be utilized toward any number of different sorts of persons. For example, the threat of relatively untraceable lethal violence can be applied toward one's spouse, whether male or female, toward one's children, toward one's daughter's boy friend, toward one's employees thereby dampening their protests regarding inadequate compensation. And let us not forget that obscenely over compensated CEO's are in a position where they can readily contract out to other unregistered gun owners in an effort to keep recalcitrant employees in line and of course such untraceable violence can be used potentially in order to disempower both organized and unorganized efforts to raise wages. But of course Messieurs LaPierre and Heston are correct, "guns don't kill people, people kill people!" However, the effort to register guns applies to people wherein lies the problem.

Reflections written during a cruise to Alaska
Date: 8/26/99 1:03:07 AM Eastern Daylight Time
to: the editors (The American Prospect, The Nation, The New Yorker)
from: Andréas Daniel Fogg

"Reflections during a cruise to Alaska"

August 13, 1999/Shipboard the Ms Nieuw Amsterdam off the coast of British
Columbia, Canada

Ongoing thoughts on racial tension and sex;
    Notes: Wm. Julius Wilson writes of preferential opportunities rather than presumably of preferential requirements (in the latest TAP). But it appears that one of the things happening coterminously with changes and adjustments to compensatory racial policies in the U.S. at least, involves changes and evolutions or perhaps devolutions in normative orientations. Such normative reorientations often revolve around the so called feminist struggle for equal economic and social rights.
    Perhaps most commonly associated with this change is the oft observed thought that not only do women enjoy sex, as previous generations had been unwilling or uninterested in acknowledging, but women are or are supposed to be "multi-orgasmic." Indeed amongst many males this thought is taken for granted. Yet in fact frigidity and/or varieties of non-orgasmicity continue to be thought of as problems for some significant proportion of women. And I recently noticed an invocation on a women's magazine in a supermarket which read "How to become multiply orgasmic."
The presence of this article suggests that that experience may not have been attained by all or even most women. Yet it continues to be, wisely or unwisely, sought and judged desirable by many women and many men, the more so no doubt if and when whatever it is has not been attained. Hence the source of some

tension and resentment between White and African-American men. For rightly or wrongly African American men and it is suggested significant numbers of White Caucasian men believe that Negro men have larger genitals and therefore, rightly or wrongly, are believed to be more likely to be capable of inducing the multiple orgasmic experience than are (most) Caucasian or Asian men, who, it is presumed, generally have smaller genitals. So wanted, it is thought, is the ever elusive multiple orgasmic experience that non Negroes tend to defer to Negro or multiracial men with Negro blood, in the hope that they will be able to provide to their spouse or girl friend what the dominant 'cultural' (and I use the word since I am assuming that it can be applied to the dominant values and normative imperatives of the mass market oriented media) paradigm suggests has been missing. Yet in this compulsive felt need to step aside resides a lingering sense of resentment associated with the sacrifice of possessiveness associated with an emotional loving relationship.

Using guild-like institutions to raise wages;

Such international corporate guilds could exclude members who paid below a predetermined minimal wage floor. Exclusion might include sanctions involving a failure or refusal to share crucial bits of information, expertise and technology as well as penalties involved if expelled and on as yet unadmitted members who attempted to use the "guild" logo on their products. Failure to display a guild logo might come to be understood to constitute evidence of paying sweatshop level wages.

Incorporating state and federal prisoners into the work force

One would think that if the law allows private industry to use state and federal prisoners to work for them at sweatshop or below minimum wage levels, that the resulting effect on the economic wage demand pool is likely to be to decrease the magnitude of demand. One would think that this decrease would be caused as workers earning above minimal living standard wages lose their jobs to prisoners forced to work for below minimum wage rates. The only circumstance in which such an effect might not occur, it would seem is if and when the 'free work force' was at 100% employment (and low paying jobs were going unfilled), that is, if unemployment was at or below 0%, that is, all of the work force was occupied and the society's work was not getting done.

Less than obvious benefits associated with encouraging art;

Given the discrepancy between "photo-realism" and social realism, and the fact that to the naive observer, the two can easily be confused, it appears that the questions of what art is good art, what art is bad art, what "art" is not in some sense art at all, all need to be considered. Should answering such questions be a task only for the mass market? If not and if the gov't should intervene and selectively subsidize, then what should the criteria for such interventions consist in?

It is suggested that the primary economic benefits associated with the presence and widespread availability of genuinely good, of "eufunctional" art involve improved societal mental health including higher academic and occupational achievement levels, more efficient economic production, fewer divorces and reduced psychiatric treatment costs. Such a theoretical argument suggests that the psychiatric community itself might well become involved in federal efforts to subsidize, spread and encourage the arts, including painting, dramatic arts (theater), cinematic and all manner of literary arts. In referring to the psychiatric community, clearly the expertise associated with the so-called consciousness raising varieties of depth psychiatry must needs be included since reliance upon psychopharmacology without an accompanying theoretical vision of content oriented mental health would not be unlike offering a sleeping pill to someone suffering from narcolepsy.

TV journalism and the process of democratic legislation;

The question arises, "What would be the impact on society if one or more television networks offered regular programming which sought to examine both the arguments and evidence (data) for and against proposed pieces of federal, and, on critical occasions, state policy legislation. To some extent, such examinations occur from time to time in the NYTimes and various specialized professional academic journals. But the question arises, what if such coverage occurred, for example, on CNN? How much of the viewing audience share would be retained? Would such a move be opposed by academics on the grounds that its implementation would diminish their power to manipulate the electorate? But wouldn't a move to trust the populace to empower itself by watching such enlightened programming result in an increased demand wage pool? And in increased corporate (and small business) profits?

Art evaluators may need the equivalent of a bar exam;

Empowering psychiatrically (and artistically) trained evaluators to play a role in selecting art and artists to be subsidized is roughly analogous to limiting the practice of law and the occupation of the judicial branch of the government, to those who have mastered the history and content of the law sufficient to be able to pass the Bar Examination or its equivalent.

August 14, 1999/on ship near Juneau, Alaska

Pigment and toilet training;

One of our earliest drives, as human infants, is to play with our feces, perhaps including a wish to smear the stuff on our bodies. This drive is quickly suppressed and then driven from consciousness during the process of toilet training. Its remnant seems to be found in most people's conscientious wish for cleanliness. When, however, one looks at persons with relatively more pigment in their skin, whether African, African American, Indian, Hispanic or for that matter, a dark skinned Italian, one subliminally, unconsciously, irrationally "thinks" or feels that such an individual became dark-skinned as a result of having played with their feces, having smeared it on their skin. As I say, this is not a rational belief but rather a sort of gut feeling that can perhaps essentially only be dismissed as a result of repeated physical contact resulting in the disconfirming discovery that the darkness has not been caused by any malfeasance, neither is it transferable. But absent such disconfirmation, the referred to unconscious perception sometimes has an ambivalent bipolar sort of impact. On the one hand, individuals perceived to be darker are envied because it is felt that they have successfully followed the drive to explore feces and disobeyed the mother's command to "be clean." At the same time, however, they are unconsciously despised for having broken the now internalized imperative to avoid and compartmentalize all contact or reference to feces, the anal part of the body and any and all anal functions.

Ashore in Juneau, Alaska

On William Julius Wilson's article in TAP (Sept.-Oct. '99); affirmative action and its problems viewed from Alaska;

Wilson claims that African-American and Hispanic persons, who often are characterized by having lower standardized test scores than Whites and Asians, often may compensate for these lower scores by displaying more community involvement and more leadership characteristics. Re leadership qualities Dr. Wilson may indeed have a point. However, several observations need to be made. First bullying and domination and intimidation, that is bad leadership, are often confused with simple or presumably good leadership that is, individuals in a college or high school egalitarian situation are all well aware that assuming a position of leadership which is to say claiming credit for an enterprise's success, while blaming failures on "ordinary" participants shortcomings (certainly not their own) is likely to improve the appearance of their resumes and their prospects for future professional and academic success as well. Hence, in such situations, persons who blame their relative lack of success on racial or cultural discrimination are likely to seek to invoke Caucasian and Euro-American guilt in the service of their endeavors to successfully claim the substantive credit for some valued project or activity, which is to say, as some of the mostly Republican frat boys who used to (and probably still do) buy prewritten term papers, do, "Please let me win, I'm a nice guy" or in this case, "Let me call myself a leader!" Or, "You hate me because I'm Black or Hispanic and that's why I'm not a success in my school work and you should feel guilty because the reason I'm not a success is because if I succeed I'm afraid you will make me fail anyway or lynch me or rape me or my girl friend and you should feel guilty about all that and you do, I know it, therefore let me please my mama and brothers in the hood by being able to say that I am a leader that is let me tell White boys what to do. Don't make me have to eat crow and be even for perhaps five or ten years, an ordinary working guy who takes orders from some White boy that is someone who doesn't get to tell anyone, not even other Blacks or Hispanics what to do."

The problem is that leaders who are emotionally unable to be effective non supervisory workers will never be able to be effective supervisors, managers or for that matter, teachers.

In this regard, the thinking of many macho African American and Hispanic working people (usually but not always, men) is apparently, "the best way to avoid being (unfairly) dominated and abused by mainstream Caucasians is to co-opt their efforts to put (us) down and dominate us, by, of course, refusing to accept any role other than that of superior dominator. That is, to withdraw and avoid any relationship, whether occupational, professional, intellectual or social, in which a non-Hispanic or non-African-American person appears to hold a superior or more powerful position (status). Ordinarily such subordinate occupational positions are accompanied by compensatory economic monetary compensation i.e. wages or salary. However, it may be the case that working class Hispanic and African American's cultures involve an orientation around a sort of subsistence level reference point such that receiving wages is not regarded as qualitatively adequate compensation for the affront to the machismo like self image that may often accompany cultures designed in the past to support relatively subsistence like (poorer) standards of living.

For example the working class man from a subsistence level culture may believe that "being a man" requires him to respond to and satisfy the sexual overtures of any and all women who extend overtures in his direction. Should he suddenly find himself the recipient of a markedly larger salary he is likely to be confronted by a markedly larger number of such overtures, to which, if he responds positively, he is likely to find that his family may desert him and he may be unable to continue the level of work necessary to continue to earn that sort of compensation.

Notes: Gold in Juneau hills not being mined; Chomsky's critique of Lasswell, The real and recognized value to society of salesmen and writers;

First, my tour guide to Juneau and Mendenhall glacier, who drove a school bus painted light turquoise green, observed that there remained unmined gold in the hills above Juneau, remaining unmined perhaps because the value of Gold itself has been allowed to float against other commodities, commodities measured and priced in paper dollars against which gold is also allowed to float. Hence, as a result of this move, society has realized that lots of commodities that can be purchased with paper dollars are worth far more than some fixed amount of gold. Thanks to the Nixon Administration and Herb Stein, if I remember correctly. But the tour guide kept referring to items like large power boats and houses as 'belonging' to himself or his friends. Perhaps this was the case yet his serving as a tour guide in a somewhat dilapidated bus that he wasn't entirely sure would start, seemed oddly inconsistent with his owning an ocean going albeit small cabin cruiser.

Chomsky's criticism of Lasswell;

Noam Chomsky once criticized the noted political scientist Harold Lasswell as "someone who served power." As someone who at one time read a great deal of Lasswell to what seemed at the time enormous intellectual profit and benefit, I did not take kindly to this report, observing to myself thoughts such as "Chomsky is arrogant!" and "Is Chomsky implicitly seeking to overthrow and replace power holders with 'good socialists'?" and "What is Chomsky's goal in dealing with power holders?" "Doesn't Chomsky realize that by gaining the respect of power holders Lasswell attained a position from which it became possible for him to credibly influence and even lead them?"

However, it should be noted in Chomsky's defense that if the nobility in England had not forced and I use the word advisedly, the King to accept the Magna Charta, there would likely never have arisen anything like the middle class based society that eventually emerged in English influenced and based cultures. Note that in Hispanic, Russian and African cultures the ability of a middle class to oppose a ruling class remains problematic and perhaps as a result such societies suffer it is theorized, reduced economic and technological growth relative to English and say German, Dutch and French based cultures.

The point that I am attempting to make is that the current American trendy emphasis in favor of achieving consensus behind the scenes away from the public media spotlight and avoiding wherever possible public argumentation, confrontation and conflict, may well amount to an acceptance of the political domination of the wealthy elite ruling class, which domination effectively increasingly renders irrelevant the political knowledge and judgment of both working and middle classes in developed corporate dominated society. For example, say eight or ten years ago, I was friendly with a warehouse worker who worked at the local branch of the company with which I am affiliated. This worker, a large man who played football in college, at that time enjoyed drinking beer with his friends, of which number I was included, and arguing vociferously about political matters. It happened that this fellow was somewhat conservative. Since then he married, was transferred and promoted to supervisor, then transferred and promoted again to Warehouse operations manager. Recently he visited our location and it emerged that mysteriously he had no discernible political opinions, at least that he was willing to discuss with his old friends while I was in the room while at work. This appears to be the impact associated with rising in the corporate hierarchy and no doubt partaking of some of the higher more extensive sorts of innovative compensation that had been mentioned vaguely to the author in response to his request for a significantly higher level of compensation.

But the point is, if subordinates are effectively "bought off" so that they no longer are willing to venture societally relevant political opinion to their peers, then isn't or hasn't corporate dominated society effectively destroyed its previously effective interpersonal feedback mechanism? And if this is the case, and it appears to be substantively true, then isn't society presently in danger much like a ship near a rocky coast without either light or radar on a stormy foggy night?

Salesmen, writers and society;

Finally in light of these comments it becomes apropos to raise the question, what is the value to society of, for example, salespeople versus writers? Is it equal? One would think, given the levels of compensation distributed, that salespersons were far more important. And in fact, if no one is willing to read and discuss what writers have to say, particularly if it is critical of the status quo, then perhaps this judgment reflects that fact. But if the autonomous struggling writer's product is of no interest to corporate people, since they appear primarily concerned to avoid offending the hierarchy of corporate authority above them, then perhaps there is something fundamentally wrong with either the corporate system or the way most of the corporate players are playing the game. Critical feedback of society and the corporate establishment must of necessity involve some danger, since real economic interests may come under attack. Yet society depends on the existence of such courageous criticism in order to avoid mistakes or even disasters. So that writers who read and observe and are willing to criticize the powers that be have much to be proud of and they certainly are not dominated whatever their racial or cultural background, whereas the corporate toady who goes along with his superiors to the point where he is unwilling to express any political opinions has allowed his mind to appear if not become enslaved and dominated by the established economic powers. The toady likely has more money and power over fellow workers, but it is unlikely that he or she has more or perhaps any genuine self respect.

August 18, 1999/on the ms Nieuw Amsterdam, off the coast of British Columbia
Regarding the teaching of Evolution and Creationism in the public schools;

The U.S. Constitution suggests, declares that the State shall not allow or establish as its own any single given religion. It is suggested that what "establish" means is in effect to declare that any one religion or religious view or theory has predominance or is true relative to any other religious account. There is, it seems clear, a qualitative difference between religious accounts, including the so called Creationist account derived from the book of Genesis, of the origins of the world and humankind and life itself and scientific sorts of such accounts such as evolutionary scientific theory. Scientific theories are based upon accumulated data whose existence and accuracy are capable of being observed and whose accuracy can be checked and validated by relatively large numbers of scientific workers. When such theories are presented to the public, usually in universities or other institutions of higher learning, supporting as well as disconfirming data are presented as well.

Religious mystically and mythically oriented accounts such as the account in Genesis as well as the accounts of other religious groups could theoretically according to the Constitution, it is argued, be taught in the public schools without making a claim that such accounts were scientifically "true." For example such accounts could be taught as Anthropology, Comparative Religions or History of Religions curricula.

August 19, 1999/on Ms Nieuw Amsterdam, docked at Vancouver. British
Columbia

The media may exacerbate paranoia;

If you allow yourself to be deterred from thinking, speaking or writing something because some synchronous disaster has occurred somewhere in the world (brought to your attention by the media), then you are unlikely to take any sort of risks since disasters are ubiquitous and taking an overly egocentric approach causes paralysis of the will, of even thought and action, since you will, under such an interpretative scheme, blame such mishaps on any innovative course of action that you have recently tried.

Economics, violence and paranoia
Date: 8/31/99 11:31:34 AM Eastern Daylight Time
to: the editors (The American Prospect, The Nation, The New Yorker)
from: Andréas Daniel Fogg
Letter from Somerville August 27, 1999

Is the fear of violence from wealthy economic interests merely paranoid?

What actually happens and the interpretation placed on it are two entirely different things. Sweatshop workers are literally locked up. Slavery exists in this century, although not necessarily in the US. I think it was Van Morrison or maybe Van Halen who wrote a popular song entitled "Nobody gets out of here alive!" Then there was that novel by the lawyer, Grisham?, in which the protagonist joined a firm but was apparently threatened with death if he left, perhaps it was called "The Practice" or "The Firm." Closer to home, an employee who attempted to leave my company for another position shortly after I joined it, died in an auto accident. Then there was the notorious story about the woman, Karen (?) Silkwood, who was going to testify against nuclear power and was killed again in an auto crash apparently on her way to testify. Of course lots of others have quit without suffering any mishap. Then you have all of the violence directed at union organizers by management in the past. Currently this sort of violence has been in a sense ratified and written into the law, so that union organizers apparently can be fired at will, if only for other reasons.

But you're right; this line of speculation is somewhat paranoid. But then some degree of paranoia may be characteristic of the relatively powerless. And one of the characteristics associated with the widening gap between the rich and the poor, and the diminished relative presence of the middle class, is that the working class increasingly perceives itself to be relatively powerless.

August 30, 1999

Perhaps this "paranoia" explains the media's apparently collective decision to avoid presenting the controversy about global warming to the public in terms that it can understand. This decision, apparently justified in terms of an alleged need to maintain peace and the ability to proceed as if the public need not be involved in attempts to forge or remold consensus, may in fact amount to acquiescing to "paranoid" fears which may in fact not be paranoid at all but rather justified. In this regard, I regret the loss of life associated with a recent accident in the Boston area in which a large sport utility vehicle, an Explorer, flipped over on the freeway while changing lanes. However, the perception that these polluters and global warmers are ultimate sources of safety and security needs to be changed

In this regard, the possibility of a presidential confrontation between George W. Bush, who apparently has received a lot of monies from oil interests, and Al Gore, may well provide the country with the opportunity to view enough of the evidence about global warming sufficient to modify the prevailing consensus. Air travel, which a recent report indicates is likely to double or triple in volume over the next twenty years, is a significant cause of global warming, its incidence of usage and pollution can be influenced by increasing its cost either through corporate consensus and or through public taxation. The same can be said of auto emissions, which also are a significant cause of the warming tendency. But the only way that attitudes can be altered is if they are addressed in the media, that is, if and when respected public figures are willing to risk retaliation by speaking out. The more public figures who speak out publicly in forums which are covered by the media, the safer such gestures are likely to become. Once global warming becomes a respectable, acceptable, moral public cause, the ability of the oil fuels industry to enforce silence through the threat of implicit violent or economic or occupational retribution is likely to vanish.

Status dissonance, inconsistent self esteem relative to societal situs, mental illness
Date: 8/31/99 11:31:15 AM Eastern Daylight Time
to: the editors (The American Prospect, The Nation, The New Yorker)

from: Andréas Daniel Fogg
Letter from Somerville August 26, 1999

A possible locus or source of tensions which lead to various degrees of mental illness and mental illness symptomatology may lie in dissonant messages coming
from on the one hand the affected individual, that is the so called patient, who
may often suspect himself of possessing degrees of importance totally unrecognized by the members of the surrounding society, and the surrounding society
which as an aggregate is likely to totally ignore or be unaware of what appears to
the patient to be his or her own acute, even frightening and obvious self importance. Indeed, such patients may often feel impelled to cooperate with such disparaging assessments when they come from individuals upon whom they may be
emotionally dependent. Indeed, such relationships, including relationships with
mental health professionals are often dependent upon the continued display of
relative occupational incapacity and gross levels of personal helplessness.

August 30, 1999

One of the aspects of US culture that perhaps makes it appear attractive and
valuable, and worth investing in and emulating, may well be the fact that we as a
nation manage to tolerate and protect the rights of virtually all cultural, ethnic,
religious and racial groups. One of the ways in which we do this includes the utilization of passive tolerance in the presence of social and competitive tensions. In
other words, if someone sits quietly at the table or in the room in which a social
interaction occurs, and that someone is resented but neither verbally nor physically attacked, that is, that person or persons are allowed to be seen, to live peacefully, then a sort of triumph of toleration has occurred. The fact that that person
may be resented by the members of the majoritarian mass society as a result of
upwardly mobile pretensions that may or may not be justified, suggests that in
mass cultural contexts, such as occur in mass media outlet situations, like television and to some extent radio, such acts of toleration, which include implicitly a
posture of humility on the part of the minority member in question i.e. he or she
speaks when the interviewer, who speaks for the majority members of the audience, speaks to her or him, despite the fact that the interviewee possesses some
sort of status characteristic which in and of itself may place him or her ahead of
the interviewer in terms of their relative value to society. However, that value
may be relatively incomprehensible to most of the members of the society,
whereas the value of the interviewer, who is able to simplify the complex nature
of what the interviewee does so that it is in some sense comprehensible to the

public, is readily apparent. However, such a triumph of toleration is possible in garden variety restaurant situations, for example, in which racial rivalries and even hostilities may be acknowledged but not allowed to escalate to the point where polite decorum is violated or to the point where anyone's safety is endangered. Indeed the attempt on the part of some Caucasians to actively take the part of the African-American, in acts of sort of genetic altruism, may result down the road in reluctant feelings of regret and self betrayal. Indeed, having a conversation need not imply that one wishes some sort of permanent genetic alliance, in which the melding of genes needs must occur. Such an assumption on the part of African Americans, i.e. if you talk to me that must mean that you want to sleep with my "sister" (or me) seemingly can lead to misunderstandings and hostilities generated by what may be perceived as a rejection.

A definition of male Black/White interactions;

For example, it has been observed that some typical conversations between African-American men and Caucasian men end with the African American man saying, instead of good bye or so long or see you later or take it easy, instead many tend to end such interactions by saying "OK." As if to say "I give you permission to leave now (even though you haven't given me any money or social commitment). Following such a "dismissal" the Caucasian, at least in the case of the narrator, tends to feel personally undermined and resentful. This resentment tends to extend emotionally to African-Americans as a group; indeed, sometimes it seems as if many of them seem to be aware of the subtle subversion of Caucasian identity (and presumed implicit superiority) that had occurred.

Indeed, we may as a society and as persons who speak for society wish to reexamine our assumptions vis a vis the ethnic, racial, religious status or pecking order. For example, does such a status order exist? If so, should it exist? Is it inevitable that we classify people by the relative general importance attached to their racial or ethnic or religious grouping? If so, is it inevitable that majority members will be resentful of minority members who personally defy the majoritarian preferred status hierarchy namely that majoritarian members should be seen as more important and more specifically in control of social interactions. Is it desirable to differentiate personal status or importance from whether or who is in control of a social interaction? That is, might feathers be smoothed if, for example, a highly touted minority group member were to behave with humility toward majority group members with whom he interacted? Such humility might include verbal self deprecating gestures in the Japanese and, for that matter, pre Israeli Jewish mode for example. All this is apropos of Caucasian/African-American interactions in which in many instances, the African-American often seems to assume that he is a superior being and in control of the interaction, hence the use of the dismissive term, "OK." In earlier years during the civil rights era, an African American who showed humility toward Caucasians was dismissed derisively by his racial mates as an "Uncle Tom." But such dismissals of humility occurred before significant numbers of American Negroes achieved relatively high levels of socioeconomic mobility, whether in the communications business, entertainment or professional sports, where some are currently pulling down enormous salaries, which, if their identities are ascertained, entitle them inevitably to a considerable amount of status. The question is, if such a highly paid individual demonstrates humility in interactions with Whites or Asians, is he guilty of being an "Uncle Tom?" Rather, wouldn't such displays of humility tend to ease racial antagonisms felt by less economically advantaged members of the majority community and reduce the possibility of a civil rights backlash such as occurred after the Reconstruction era which followed the American Civil War?

August 31, 1999

More generally the question is how should the general problem represented by the three archetypical cases, the Tutsi relative to the Hutu, the Armenians relative to the Turks, and the Jews relative to Hitler's Germans and anti-Semites in general, be dealt with. That is, these cases involve a minority group achieving and earning and holding disproportionately more socioeconomic success than the proportion achieved by members of the surrounding majoritarian community. Is the solution to resentments held by the majoritarian community to insist that success should be achieved at equal proportionate levels? That is, should the policy be that twenty per cent of Tutsis and twenty per cent of Hutus should be enabled to achieve a given, similar level of wealth and status? Similarly with Jews and Gentiles and Armenians and Turks? When the question is posed in this way the answer appears to be negative. This would seem to be the case since there are two basic interpretations which attempt to explain the relative differential levels of success. One is genetic and the other is cultural, that is, that the more successful groups practice cultural processes which entail an adaptational advantage. The substance of cultural practices and advantages can be learned even "stolen" by those who are open minded enough to take advantage of them. If the preferred interpretation leans toward the genetic then solutions range from genocide, practiced in the past by all three resentful groups against their more successful neighbors, to sexual sharing and blending of the gene pools. But where the rivalries and resentments are intense as they often are, inter group sexual alliances are likely to be anathema that is avoided, unless they involve gross humiliation such as the forced prostitution and rape practiced by the Nazis and in a different case, the Serbs against the Kosovars.

But, if disproportionate success should not be prohibited, but rather seen as emblematic of legitimate group and self-actualization, then the problem is how to reduce and civilize the resentments felt by the less successful majoritarian members.

All this is presuming that the successes referred to are deserved and not merely a result of dysfunctional legal quirks which funnel sociologically dysfunctional disproportionate levels of economic success to a relatively undeserving few. It may also be the case that minority status itself may be a prerequisite to such disproportionate levels of success. For example, émigré minority Chinese in southeast Asia tend to be economically more successful than surrounding Asians such as Malaysians and Indonesians, whereas when Chinese live in China they do not constitute a minority and the levels of success and poverty are spread proportionately throughout the society. Similarly, the folk wisdom that there is no such thing as a poor Jew does not apply anywhere, but particularly in Israel, where Jews constitute the majority. But the suggestion in general is that successful and relatively unsuccessful minority group members whose group is envied and resented, should in general make efforts to recognize and respect perhaps allow the members of the majority the right to initiate conversation, in general recognize, that their success and physical well being as minority members, is contingent upon not unduly insulting the self conceptions and self esteem of members of the majority group or groups.

Re: economics, violence and paranoia
Date: 9/3/99 12:00:42 PM Eastern Daylight Time
Dad,

The point is that one or two coincidental, planned or unplanned accidents, in an atmosphere dogged by overtones of paranoia, paranoia can also be thought of as unbounded, undirected libidinal energy, can result in the imposition of a paranoiacally generated intimidatory effect, such effects can, and I believe do and does, support a harmful, environmentally harmful consensus.

Re: status dissonance, inconsistent self esteem relative to societal situs, m...
Date: 9/3/99 12:08:35 PM Eastern Daylight Time

Dad,

I'm thinking. There is it seems a difference between the basis of the Tutsi economic domination, versus the strength of the Jews and Armenians, which seems largely to be based upon scientific and business intelligence. The Tutsi strength, I suspect, is partly based upon their physical stature relative to the Hutu. That is the Tutsi are markedly taller than the Hutu. Now we seem to be creating an economic elite of Tutsi like American Negroes whose economic accumulations are largely attributable or have as a prerequisite large size accompanied by athletic ability. As someone of below average height, this makes me uneasy, but also on general principles.

More later....

Darwin's indirect effect on sexual mores, Kubrick's last film
Date: 9/7/99 12:57:37 AM Eastern Daylight Time
to: the editors (The American Prospect, The Nation, The New Yorker)
from: Andréas Daniel Fogg
September 4, 1999
Letter from Somerville

As pointed out, the scheme which involves inter ethnic or interracial genetic transmissions often utilizes fantasies of rape and prostitution, even forced prostitution, in order to transcend the inner group's resistance to sexual fraternization with out group members. This fantasy scheme is facilitated by the gross discrepancies in wealth which the present distributional system is utilizing. Thus, on the one hand, racial and ethnic group feelings of envy and admiration, even jealousy, can be much more easily handled either actually or in fantasy, through inter group shared sexual behavior, such fantasized or actual behavior is in fact much more easily accomplished, than for example, learning how to play the trumpet like Wynton Marsalis, or writing or reading and understanding and being able to discuss any adult level treatise on Sociology, Economics or Physics. And Darwin and his current advocates, who often may be confused with the so called Social Darwinists, seem to endorse the idea of relatively promiscuous sexual couplings as evolutionarily functional. This seems to be the case, although perhaps I misunderstand the import of their observations. Thus, for example, when a Darwinian observes that such and such a mammal or bird seems as a matter of course to cheat on her mate by consorting, i.e. either mating or flirting with males other than her spouse, then one possible implication for humans is that strict monogamy constitutes a sort of evolutionary dysfunction. Carrying this implication one step further one arrives at the conclusion that an evolutionarily enlightened human has a responsibility to be sexually promiscuous, indeed, the more promiscuous the better.

Putting this thinking into the context of racial relations in the United States, one may well observe that or at least some have claimed that precisely such principles were utilized by some White slave owners prior to the Civil War. This allegation cries out for historical research. For if it was true that such thinking was utilized, i.e. that Negro slaves were encouraged to couple toward the end of creating evolutionarily more functional field hands, and were encouraged to ignore marital vows to this end, then such a paradigm, which seems to be consistent with Darwinian thinking, may have worked its way into the formulation of current secular American sexual norms and mores.

A mechanism which would facilitate such an implicit destruction of the family unit would not be inconsistent with the presence of a relatively small number of extremely wealthy individuals, professional athletes, entertainers and the corporate elite, whose wealth and status would theoretically allow them to reward sexually promiscuous behavior, either by giving significant monies to their own partners, or to associates who demonstrated such behaviors with others. Such a supposition seems preposterous in light of the furor over the President's recent sexual escapades, however, it is well to note that that escapade did not involve evolutionarily effective interactions, that is, it involved sexual behaviors that could not result in reproduction, the primary sort of action that a Darwinian is interested in.

A definition of paranoia;

Paranoia may be defined as a state of mind or behavior caused by relatively unbounded significant libidinal connections. That is more plainly, paranoia may be caused by insufficient interpersonal human connection or relationships. For example, if the most important people in a persons life are television and cinematic personalities, that is, if an individual values the opinions of such persons far and away over and above the opinions (and gestures) of more ordinary persons with whom he or she can discourse (talk) and interact (including touch), then such a person is in fact according to this definitional theory, likely to be significantly paranoid. Whether such a tendency is diagnosed and treated depends in large part upon the manner in which it is manifested as well as upon the society's current inclination to treat or ignore these problems. It should also be noted that a certain degree of paranoia is likely to make the population relatively amenable to mass media generated social and political control.

September 6, 1999

Observations stemming from viewing the Stanley Kubrick film, Eyes Wide Shut;

The film seems at first to be some sort of a political metaphor, although it is conceivably possible that some such events similar to those depicted in the film have happened or for that matter continue to happen. There have been reports about the so called "Bohemian Club" which suggest that such events might be possible. However, the events depicted are certainly possible and important as fantasy or dreamed material. In either case, what is involved in the masked orgy, to which only apparently wealthy individuals arrive at the mansion on the outskirts of town in limousines, is a sort of acting out of the Darwinian dictum "blind variation and selective retention."

That is, the participants, whom some segments of society has dubbed "important" or recipients of the grace of God, or even, in Nietzschean terms, "supermen," are deemed, because of their wealth which presumably represents evidence of their evolutionary desirability, and because they are willing to participate in extramarital copulatory orgies, i.e. their ability to transcend "bourgeois morality, "ubermenschen."

Note that because all participants are masked, selection of partners is identity blind i.e. utilizing "blind selection." Hence it is not surprising that this film came from a novel written apparently by a psychoanalyst, who would be familiar with "enlightened" critiques of what is often termed repressive religious based moralities. It is not clear from the film whether the author of the novel, or Kubrick himself, was attempting to ridicule the protagonist's marital moral fidelity or to praise it and ridicule the practices attributed to the wealthy anonymous elite. The story is simply presented.

That said; note the earlier observations to the effect that the existence of a relatively small number of wealthy individuals at the top of the income spectrum constitutes in and of itself a challenge to the notion of the monogamous moral family unit. That is, when great expensive commodities are continually dangled in front of the eyes of the societal majority, as they are on television, the temptations on the working and middle classes, indeed, perhaps upon most of the non wealthy members of the society, to violate marital vows, even to dispense with marriage itself, which already exist, are multiplied. There is some question whether the groups of wealthy disguised, powerful individuals, who clearly do not believe in bourgeois morality, represent either a fascist or corrupted Marxist elite. The film goes into no detailed descriptions whatsoever as to the political concerns and objectives of the members of this secret group. The absence of such detail suggests in fact that the group is primarily if not exclusively interested in preserving its own power and indulging in debaucheries (most of the women involved in the orgy, it is suggested by the film, are young shapely prostitutes) such as those depicted. This lack of larger dedication to the good of society and humanity suggests in fact that these individuals either are explicitly fascist or if originally Marxist that they have allowed themselves to become de facto fascists.

Further it is not clear, either from the film, or for that matter, in general, whether the transcendence of ordinary sexual morality is a necessary prerequisite for membership in the higher income echelons of the American and international corporate elite. It would of course be interesting to speculate and investigate such questions, however, it is clear to the narrator, at least, that even at the lower levels of corporate organizations, management guards its privacy and doings and pre-rogatives jealously and carefully. Neither is the narrator privy to what goes on behind the closed doors of the so called country club elite. Perhaps some other researchers have access to this sort of information.

Further comments about Kubrick's last film, East Timor
Date: 9/8/99 12:13:51 PM Eastern Daylight Time
to: the editors (The American Prospect, The Nation, The New Yorker)
from: Andréas Daniel Fogg
Letter from Somerville September 7, 1999

Kubrick;

Note that in Kubrick's film, the actual masked orgy is preceded by what appears to be a religious ritual, accompanied by monastic like music and chant-ing, in which a viewer inferred that a group of representative women appear to ask permission of a single male "religious" masked leader, that is permission to make sexual advances to apparently any of the masked men assembled at the gathering. This ceremony is followed by the women disrobing, except for their masks, and proceeding individually; to each accost a different single masked man. Hence the orgy depicted does not involve men "raping" women.

East Timor;

It appears from the news reports that anarchy reins in East Timor. It is appar-ently being encouraged by the Indonesian armed forces. The US needs to make clear to the Indonesian government and to the World Bank and the IMF that our government does not support this outrageous and antidemocratic, illegal and immoral flaunting of the rights of the East Timorese people to both live in peace and to express their wish for independence democratically, particularly since the region was, it appears, seized by force by Indonesia as recently as 1975. Hence, from here it appears that either a local multinational or international force needs to be called in to neutralize what appears to be an Indonesian military force that at best has no regard or respect for the opinion of the central Indonesian government neither for the political will of the vast majority of the East Timorese people. Hence the Indonesian government needs to be told that unless it requests the intervention of such an external military force into East Timor as soon as possible, that the US and the UN, the World Bank and IMF will all be forced to reconsider, probably even cancel all financial assistance to Indonesia for the foreseeable future.

In the event that Mr. Habbibie (?) cannot be convinced to ask the outside world for such assistance, some other legal justification for international intervention needs to be identified

Corporate media merger and the free press, Palestinian refugees
Date: 9/13/99 9:58:45 AM Eastern Daylight Time
to: the editors (The American Prospect, The Nation, The New Yorker)
from: Andréas Daniel Fogg
Letter from Somerville September 10, 1999

Thoughts on the proposed merger between CBS and Viacom;
    What function does this proposed media merger serve other than to achieve the centralization of power over yet more of the media market? If for example there seemed to be a need for the CEO of Viacom to have a "lock" over more of the market, then such a merger might be justified, but the justification would be totalitarian in nature. But no one has made any sort of argument in this direction. Even if they did it would seem to be bogus since the direction of the move is away from more freedom of choice toward less freedom of choice (of programming).
    Do we secretly, as Erich Fromm suggested so many years ago in his book, Escape From Freedom, wish to avoid the difficulty of making our own choices re entertainment and the selection of political candidates and political positions? Or, is this move toward consolidation merely part of a political cabal which seeks

control over the hearts and minds of American citizenry and citizens of the world? If so, what is the political orientation of such a cabal? Is it enough to merely assume on the basis of superficial evidence that such would be totalitarian media moguls are "on the right side?" And what happens if such moguls begin to radically differ from significant numbers of the electorate, are we to expect that they will, upon having consolidated power humbly welcome the expression of dissenting views? Such an expectation, given the history of totalitarian movements would certainly seem to be naive. And, once such consolidation of control is legally ratified it is unlikely to be easily reversed in the event that the holders of decision-making power at the apex of such organizations attempt to abuse or misuse their power. And, the history of totalitarian political organizations suggests that the leadership of such organizations typically falls into the hands of cruel, unethical and ruthless manipulators i.e. those such as Stalin, for example, whose lust for power empowers them to push those with more moral and ethical dispositions aside.

Then there is the blanket observation which seems to justify the publication and distribution of books and movies that are in the poorest taste and which seem to have little or no redeeming social value, namely, that they sell a lot. Surely there should come a time when gross revenues are evaluated not merely in terms of their magnitude but also in terms of the quality of life upon which they are based? And, indeed, upon the quality of life that they in a sense inspire and reinforce. Thus it is well to note, in considering what artistic vehicles need to be encouraged, that life often tends to imitate art or in this case "art." Hence just as the artist or novelist or film producer deserves some of the credit for the behaviors that he or she encourages, similarly they in the event may deserve some of the blame. Hence the artist, particularly the artist who utilizes media for purposes of distribution, needs perhaps to keep in mind the dictum of the physician, namely, "above all do no harm."

The adjudication of military interventions;

We need to keep in mind that the evidence used to justify military interventions has in the past been faked. Consider for example, the justification for the Spanish American War at the beginning of the twentieth century. Therein, if my history serves me correctly, US agents sank a ship, the "Maine," and then blamed its demise on the Spanish and actually attacked Spanish interests as a result. Going to war can and often involves the blatant manipulation of public opinion. And of course, when the press and the media are controlled by one or merely a few political interest groups, the manipulation of public opinion becomes relatively easier, and, of course, potentially subject to corruption and abuse. Hence the preservation of a genuinely free press is likely to constitute a greater guard against unnecessary and unjust military adventures than an attempt to turn the problem over to some legal court which would inevitably also, indeed all the more if it had sole authority, be subject to economic and other intimidatory pressures.

Of course it is important that journalists be responsible accurate reporters. To this end journalistic credentials need to be handed out based upon writing experience at the least. However, the availability of a diverse, independent group of journalistic media inclusive support corporations is likely to serve as a sort of check and balance mechanism which theoretically would ensure against the potential high jacking of public opinion by a media mogul powerhouse whose power had been allowed to grow to the point where it would become virtually impossible to convincingly contradict its pronouncements in the public media sphere. Such power would likely seem benign to viewers at first until that is its use began to be abused. Then a remedy would be sought but achieving the overthrow of such concentrated power once it were established would be all the more difficult, perhaps nearly impossible.

September 12, 1999

The Palestinian refugee problem;

A suggested solution is to give each refugee family a free choice as to whether they wish to return to the land they call Palestine, or, to emigrate elsewhere. Such a choice would include estimates of the likelihood of finding work in specified areas at the then present time. For example, the problem could be handled by the Palestinian Authority in conjunction with the UN agency responsible for helping refugees. Together, they could ascertain which countries would be willing to accept how many Palestinian refugees as well as what the employment prospects are and are likely to be in those countries. Then, as part of the settlement, Israel, since she served as a contributing cause of the original problem, although not the sole contributing cause, and the Palestinian Authority, assisted by Arab brethren nations and UN revenues designated to aid refugee resettlement, could finance the resettlement of the refugees. It is likely that, larger subsidies should be available to refugees who chose to immigrate to destinations other than their original homeland. Israel and Palestine are/is a crowded place already. Hence there is a need to provide an incentive to returning refugees to choose a destination other than their original homeland.

September 13, 1999

Indonesian troops in East Timor;

It might be worth considering the possibility that the UN ask Indonesia to withdraw its forces from East Timor gradually immediately prior to the entry of the UN sponsored peacekeeping force.

Origins of anti Timorese antipathy are what?

Date: 9/13/99 10:12:27 AM Eastern Daylight Time

Dad,

It may be well to examine what exactly constitutes the original antipathy against the East Timorese. The region has been described as impoverished yet a deal to apparently appropriate East Timor's off shore oil reserves was struck some years back between Australia and Indonesia, according, I think, to Chomsky. Could it be that the antipathy is due to the military weakness of the state combined with the fact that East Timor legally had and has rights over some then as yet unexploited oil reserves?...

Violent films and post traumatic stress disorder, raising media taxes

Date: 9/22/99 11:58:36 AM Eastern Daylight Time

to: the editors (The American Prospect, The Nation. The New Yorker)

from: Andréas Daniel Fogg

Letter from Somerville September 14, 1999

Psychotic like realistic graphic violence may be effectively imbuing post traumatic stress disorder in significantly large numbers of filmgoers. Further, a small number of viewers may be allowing themselves to react to and adapt to this trauma by directly imitating it, instead, for example, of overreacting to it by perhaps obsessively compulsively emphasizing non assertiveness.

Origins of anti-Timorese sentiment;

I think Chomsky has asserted that the allegedly impoverished East Timorese State actually has legal rights to an off shore oil field whose rights, it was alleged, were recently divided between Australia and Indonesia. Could it be that the antipathy toward the East Timorese on the part of the Indonesians is the product of several factors. East Timor was a Portuguese colony prior to its seizure by the Indonesians, most of whom had been citizens of the Dutch ruled Dutch East Indies. Then the combination of having access to wealth coupled with military weakness may invite attacks which are motivated by the possibility of getting away with significant seizures of wealth. Then, I am also under the impression that the original seizure of East Timor was directly encouraged by Henry Kissinger's American State Department as part of an effort to promote a counter balance to Chinese power in the region. Note that the invasion of East Timor, which occurred in 1975 or 1976, occurred after the Kissinger Nixon rapprochement with China, which if memory serves me, occurred in 1972.

September 20, 1999

Are CFC's used in the manufacture of computers?

A drinking buddy, musician has suggested that CFCs are integrally involved in the manufacture of computers. This suggestion, or accusation, cries out for either refutation or corroboration.

September 21, 1999

Origins and discussion of the concept of ego psychology;

Could it be the case that ego psychology and apparently its accompanying ethics derive from a sort of hypothetical vision of what behavior should be like in a classless society? Note that one of the primary motivations fueling the affirmative action/civil rights movement is an attempt sometimes it is thought or asserted, to create a classless society, other times it is more commonly suggested that the attempt is to create conditions which will allow for truly equal opportunities for upward socioeconomic mobility, that is for opportunities for mobility that are statistically identical regardless of race, culture or religion or ethnicity. There is, it appears some confusion in the public mind, if such an entity can be referred to, as to whether the goal is a meritocratic based set of social classes or rather a purely classless egalitarian society. Note that the traditional notion of class was based perhaps as much upon inherited wealth as it was upon merit. This traditional notion of class is thus quite qualitatively different from the meritocratic notion of class (in which it is hoped, class position is based solely upon merit). That is under the meritocratic ideology, it is thought to be desirable to remove inherited wealth from the process of determining adult social status. There seems to be a sort of schizoid double bind here wherein successful members of society, particularly those who are so called self made men or women, take pride in their position in society; yet they seem to find no inconsistency in using their wealth in order to help ensure the successes of their progeny. And everywhere, or most everywhere, the imperative seems to be "get ahead, get as far ahead as you can."

But it is asserted that the goal of deliberately attempting to ensure statistically equal rates of socioeconomic success regardless of culture, religion, ethnicity or race seems to be futile or even harmful. The weaker strategy of attempting to encourage members of less successful groups to strive for (and achieve) success is preferable and different in that this weaker strategy tends to be less radically critical of the system's criteria of success. That is the strong affirmative action case involves a substantial subversion of the social order in that members of less successful groups are told straight-out collectively, "it's not your fault that you as a group are less successful, it's the system's fault." Hence this approach engenders hostility toward the system and toward members of more successful groups. Hence this approach, before it was criticized even debunked by largely conservatively oriented political critics (but also by some generally liberally oriented critics, such as this writer), could have been accused probably correctly of sparking significant amounts of civil unrest.

The problem with ego psychology seems to the writer to involve its similarity to basically, endorsed pushiness. I.e. ego psychology seems to assert that strength and intimidation should by all rights play a large role in determining who by all rights should succeed. It seems to turn the dictum "and the meek shall inherit the earth" on its head to read "and the strong shall inherit the earth." But perhaps I am missing something here. And of course when this version of ego psychology is used in conjunction with so called affirmative action, affirmative action in which criteria of merit as well as those of social class are subverted in favor, toward equality of result, and of strength of perceived drive for self advancement; then we have situations in which merit is likely to be regularly overlooked in favor of unabashed statements of self advancing self esteem. Humility ceases to be a rewarded social value. And eventually merit also is likely to become a diminished social value. It is possible to make a strong argument for the case that a certain amount of humility usually, necessarily accompanies real merit. For the corrupted ego psychologist, computers will serve as alternatives to human skill, knowledge and merit. Computers, after all don't express resentment when they are not adequately, relatively compensated. And of course in the world of affirmative action only members of the so called disadvantaged groups are allowed to express resentment. Those members of successful groups who are regularly being ripped off by the successful members of the system are told to compare themselves with the less successful members of society and to count themselves well off, apparently leaving the lion's share of the spoils to the unabashedly assertive.

Of course it is important to distinguish between well thought out changes in society's criteria for success, such as for example, an increased emphasis upon the society's devotion to the arts, and the triumph of egotistical ambition. The former is to be desired and sought after. The later leads to the deterioration of the quality of life.

September 22, 1999

Predicting the impact on corporate profits of legislation raising taxes and or licensing fees on media based corporations;

Presuming that the pool of corporate monies available for salaries would shrink as a result of the increased costs of taxes and licensing fees, and assuming that relatively quickly the result of this across the board contraction would result in reduced corporate salaries, since the assumption is that the cause of these exorbitantly large salaries is a surfeit of available cash, which is then drawn competitively into the salary pool, then as soon as salaries were proportionately reduced, corporate profits per share, earnings per share, would likely remain constant or even increase, since the assumption is that a resultant increase in the overall societal wage pool—as a result of increased popular funding for Medicare, Medicaid, education, social security, even subsidies for medical insurance available to the general working population, would result in increased general spending which would positively impact on corporate profits in general, if only indirectly on media corporate profits. But consider that corporate media profits in the case of GE for example, are impacted by general spending. Consider also that general spending that does not involve an increase in private debt is likely in general to entail less peripheral costs such as bankruptcy costs to banks as well as psychiatric costs associated with a significant proportion of the population living beyond its means.

Finally it is important to note this predicted positive benefit associated with raising taxes on media corporations is only likely to follow if the increased tax revenues are channeled back into the public coffers and thence into public benefits. If as the Republicans wish, the resultant surplus is returned in an equal across the board tax cut, all predictions for increased benefits to corporate profits and the societal good are off.

Part Five: Fall

Conservative quest for security, forgiving third world debt
Date: 9/28/99 1:06:55 AM Eastern Daylight Time
to: the editors (The American Prospect, The Nation, The New Yorker)
from: Andréas Daniel Fogg
Letter from Somerville September 23, 1999

A missile defense shield and the Republican quest for ultimate security;

One of my father's favorite sayings is, "Nobody has it made." George W. Bush and the Republican conservatives who support a rejuvenated effort toward a missile defense shield and a sort of fortress American mentality i.e. worry about ourselves and let the rest of the world go to hell should take note. The drive for a new star wars defense goes hand in glove with the move toward gated defended wealthy enclaves designed to keep workers who might catch on that they are being exploited and treated unfairly away from those who reap the large scale rewards. It's the same principle. Indeed I have experienced such thoughts myself during idle moments when speculating about how I would feel if I were to succeed big time. But the move to take huge rewards and then seek to avoid social accountability toward those who continue to be poor by attempting to make oneself and one's wealthy associates invulnerable to resentment generated attack indeed to hide from contact with workers is when you stop and think about it emotionally stultifying and life draining. And it cannot lead to the long term growth of profits either. The only economic move that can lead to long term bubble free increases in corporate profits involves moves to raise wages and at the same time ensure safety from competitive retaliation.

September 28, 1999

Whether or not or how the IMF should forgive third world debts;

If these debts are merely unconditionally forgiven, then no positive socioeconomic purpose will be accomplished, as likely as not third world "elites" will pocket the IMF and World Bank funds and the IMF (largely US, European and

Japanese) tax payers will be forced to foot the bill. On the other hand, if conditions must be fulfilled, purposeful, lasting redistributional conditions, like funding for public education and/or subsidizing public health insurance, for examples, before the debt is forgiven, or partially forgiven, then at least some positive locally oriented pro growth strategy will have been implemented which will result in western and Japanese taxpayers paying for the establishment of a set of conditions which will allow for continued local growth and relative self sufficiency. In considering this problem, the observation that many poor third world nations are essentially kleptocracies should be resolutely kept in mind.

Fictional vignettes
Date: 10/4/99 12:16:21 PM Eastern Daylight Time
to: the editors (The American Prospect, The Nation, The New Yorker)
from: Andréas Daniel Fogg
Letter from Somerville October 3, 1999

The young man who scared himself into self-effacement;
    There once was a young boy named Fred, who also happened to be close friends with another boy of about the same age as himself, who also happened to be named Fred. The other Fred had some variety of asthma which required that he regularly receive a series of apparently painful injections. The asthmatic Fred was an enthusiastic basketball player whose hero was the Celtics star, Bob Cousy. The asthmatic Fred also had a favorite song which he liked to sing over and over again to his friend, the then healthier Fred, while they would play catch. The song was "The Ballad of Roger Young." Roger Young, according to Fred, had been a war hero; it was not clear in which war he had fought in "with forty-seven bullets in his stommma_ik" and died a hero. Anyway once in the probably fifth or sixth grade the two Fred's had been hanging out together in the asthmatic Fred's bedroom and they got into a sort of a fight or altercation, over who knows what. It was the only time that they ever fought. The non asthmatic Fred "won" by getting the other Fred in a head lock and squeezing as hard as he could until the other Fred I guess gave up. The winner had, until that time taken pride in the number of chin-ups that he could do, but after this incident, which scared him immensely, he just stopped doing chin-ups entirely. I guess he was afraid that he had been trying to kill his friend and from that time forward became overly afraid of expressing anger or rage at any other males. It was as if he thought that if he allowed himself to express anger that he feared that he would be unable to control

his rage. And, since he had stopped doing chin-ups and for a long time much heavy exercise at all, he also feared that if he was lured into an altercation that he would be defeated. So the fear of being unable to control his own anger led to a deliberate strategy of being weak. And being weak in turn tended to result in other males not respecting him. It wasn't until much later that he discovered the mood enhancing pleasures of lifting weights.

Is there any positive psychiatric, social or artistic purpose to be potentially served by producing or presenting or legitimating as art paintings or sculptures which might seem to cast disrespect upon some religious group or religious figure?

I have not yet seen the controversial exhibit at the Brooklyn Museum of Art, but I would like to see it and intend to see it before it leaves. And since not seeing it has not stopped the Mayor of New York City from attacking the work and its presenters, I feel that some words need to be written in defense of works which might tend to cast disrespect upon one or another religious institution. First place, this work which might tend to cast disrespect upon the Virgin Mary (but might not, it turns out) raises the question as to whether the Virgin Mary, or a Virgin Mary might be black. Then there is the use of elephant dung, which in some cultures it has been alleged indicates respect, but in western culture does not. Still the larger psychiatric question arises, if the artistic community is not allowed to criticize religious institutions, and the media is not allowed to criticize religious institutions, then will religious institutions still manage to remain relevant and in touch with contemporary social and spiritual needs if the political system successfully insulates them from any and all public criticism?
Probably not.

As for the relative justifiability of criticizing the Virgin Mary, there are both good things to say about such criticisms and bad things. For example, reverence for the Virgin might convince fathers, uncles and brothers to refrain from molesting and violating their daughters, nieces and sisters. Such a result should no doubt be considered positive. On the other hand, reverence for the idea and ideal of virginity can have statistically speaking, according to a psychiatric friend I know, considerably confusing effects upon some young women. Some may grow up to become old maids, mental patients, perpetually celibate despite wishes to the contrary, some may even become prostitutes in a sort of compulsive overreaction to the cult of the Virgin. In Catholicism, virgins and nuns in general seem to avoid giving themselves to any one man other that is than Jesus. This tendency in some Catholic communities tends to lead to a high level of repressed sexuality which tends to find expression in overly excited and not particularly the healthiest ways. For instance, heavy drinking among the Irish (which drinking may also lead to creative writing and poetry), among Italians some think, compulsive womanizing. Then you have Mardi Gras in Louisiana which gets you ready for Lent. All this repression and reaction against repression may or may not have its roots in the Church's insistence that Catholic priests remain celibate and unmarried. If the culture's primary vehicle for expressing itself, the mass media, refuses to recognize that this celibacy issue is a legitimate object for a public critique, then the largest single religious grouping in the United States is likely to find itself increasingly irrelevant to its own parishioners. Indeed some have suggested that this trend is already in evidence. That is, it has been suggested that increasingly significant numbers of Catholics simply refuse to follow the dictates of the Vatican.

These are the views of a psychiatrist friend. They are not necessarily the view of the narrator.

The psychiatric friend goes on to criticize the Jews as being too entranced with their own self importance, the Muslims as being overly protective of women, and the Protestants as being dourly lacking in a sense of humor. He feels that a significant problem with media programming in the US today lies in its inability to connect characterizations and character strengths and weaknesses with religious and ethnic and cultural affiliations. Perhaps as a result, he suggests, media presentations have ceased, with a few exceptions, to be much more than a sort of attractive but valueless "candy for the eye." And the Mayor of New York wants to get votes by ensuring that nothing relevant to today's citizens' concerns gets expressed in museums that receive public funding.

Vegetarians and meat eaters dealing with separation anxiety;

I once ran into someone who might have been an old acquaintance who I had not seen in perhaps seven or eight years. He had been a vegetarian and when I spoke to him he pointed at the meat on his plate and refused to speak with me. It was as if he had been suggesting that he had somehow betrayed me by eating meat when I wasn't around? Such a suggestion is absurd, as if one were hypersensitively afraid of cannibalizing his friend "by accident" in their absence. This point was actually suggested in a movie called, I think; Weekend, in the late sixties or early seventies. I think it was a Godard movie. At any rate, I have found that one way of demystifying and desanctifying old friendships and relationships which haven't gone anywhere in part as a result of lengthy temporal and physical separations, is to deliberately eat meat before renewing such relationships. This action seems to have had, in one case, the result of placing what had become a sort of idealized friendship into a more mundane perspective out of which new and ongoing concerns can be evolved and addressed.

The borrowed sleeping bag;

An individual who had experienced sexual potency problems borrowed his younger male cousin's sleeping bag to go abroad for the summer. The younger cousin was the aforementioned Mr. Quincy's exceedingly good looking son, the one with two Porsches. During the trip he met an old college buddy who was serving as an officer in the Air Force. He, the officer buddy, and a younger guy shared a single basement room over the course of the summer. While working on an archaeology dig at the Dung Gate on the edge of the old city of Jerusalem, some friendly soldiers briefly loaned him an army forage hat. Later, during the trip he met a beautiful young woman, and perhaps with the help of his cousin's sleeping bag and all of the other intervening events, including about four weeks of study of the local language, his potency problems disappeared. Perhaps the problem would have disappeared anyway. He returned the sleeping bag at the end of the trip.

Peripheral social psychological functions associated with the US "star" system
Date: 11/3/99 11:53:34 AM Eastern Standard Time
To: the editors (The American Prospect, The Nation, and The New Yorker)
From: Andréas Daniel Fogg
Letter from Somerville October 18, 1999

One of the most salient peripheral characteristics associated with the US system of cultivating and over paying public celebrity personalities has to do with the observed fact that in many cases, ordinary persons tend to either directly identify with one or another of the "stars" or to identify someone that they know or know of with such personalities. Hence, it is implicitly thought, "the real stars" that is the relatively ordinary persons that the individual knows in daily life, persons who in most cases have no as it were public identities what so ever, are protected from the glare of publicity, the tarnishes associated with scandals and the dangers associated with envy and jealousy when it is attached to relatively real people. That is, it is, it is asserted, tacitly understood that the so called stars are in fact merely public relations fabrications whose real identities in fact are often hidden from view. The point is to think about them as sort of public relations oriented artificial constructions. For successfully posing as such constructions the stars are given their enormous compensations.

All this public relations oriented posing is designed to allow relatively ordinary persons to vicariously experience a wide range of attitudes and experiences, both developmentally positive and, theoretically, negative.

October 24, 1999

One task for society as a whole is to get ordinary real people to think of themselves and their actions as having real significance and importance. This is difficult in part because much of so called mass media culture is designed to have a sort of pacifying effect, designed to render protest movements either harmless or amenable to guidance and direction from the powers that be, who it is assumed, express themselves through media based statements and imprecations. Hence one major task for therapists, social workers, social scientists, artists and writers who might have some influence over the content of media programming content and publication content in general, is to figure out some way of getting relatively ordinary hard working people to correctly value themselves and their contributions to their fellows (and fellowettes), not that is, to overvalue their contributions, neither to under value their contributions, but rather to understand and value themselves for their own personal and behavioral strengths. If such a goal were accomplished it might be theoretically possible to reverse the trend currently in place wherein the rich are getting vastly richer, progressively, than the overworked workers. In this regard statements to the effect that ordinary workers are just as deserving of being exorbitantly over paid are clearly utopian and out of bounds. Better to give up the struggle to end class conflict and class divisions entirely, in favor of attempts, traditionally liberal attempts, to incrementally lessen the burdens of poverty imposed upon the poor and those who personally have been victimized in part by the difficulties associated with being poor and downtrodden. This can be done by making higher education for workers relatively better and cheaper, by making health care cheaper and better for the poor. The obvious way in which these goals can be accomplished is through national and state level subsidizations.

Speculations on the observed positive correlation between breast cancer and higher socioeconomic status amongst women;

It would appear that the wealthier and more occupationally successful women get, the less likely they are to tolerate being treated as sex objects by their husbands or spouse equivalents. In fact, perhaps, the less likely they are willing to allow themselves to think of themselves as being in any way "less than men" or as having any particular duty toward men in general. This reaction to the old heterosexual role, a reaction in which the old role is given the boot, may in part come about as a result of overreacting to the global imperative to curtail population growth. This is perhaps a naive view of women's liberation, perhaps it is also realistic. Such women may feel that any physical contact with men is to be avoided and as a result may experience levels of anxious self confusion and latent personal distaste which taken as a whole may result in the perceived correlation

October 25, 1999

A need to change the traditional definition of heterosexuality;

The traditional definition of especially monogamous heterosexuality, but of heterosexuality in general revolves around women or a woman on the one hand being taken care of and supported by her man and, on the other hand, a woman, the woman in the archetypical heterosexual relationship, obeying her man. According to the old archetype, being taken care of and obeying constitute the "good woman's" extent of responsibility toward her man? In an effort to get away from this archetype and in order to incorporate the new realities wherein a man often must obey his woman and may indeed find himself either completely or partially dependent on her for support, the old archetypical definition has been thrown out by the new feminism.

However, in this act of rejection, the basic idea that one of the responsibilities of womanhood may include a need to find, love and sustain a man has also been thrown out (in many cases). That this has happened is understandable given the noxiousness and degradation associated with the old point of view. However, from the point of view of the mental health of both women and men and children this ideological abandonment of a liberal view of heterosexuality is probably quite sociologically speaking damaging.

In fact the rejection of the heterosexual dyad as being a central part of the societal nexus is also consistent with a social paradigm that has become central to the expression of information in this age of mass media. That is, millions of men and women consider themselves involved in fantasy with the beautiful stars and consciously or unconsciously opt for such physically unencumbered relationships over more down to earth satisfying relationships with real persons of the opposite sex. No doubt they are telling themselves that eventually they will become stars themselves and eventually rate a star for a partner. Or they are being fed on homosexual or lesbian subcultural support group reinforcements and negative sanctions which tend to teach them that they have no real need for the company of the opposite sex in any case. For example, the implicit and at times explicit message in many homosexual and lesbian subcultures is likely to be "Of course you realize that you are essentially, biologically a _____ (fill in the blank, either a homosexual or lesbian) and exclusively a _____, because if for any reason you might even consider being anything other than a _____, you will discover that you will soon lose all of your friends who are members of the group (and perhaps your job as well since it is granted as a perk associated with your continued maintenance of your _____ identity). It would be interesting to determine how many of the high tech information processing jobs involve either semi-erotic or semi-homoerotic ties between these relatively elite workers and their even more elite supervisors.

In either case many of the long term needs of society are losing out. And of course the group defined as "the stars" includes the small percentage of individuals who are making the enormous salaries, which, as has been pointed out, enable them theoretically to support fantasized or real sexual dalliances with vast numbers of the poor who, starved for real self esteem, are willing to "share" the affections of the rich with vast numbers of others. None of this sort of arrangement offers many real social rewards. It has probably come about as a result of the media having successfully transformed the individual into a sort of collective mass whose individual traits have become lost in the shuffle.

October 26, 1999

Fictional observation in the department of ghostly coincidences,

I know someone named 'Schwartz' who was writing an e-mail letter on the Sunday morning before Payne Stewart's plane went down. He signed the letter Mark Schwartz, and then, used AOL's spell check to check the letter. AOL's spell check said that 'Schwartz' should be spelled 'Stewart.' Apparently they think, as does apparently, the mass culture, not withstanding the feelings of Schwartz's everywhere, that Stewart is a much more appropriate name than Schwartz. As Pat Buchanan says, "Let the melting pot do its work" whatever he means by that. And the question arises, by the way, what does he mean? Could it be that all of this cultural homogenization actually has some negative side effects? Might it be the case that all of these media big wigs have, as an old friend used to say, "Their heads stuck up their you know what's?"

Health insurance....televisual culture. rage...education
Date: 11/16/99 11:07:02 AM Eastern Standard Time

to: the editors (The American Prospect, The Nation, The New Yorker)
from: Andréas Daniel Fogg
Letter from Somerville November 9, 1999

A strategy for challenging the health insurance status quo establishment;

Consider the possibilities for success associated with issuing a public challenge to the collective private health insurance industries. Such a challenge would ask them to publicly defend the justifiability and necessity associated with their continuing to collect the middleman based current percentage of the nation's health expenditures.

In other words, the idea is that this or the next Democratic Presidential administration would attempt to systematically chip away at and reduce the percentage of the nation's private dollars devoted to bureaucratic processing by non medical personnel of the nation's health dollars. In the past, the health insurance industry has been able to resist change by claiming that any changes would detract from the public's ability to freely choose their own doctors.

November 11, 1999

Fiction: hypothetical illustration of what C.S. Lewis might have meant by the term that "hideous force."

This didn't happen, but if it did happen, it would illustrate what I am talking about. A young boy goes sledding on a hill that is new to him. It is steeper than anything he has been on before. His parents had told him that afternoon to "go out and do something!" At the bottom of the hill, perhaps two hundred feet from the beginning of the relatively flat runoff, is a potentially menacing clump of large boulders (one of them is like ten feet by ten feet by ten feet) and trees. The boy gets on his sled and heads straight down the slope; actually it is closer to being a cliff than a slope. He has never gone that fast on a sled before. Then he notices that he is headed straight for the clump of boulders and trees. He tries desperately to steer the sled away to the left. He tries and tries but the sled, seemingly possessed by either a mind of its own or perhaps Lewis would suggest, by a ghostly power, refuses to change course. The boy, only about eight or nine years old is terrified. Finally, he gives up trying to steer the sled and throws his body into the air and off the sled. The sled crashes into the boulders and he lands on the ground shaken but unhurt. He wonders about what had happened to the sled, in fact, he is probably still wondering about it years later. Is this what people mean when they say that "everything is determined?" Or should they more correctly point to Shakespeare and say that there are "more things in Heaven and on Earth than are dreamt of in your philosophy, Horatio!"

The boy's friend, Eddie Westwood, who had walked to the hill with him, watched the first run from the top. But by the time the boy had picked himself up and climbed back up the hill, Eddie had gone home. So he did not see the second run. This time, the boy set a course far to the left of the clump of trees and boulders and stayed on the sled until it stopped. Then he went home and avoided talking about the incident to his parents or sisters, or, for that matter, to anyone else.

November 14, 1999

Dealing with rogue potentially or actually nuclear empowered states;

It would appear that the need to remind nuclear powered states of their responsibilities toward both each other and the other countries of the world, humanity and life in general, might be best exercised through a consortium of nations speaking together, perhaps organized for the express purpose of seeing to it that nuclear power is used only for peaceful purposes. Perhaps what is called for is a UN based agency created explicitly for this purpose. On second thought, perhaps the UN Security Council is such an agency.

At this point it seems advisable to voice my own personal doubts about the wisdom associated with the Republican move to obviate the nuclear test ban treaty.

It would appear that the trend of US foreign policy needs to be moving away from scenarios wherein the actual option of using nuclear weapons becomes more likely.

But reopening the option to test nuclear weapons, which obviating the test ban effectively accomplishes, in fact makes the use of nuclear weapons and the acquisition of nuclear weapons by previously so "unempowered" states relatively more possible and therefore likely. Therefore, if you accept the basic premise that humanity and the planet must needs seek to avoid any further actual utilization of nuclear weapons against living creatures of any sort, then you would probably vote against those Republican, or, if there are any, Democratic legislators who voted to cancel the nuclear test ban treaty.

And on the subject of nuclear empowerment, one method for seeking to avoid the further proliferation of nuclear weapons is to, as a matter of US international policy, seek wherever possible and feasible, to psychologically as well as economically empower such states before they feel the need to test nuclear weapons. One of the areas in which such empowerment can occur lies in the question of the determination of third world corporate wages. So long as the corporations continue to play one poor country off against other poor countries (and states) contriving to perpetuate a lower and ever lower diminishing international wage spiral, such countries will eventually begin to see themselves as economically powerless and eventually they are likely to turn, as have the North Koreans, to the threatened acquisition of nuclear weapons if only as a sort of economic bargaining chip.

Meanwhile we have the problem of Pakistan, which has already acquired nuclear weapons and seems unable to organize and sustain itself as a functional democracy.

Reports indicate that democracy in that state had coexisted with vast quantities of theft, that the country had become a sort of kleptocracy. Hence, it would appear that merely restoring democracy in Pakistan will not solve that states problems. Some sort of outside coaching as to how to run that state seems to be needed. What that coaching might consist in and who should offer it remain open questions.

Perhaps a UN investigative committee should be sent to Pakistan with a mandate to conduct extensive interviews amongst both powerful and ordinary citizens in order to ascertain both what the status quo has been and what can be done to better the situation.

Fiction: changing interactive norms influenced and justified by so called psychological wisdom;

A supervisor informs me to the effect that sharing is considered a sign of emotional adjustment and maturity. And, coincidentally enough, I notice two associates who are actually cousins, pointedly sharing little baglets of sweet snacks with each other and me at breaks between work. They tend to laugh, even giggle, whenever anyone eats a banana. It is as if they had been told or heard that such sharing is a sign of emotional maturity. It is also of course a sign of economic security. However, in their cases, sharing apparently does not extend to readily allowing others to spend time with attractive women. One of these boys, they are both in college but continue to live at home with their parents, as do so many of their peers, states authoritatively in a loud voice that he can have any woman he wants to "with his right hand!" He means, I think, that he can have them in fantasy by masturbating while thinking about them. This statement is a sad even pathetic comment on his attitude and to the extent that it reflects the attitude of a generation which has given up on having any sort of sexual experiences before marriage, it is sad commentary on that generation as well. This same young man has said that "there is nothing wrong with a young guy having sex with his cousin," seemingly implying that he had a sexual relationship with his (male) cousin (who works at the branch, and with whom he "hangs out" a lot.) This same young man had made complaints about the "fact" that, at age twenty, he was still a virgin, until the narrator told him that he was under no real obligation to tell anyone about the actual results of what had happened on his dates. Then, the statement about his having sex with his cousin, and being (in the vernacular) "gay," was revealed to be another "joke." Note that the psychologists who counsel such young men have tended to express extremely permissive, even encouraging attitudes toward the expression of homosexuality. And probably as a result of such expressions, the danger that any heterosexual contact is likely to include the possibility that that partner had been exposed to HIV through contact with a male who, giving in to the encouragement of the supposedly wise psychologists, had also indulged in homosexual coital relations is greater. (I am no great fan of actively homosexual "gay" men, however, I find that in many cases their company, for regular, intermittent, ongoing periods of time at least, can be quite supportive and is preferable to the company of either covert homosexuals who feel compelled to boisterously assert their preferences for any and all good looking women, or in some cases, even to the company of perfunctory heterosexuals who spend considerable portions of their time denying their own interest in the affairs and doings of other men as a matter of principle.)

It is indeed amazing how some psychologists can empower relatively ordinary young men to do what most people would assume to be foolish or inappropriate behaviors. For example, when I was an undergraduate, there was a tall, thin, somewhat nerdy philosophy student who would spend most of his time in class with his legs crossed, gently and regularly moving his suspended foot up and down say maybe twelve or fifteen inches in each direction. I used to find this practice extremely annoying, as if he were in effect masturbating in class, as if, if his example were followed the whole class would degenerate into some sort of "gang bang." But I suspect that some shrink or other had told him that that this practice was an acceptable way to deal with anxiety and or sexual excitation.

So my two friends think that they get along well because they ostentatiously share their Twinkies and cupcakes. But one also proclaims his "interest" in, (in a sense lays claim to) all the good looking women who walk by, seeming perhaps to imply that they are "his" or else he may get angry and possibly violent. And he repeatedly makes loud violent threats directed at no one in particular which he claims are merely "jokes." I notice now in retrospect, that even though I have called both of these individuals "buddies" in the past, I can't seem to remember ever having touched either of them, neither do I feel any wish to touch them. Perhaps this lack of a wish for non sexual contact occurs coterminously with extensive suggestions that one has a wish to engage in sexual contact with the other or perhaps me or perhaps some woman or other. Perhaps the lack of a shared history of non sexual contact also correlates with generalized joking expressions of violent threats such as "do you want to step outside, ha ha!" "I'd like to beat the crap out of so and so" or supposedly joking, one cousin to the other, "step outside and I'll break you in half!" (such violent sentiments are pronounced in a loud, humorless flat voice, as if deadly serious and then disavowed as "jokes") and with fear engendered by intermittent generalized violent gestures and rhetoric. (They have both, as have so many of their generation, studied karate for numerous years.) These sorts of violent statements, it would seem, revolve around a sort of sexual identity confusion such that such individuals often feel the need to display the rhetoric of violence toward other males lest they fear that they might be mistaken as sexual "deviants." They have a list of the top ten best looking women in the branch.

(Anyone who has been "groped" can easily tell the difference between a touch which seeks sexual gratification and a touch which connotes friendly emotional support.)

Touch and televisual based culture;
    Televisual culture gives viewers the illusion that they are "right there" with the television people. But of course, they are not. In fact they are frozen into voiceless passivity. They will be lucky if they are even consulted by any of the numerous polling organizations which regularly tell us how we think about the issues that the television national news informs us that it is OK to think about. So that the only way to really assure ourselves that we are not watching television in our daily lives is to elicit some direct evidence that we can in fact directly effect those with whom we interact. That is we can touch them. They can touch us. They do hear us. We do hear them. This has nothing to do with sex, as so many pop psychologists and media spokespersons would have it. After all, it is in the interests of television's continued monopoly and control over the population in fact to discourage as many independent thoughts and opinions as possible. And the best and easiest way to discourage such independence is to stigmatize independent social friendships as being expressions representative either of illicit heterosexual i.e. "cheating" relations, or, as being symptomatic of a gay or lesbian homosexual orientation.

Withholding taxes;

During a bar room discussion with an Air Force technician the suggestion is made that one way of providing tax relief on an ongoing basis is to tinker with the way in which withholding is administered. Thus, for example, a family of three could have its standard deductions registered proactively with the IRS so that only income that exceeded the allowed deductions would be withheld. Such a move would give those at the lower end of the income scale an immediate break.

Redefining education, a possibly crucial paradigmatic shift;

In the past and even today for many, education is thought of as a process whereby knowledge and facts are transmitted from teachers to students. The students who learn the most facts acquire the most knowledge, correctly, are the most successful. However, this is not necessarily the most functional way to view the educational process. For example, suppose educational success is defined as a process whereby a certain minimal number of facts are learned, however, what is also learned is "how to ask important questions both within the context of the relevant course as well as independently." So that according to this definition of education the more important product is not whether the student has the correct answer, but rather, how good are the questions that she or he is asking? Are they answerable at all, for example? Does answering them make a difference for themselves, for their friends and for society and the world at large? For some, education ends with their final examination. For others it becomes a life time involvement. Such lifetime involvements involve implicitly higher levels of social responsibility and accountability than does an attitude toward education which ends after one's final high school or college examination. As society moves toward higher levels of affluence and if and when such affluence is spread throughout the various socioeconomic classes of society, then the differences between these two conceptions of the educational process and the consequences of these differences will begin to become culturally crucial.

It is important to remember the somewhat uncomfortable fact that good and effective especially higher education tends to differentiate between those who have learned more effectively and thoroughly, and therefore are more empowered, and those who have learned less effectively and thoroughly and therefore are less empowered (in the areas taught). That is, good education does not promote equality; quite to the contrary, good education creates inequality, often inequality that had not existed prior to the inception of that educational process. Television, on the other hand is designed to purvey exactly the same message to each viewer. Television has no office hours, as do teachers and professors, there are no teaching assistants who are willing, even supposed to help students with their individual perceptions and problems. Television is designed to seduce everyone equally into passivity, or if genuine advice is offered it is usually likely to be of a sort that will not enable any one viewer to succeed in a way markedly differently from any other. So television is not designed to help any one person get ahead to any particular extent more than any other person. Television is designed so that everybody who watches can succeed equally, so that no one achieves any advantage over any one else. And when you are genuinely competing for the love of a good looking intelligent man or woman, unless you are a violent ruthless caveman sort of individual, you need to acquire all of the relatively superior advantages that you possibly can. That is the case, of course, unless you are content to have "any woman or man that you want with your right or left hand." In other words, we are all equally everything (by virtue of our abilities to identify) and nothing (because we are effectively mute) in front of the TV tube. And, being at the same time everything and nothing is extremely frustrating and aggravating. It's no wonder that relatively so many people have trouble managing their anger and that so many incidents of seemingly random generalized violence occur.

November 16, 1999

Additional notes; the other cousin has had a girl friend with whom he just recently broke off. She apparently had given him the impression that she had been sleeping with several others during their relationship. This is, of course, more fictional material. The cousin's question to the narrator, spoken in a voice that was perhaps serious, perhaps joking, was "should I kill her?" To which the narrator, unwilling to risk the likelihood that the question was or was not serious, because so many ex girl friends and spouses do get attacked and even killed, responded "no."

Another fictionalized associate who has used violent language in the past has been living without his spouse but with his teenaged son, who does not like to go to school. There has been much tension and conflict reported. Over the weekend the two had a violent physical altercation with blood shed and pain reported.

Something to be thankful for

Criticism of the WTO

Date: 11/26/99 9:16:26 PM Eastern Standard Time

We just had dinner, during which I attempted to start a discussion about the WTO meetings which are coming up this week in Seattle. I have been reading The Nation on the subject during the afternoon and yesterday evening. No one wanted to talk either positively or negatively about the WTO. Instead my two brothers in law pontificated about quantum theory and about how it had nothing to do with social science, presuming I understood them correctly.

There is a particularly interesting article in the Nation by Robert Borosage, called I think, "The Battle in Seattle." You might be able to find a similar article at <http://epn.org>. This is an interesting quote "But the new economy has not worked very well for most working people. By 1999, 200 million more people lived in abject poverty (on less that $1 a day) than in 1987. Inequality has grown both between and within countries. Only thirty-three countries achieved sustained 3 percent annual growth in GNP from 1980 to 1996. In fifty-nine countries, primarily those in sub-Saharan Africa and the former Eastern bloc, GNP per capita actually declined. Environmental despoliation is getting worse. The Nike economy saw the rebirth of the satanic mills—child labor, young women working for a pittance in export-processing zones where union organizers are routinely fired, beaten or killed." (p.20 The Nation, Dec. 6, 1999)

It's enough to get you thinking, perhaps even question authority.

Influencing the market, motivating students, an experiment suggested
Date: 12/9/99 11:06:30 AM Eastern Standard Time
to: the editors (The American Prospect, The Nation, The New Yorker)
from: Andréas Daniel Fogg
Letter from Somerville November 18

Tinkering with the Market Distribution Mechanism;
The free market laissez-faire doctrinaires tend to sanctify the market oriented mechanisms for making decisions about who gets what and how much. Whereas in fact, this view tends to obscure the fact that much of economic activity, advertising and legislating for examples, involves attempts to influence the rewards and punishments that the market will continue to hand out.

November 28, 1999
The authoritarian mentality, the relatively open mind, pedagogical orientations;
It may be fair to say that the kind of education that children and young adults receive, i.e. whether they are encouraged to question freely or instead are limited to giving answers that the teacher then acrimoniously accepts or rejects, may well influence their future adult life styles and political behaviors and attitudes.

Perhaps as a result of being involved in significant periods of socialization in which the only utilized roles are either "parent-figure" or "child" not surprisingly, such limited individuals tend to be unable to assume any roles that differ from the above named two. Thus adult roles involve neither the deliberate effectively unconditional submission to the authority of some designated parental surrogate figure, neither the imposition of such parental like authority upon subordinates. It should be noted, however, all the socialization into adult like equal, autonomous roles is of no use unless viable economically supported roles are available to sustain such behaviors. Without such roles, jobs or careers if you will, individuals educated and trained for adult like thinking must needs find themselves either classified as mentally ill, or are forced to assume (usually) subordinate roles in authoritarian like organizations. The roles assumed are likely to be subordinate since a prerequisite for assuming so called "leadership" like roles often involves the willingness to ruthlessly assert ones will one's authority so to speak, often in such a way as to quash the autonomy of ordinary workers.

Women, feminism and authoritarianism;

It would appear, perhaps, that some women, in their apparent fascination with the idea that women as a group may have a generalized orientation that is superior to that held by many men, have come to adopt an attitude that is one in which they assume that because they are women, that therefore they are above all men in generalized importance and status, to the point where men as a group are regarded as beings who should not speak unless spoken to (by a woman). This attitude may not get them very far when it comes to making actual alliances and political deals or compromises with men who might be sympathetic to some or all of their causes.

In any case, the assumption that all women are congenitally and intellectually superior to men amounts to nothing much better than a sort of reverse sexism which rests on a sort of adolescent like mentality which enthrones one's own gender and ignores or derogates the other.

Calculating the budget deficit;

I should like to raise the question as to how much of the current national budgetary deficits are held by multinational corporations who have been engaged in assembling many of their products while utilizing a process of cross border importation. So, how much of the US trade deficit with China or Mexico, for examples, has been generated by US corporate subsidiaries assembling products in those countries, using indigenous cheap labor, and then exporting those products back into the US?

Whose interests does the WTO serve?

The question needs to be raised, are current WTO rulings overly slanted in favor of private investor and corporate interests, as opposed to societal and national interests such as might be represented by the need to maintain the civil peace, to avoid environmental cleanups, to educate and sustain the morale and consumerist habits of the great bulk of the world's population.

November 29, 1999

A fictional study of a tech writer;

This tech writer was also a graphic artist. His name is Vlythill. He ironically thinks that he is a communist. However, he knows nothing of glasnost. As a loyal communist, he feels obliged to avoid any and all expressions of personal economic interest. He feels that as a matter of true belief and commitment that he must totally entrust his economic well being to the party. "The party knows best," he likes to say. So investing in independent economic interests is, for him and his wife, out of the question. Never mind the fact that along with his commitment goes a sort of compulsive political passivity, an unwillingness to question or criticize any policy based or politically oriented decisions that he thinks might have been made by the party. And, yet, still, he and his wife are perennially likely to complain about the amount of income that they are able to receive. As true believers, they assume that the party controls the conditions of their employment (despite any and all evidence to the contrary) and that the way to be a good communist is to effectively subsume one's will to that of the Party. Criticizing the Party is unthinkable. Never mind the problem associated with identifying what that will is. Rather, it is assumed that the Party is in control, exercising the grand plan to centralize more and more decision-making by continually centralizing corporate authority into fewer and fewer central corporate decision-making centers.

December 3, 1999

Vlythill on Heisenberg; Heisenberg's principle, he prefers not to call it the "uncertainty principle," is about the difficulty involved in measuring photons as they change quanta. Einstein disagreed with Heisenberg and expressed his disagreement in the famous phrase, "God does not play dice with the Universe."

Vlythill is also quite sure that Heisenberg's principle has nothing what so ever to do with social science. He, that is, Vlythill, is obviously wrong in this regard, despite the possibility that he may have grasped in some part the essence of Quantum theory as well as the context of Einstein's remark about God the Universe and dice. (What all this has to do with either the numbers forty-one or forty-two is unclear.) Of course, it is possible a.) That Einstein was wrong about God's possible reliance upon probabilities and b.) that the uncertainty theory, that making observations and communicating those observations, in the social sciences, may effect the configurations of future observations, that is, the qualities of a changing data base. Such an insight, based as it is on an idea of science more like that of Heisenberg than that of say Boyle or Newton, suggests that social science may well be of value more as a component of a dynamic socioeconomic or even political process than in so far as it is able to identify and prove absolutely perfect numerical laws or relationships.

WTO and the world economic paradigm;

All the squabbling at the WTO meeting in Seattle over the conditions under which it will be determined which countries will be able to land the relatively few number of production oriented jobs that are necessary to supply the world's needs, suggests the need to develop a different sort of paradigm which would allow the world's paymasters to dole out monies for what may turn out to be effectively a newly defined sort of work product. In order to effectively support such a product, however, a consensus would needs be built up which would effectively justify its value to society.

My initial thoughts along these lines involve the redirection of societal funds in the general direction of more professional educational support for both professional teachers and students. One of the initial insights which led to this position involved the complaint by some coworkers at the warehouse as to the absurdity of the fact that convicts incarcerated in prisons were often able to get college level educations more cheaply than were law abiding workers.

December 4, 1999

Paying high school students based upon levels of achievement, a thought experiment;

Consider, if you will, the long term consequences that would or might follow as a result of the implementation of a plan whereby high school, college and adult ed students, from the tenth grade upward, for example, were rewarded monetarily roughly along lines commensurate with the academic grades that they received. So that an A would be worth more than a B, a B more than a C, a C more than a D, and an F worth nothing. By the time an individual got to college, monetary rewards could be larger and not necessarily directly pegged to a standard magnitude. That is, some A's might be worth say a minimum of the equivalent of the course's tuition cost, or half the tuition cost. Some A's might actually be worth a positive net income over and above the course's cost. It appears on first sight that the implementation of such a principle, particularly if quality standards were enforced and not subject to mandatory, quota-like feel good, affirmative action like diminution and dilution, might have the effect of triggering a vast quantity of positive academic motivation throughout the student grouping. Levels of monetary rewards need not and probably should not be widely publicized. However, items indicative of achieving membership in the honor roll, for example, such as emblematic tee shirts, would likely serve as relatively harmless yet effective public incentives to spur achievement.

In colleges and college equivalency like courses in high school, in cases where extraordinary achievements are accomplished, yet where teachers, counselors and school psychiatrists and psychologists deem such achievers emotionally unable or unready to accept what may be quite large economic rewards, such rewards could be held aside and invested wisely and safely until such time as said individuals matured enough to receive all or portions of them. This view of achievement and its reward suggests the need to radically reexamine the way in which financial aid for college work is currently allocated.

Such a scheme of monetary rewards might go a long way toward correcting American society's relatively dysfunctional excessive fascination with athletics and sports, a fascination which may well too often occur at the expense of sacrificing efforts devoted to excelling at more cerebral yet in the long run more societally valuable intellectual work. Note too, that in racially integrated schools, in many sports, the de facto policy of bestowing public rewards upon successful student athletes but not upon successful students, amounts to accepting a policy that is in effect equivalent to a sort of pro African American, anti-Caucasian and anti-intellectual reverse racism. This is the case, despite what ostensibly responsible authority figures on both sides of the political spectrum may say. You have only to look at the racial composition of athletic football and basketball especially in the professional ranks, but also in racially integrated colleges and high schools, to conclude that at this point in history African American men tend to be better athletes in these more popular sports than are Caucasian men. So that if the society insists on only recognizing publicly achievements in sports during high school and college, then most men on campus with publicly recognized high levels of status will be, in the main, African Americans. This state of affairs tends to generate White anti-Black resentment, which resentment in turn may deter Blacks from working hard at their studies for fear of bringing yet more resentment down on their heads.

December 5, 1999

This idea of rewarding students for their work is perhaps premised on the idea that the problem with current student performances may lie more with a relatively poor ability to motivate them to think, work and interact, an inability that may well be more closely associated with televisual and to some extent Internet culture than with a deteriorating level of teaching quality.

Testing the scheme;

Implementing a scheme in which students were rewarded financially for their achievements, after those achievements were accomplished probably should proceed gradually, utilizing closely monitored experimental test case situations. Thus the apparatus of quasi experimental research designs, familiar to behavioral scientists should likely be implemented. You could have a variety of test case scenarios, including the utilization of a controlled, uniform, standard test case mechanism in affluent suburbs and relatively deprived urban and rural school districts.

Note that much of what passes for classroom verbal participation in high school and college often gets passed over when it comes time for teachers to award grades. Thus, students who in their youthful zeal to speak, lead and show off, who may succeed in stating verbally answers that may even challenge the rationale employed by the teacher or professor, may not receive top grades, in part because teachers and professors are human and may resent being shown up by uppity students, who then may find themselves at a loss during exam time as well as being the objects of retaliation in the form of mediocre grades. Professors are human and if the student criticizes the professor's or teachers questions, or foci, he or she may in effect be giving the teacher the equivalent of poor grades. Such professors may well then be excused for retaliating by awarding the "bright" offender with his or her own bad grades. All such needs to justify oneself by leading the professor and the class toward true enlightenment are likely to be placed in a more realistic perspective if and when students become aware that their primary responsibility is to do the work that the teacher or professor requires, rather than to "teach" either the professor or especially the class. Indeed, if in the course of fulfilling the professor's requirements the student also manages to raise his or her i.e. the professors level of understanding and awareness in the field concerned, then that accomplishment is more likely to be forgiven and even rewarded if said student has not also attempted to usurp the teacher or professor's authority in the eyes of the class at large.

December 9, 1999

The problem with high status media commentators;

Part of the problem involved in motivating students to pay attention to and study and write for, individual non-media located teachers and professors has to do with the magnitude of status that the society assigns such teachers versus the status assigned to the so called TV and media based "wise men and women." This differential status assignation seems to be implicitly if not explicitly implied as a consequence of the vastly incommensurate pay differentials between real life teachers and professors and the "media maven pundits." The presumed vast difference in pay implies to most that the messages of the media mavens are intrinsically more important than the messages of the real life teachers in high schools and universities. This difference is compounded by what perhaps was called the Bales power/status interaction rating schema. Under the Bales status power rating system, power and status are determined by the number of people who pay attention either directly or indirectly to what any one individual is saying or indicating. According to this schema, TV spokespersons and commentators seem to be far more powerful and important than real life teachers and professors who teach usually no more than from eight or ten to five hundred students at a time. Further, the professors tend to direct their written comments to a relatively small group of elite professors, whose importance in the eyes of the society is, to most nonacademic, nonintellectual citizens, unknown.

Hence the temptation for high school and university students is to pay more attention to the messages of the media than to the more difficult and challenging material hopefully presented by their real life professors and teachers. The result is likely to involve a diminution of student performance. The result is likely to also involve the elevation of relatively noncomplex mass cultural, "lowest common denominator" like knowledge over the acquisition of any sort of specialized knowledge, the sort, for example, that might be useful as a tool to inform and lead the production of better and more useful media originated statements.

About the Author

Not that much is known about Andréas Daniel Fogg. After finishing college he attended graduate school at State University of New York at Buffalo in Anthropology and later at University of Massachusetts at Amherst in Sociology. He is a writer who lives in Somerville, MA. In college he concentrated on the social sciences and philosophy, some economics, psychiatric theories and some literature. The author, in his twenties, voluntarily checked into a major Massachusetts psychiatric hospital as an in patient as part of a proposed anthropological participant observation research project. The idea was to attempt to see how the world looked to psychiatric patients, the assumption being that if the world engaged in nuclear war, that such a decision would partake of thought patterns characteristic of the mentally ill. During the course of this research, the author was diagnosed as being mentally ill. His writing is and has been an attempt in part to prove that he is in fact sane. For most of his adult working life he did blue collar warehouse sorts of work. He admires the work of Eric Hoffer, especially the book <u>The True Believer.</u>

978-0-595-38629-1
0-595-38629-6

www.ingramcontent.com/pod-product-compliance
Lightning Source LLC
Chambersburg PA
CBHW030309290526
45785CB00001B/281